CHARMING SMALL HOTEL GUIDES

BRITAIN

& IRELAND
1990

CHARMING SMALL HOTEL GUIDES

BRITAIN

& IRELAND
1990

Edited by Chris Gill

DUNCAN PETERSEN

First published 1988 by Papermac, a division of Macmillan Publishers Limited

This edition published 1990 by
Duncan Petersen Publishing Ltd,
5 Botts Mews, London W2 5AG,
and distributed by the Publishing Division of
The Automobile Association, Fanum House,
Basingstoke, Hampshire RG21 2EA

Conceived, designed and produced by Duncan Petersen
Edited by Fox & Partners, The Old Forge,
Norton St Philip, Bath BA3 6LW

A CIP catalogue record for this book is available from the British Library

ISBN 1 872576 00 1

Typeset by Lineage Ltd, Watford, Herts
Originated by Regent Publishing Services, Hong Kong
Printed by G. Canale & C. SpA, Turin

Contents

Introduction

Here is a new accommodation guide series with a singular focus on places which are both charming and small: in Britain, for example, the recommendations have usually fewer than 15 rooms, rarely more than 20.

The *Charming Small Hotel Guides* look different from others on the market; their descriptive style is different; and they are compiled differently. They are, in fact, designed to satisfy what we believe to be the real needs of today's traveller; needs which have been served at best haphazardly by existing guides.

Our entries employ, above all, words: they contain not one symbol. They are written by people with something to say, not a bureaucracy which has long since lost the ability to distinguish the praiseworthy from the mediocre. The editorial team is small and highly experienced at assessing and writing about hotels; at noticing all-important details. Every entry, however brief, aims to give a coherent and definite feel of what it is actually like to stay in that place.

Although we have made use of reports from members of the public, and would welcome more of them (see box) we have placed great emphasis on consistency in our selections and our descriptions.

These are features which will only reveal their worth as you use your *Charming Small Hotel Guide*. Its other advantages are more obvious: the use of colour photographs to depict a hundred or so of the entries, which, from the outside at least, are particularly appealing or interesting; the ease of reference, with clear geographical designations for all entries.

Where small really is beautiful

Small hotels have always had the special appeal that they can offer the traveller a personal welcome and personal attention, whereas larger places are necessarily more institutional. But the distinction is clearer than ever in the Britain of the 1990s.

The traveller who returns to Britain now after an interval of a decade will notice many changes, and not least among them will be the transformation of the hotel scene. There has been something of a renaissance of hotel-keeping in Britain and Ireland, and in particular an influx of new people into the business who bring to it little or no professional training, but abundant enthusiasm, strong motivation and crystal-clear ideas about what constitutes a good hotel. Since these ideas are usually based on experience of the customer's side of the reception desk, they are often right.

The establishments described in this guide are simply the 300 hotels, guesthouses, inns and bed-and-breakfast places that we believe most discriminating travellers would prefer to stay in, given the choice except that we have ruled out 20 or 30 which are now so expensive as to be beyond the pockets of ordinary people who lack expense accounts. Even so, some undeniably pricey places are included the top mark is around £40 for bed and breakfast; but there are, equally, plenty of places costing only half or a third of that.

Our ideal hotel has a peaceful, pretty setting; the building itself is either handsome, appealing, historic, or has a distinct character. The rooms are spacious, but on a human scale not grand or intimidating. The decorations and furnishings are harmonious, comfortable and impeccably maintained, and include antique pieces meant to be used, not revered. The proprietors and staff are dedicated, thoughtful and sensitive in their pursuit of their guests' happiness – friendly and welcoming without being intrusive. Last but not least, the food, whether simple or ambitious, is fresh, interesting and carefully prepared. Elaborate facilities such as saunas or trouser-presses count for little in these guides, though we do generally list them.

Of course, not every hotel scores top marks on each of these counts. But it is surprising how many do respectably well on most fronts – and it may be particularly surprising to our imaginary traveller returning to Britain after a decade that it is small hotels which are in the forefront of the steady improvement in cooking standards.

How to find an entry
In this guide, the entries are arranged in a sequence starting in the extreme south-west (Cornwall) and working through the counties in a generally north-easterly direction. Ireland comes last in the sequence.

To find a hotel, simply browse through headings at the top of the pages until you find the area you want to visit. Or, to locate a specific place, use the index which lists the entries alphabetically, along with their locations – usually a village, town, city – or neighbouring village, town or city.

On pages 10 to 13 there are, in addition, maps showing the location of all the entries.

Reporting to the guide
The guide is greatly strengthened by reports from people who have stayed in the hotels recommended here, or who have found other places which seem to deserve an entry. On page 216 is further information on reporting to the guide.

Introduction

How to read an entry

At the top of each entry is a coloured bar highlighting the name of the town or village where the establishment is located, along with a categorization which gives some

The factbox given for each hotel follows a standard pattern which requires little explanation; but:

Under **Tel** we give the telephone number starting with the area code used within the country; when dialling from another country, omit the initial nought of this code.

Under **Location** we give information on the setting of the hotel and on its parking arrangements.

Under **Food & drink** we list the meals available. A 'full' breakfast is a traditional hot meal of bacon, eggs and so on; such a breakfast may be available at extra cost even in hotels where we have not mentioned it.

We also say what licence the hotel possesses for the sale of alcoholic drinks. A restaurant licence permits the sale of drinks with meals, a residential licence permits the sale of drinks to those staying in the hotel, and a full licence permits the sale of drinks to anyone over the age of 18 during certain prescribed hours (basically lunch time and the evening).

The **Prices** are per person, including tax and service for 1990 wherever possible. Normally, a range is given, representing the smallest and largest amounts you might pay in different circumstances – typically, the minimum is half the cost of the cheapest double room in low season, while the maximum is the cost of the dearest single in high season. Thus, with an appropriate allowance for inflation, you can usefully estimate the cost of rooms in years following publication. If no clue to its character. These categories are as far as possible self-explanatory. 'Country house hotel' needs, perhaps, some qualification: it is reserved for places whose style is appropriately gracious.

bed and breakfast price is given, this is because we understand that dinner is inescapable. After the B & B price, we give either the price for dinner, bed and breakfast, or for full board – or, instead, an indication of the cost of individual meals. After all this basic information comes, where space allows, a summary of reductions available for long stays or for children.

Our lists of facilities in bedrooms cover only mechanical gadgets and not ornaments such as flowers or consumables such as toiletries or free drinks.

Under **Facilities** we list public rooms and then outdoor and sporting facilities which are either part of the hotel or immediately on hand; facilities in the vicinity are not listed, though they sometimes feature at the end of the main description in the **Nearby** section, which is necessarily selective.

We use the following abbreviations for **Credit cards:**
AE American Express
DC Diners Club
MC MasterCard (Access/Eurocard)
V Visa (Barclaycard/Bank Americard/Carte Bleue etc)

The final entry in a factbox is normally the name of the proprietor(s); but where the hotel is run by a manager we give his or her name instead.

Unfamiliar terms
Some overseas visitors to Britain, particularly from North America, may be mystified by the terms **'self-catering'** and **'bargain breaks'**. The first means that cooking facilities such as a kitchenette or small kitchen are provided for making one's own meals, as in a rental apartment. The second means off-season price reductions are available.

Master location map

Isle of Man

Manchester

Liverpool

Swansea

Cardiff

Bristol

Bath

Plymouth

Penzance

(Continued on following two pages)

Newcastle
upon
Tyne

54

49   50

York

Leeds
47

Lincoln

39   40

45

Birmingham   Norwich

Coventry   43
38   36   Cambridge   44
        Ipswich
    37
34
        42 41
    35
        London
16   23   24
    18   21   22   Dover
Southampton   19
Portsmouth   20
    Brighton
17
Isle of Wight

D MIDDLE ENGLAND
                                    Page No.
32 Hereford & Worcester
....100-105
33 West Gloucestershire .106-108
34 Cotswolds.................109-120
35 Oxfordshire................121
36 Northampton 122
37 Bedfordshire 123
38 Warwickshire..........124-125
39 Derbyshire 126-128
40 Lincolnshire...................129

E EAST ANGLIA AND REGION
                                    Page No.
41 Essex.....................130-131
42 West Essex 132
43 Cambridgeshire 133-136
44 Suffolk....................137-139
45 Norfolk....................140-145

B SOUTH EAST ENGLAND
                                    Page No.
17 Isle of Wight...................55
18 Hampshire.................56-58
19 West Sussex.................59-64
20 East Sussex.................65-70
21 West Kent...................71-75
22 East Kent....................76-78
23 Berkshire.......................79
24 London 80-83

11

Master location map

Londonderry

Belfast

Dublin

71

70

69

67

64

65

66

68

63

Lewis

62

Harris

Skye

61

Inverness

Aberdeen

60

Fort William

59

Dundee

Mull

Perth

57 Edinburgh

Glasgow

58

56

West Cornwall

Restaurant with rooms, Helford

Riverside

This pair of charming whitewashed cottages in a seductive spot beside a tidal creek has strong echoes of the French country 'auberge', with its flowery terraces, beamed cottagey dining-room and simple but pretty bedrooms. The cooking of previous owner George Perry-Smith enjoyed a wide reputation in the area; the new proprietor Susie Darrell has not yet had sufficient time to acquire the same recognition, but makes good use of local fresh fish and organically grown vegetables. Dinner is at a fixed price despite a wide choice of dishes.

Nearby Glendurgan Garden, one mile (1.5 km); Lizard Peninsula.

Helford, near Helston, Cornwall TR12 6JU
Tel (032623) 443
Location 12 miles (19 km) E of Helston in village; with garden and ample car parking
Food & drink breakfast, dinner; light lunch, picnic by arrangement; restaurant licence
Prices B&B £37.50-£90; dinner £24
Rooms 7 double, all with bath; all rooms have central heating, colour TV
Facilities sitting-room, dining-room
Credit cards not accepted
Children welcome; camp beds, cots and high tea provided – under 10 not allowed at dinner
Disabled access possible but difficult
Pets not accepted
Closed mid-Nov to early Mar
Proprietor Susie Darrell

Country hotel, Mawnan Smith

Nansidwell

A Devon-based hotelier recommends this turn-of-the-century house, long since converted to a hotel but only since 1988 in the hands of Jamie and Felicity Robertson – he an ex-London restauranteur, she an ex-banker. The stone-mullioned house has a glorious setting, in large sub-tropical gardens with the Cornwall Coast Path only a stroll away. To this sound basis the newcomers have added cosy but tasteful traditional decoration, home-like trimmings (plenty of magazines and fresh flowers, constant open fires) and ambitious French cooking.

Nearby Glendurgan Gardens, 1 mile (2 km).

Mawnan Smith, Falmouth, Cornwall TR11 5HU
Tel (0326) 250340
Location 0.5 mile (0.8 km) SW of village, SW of Falmouth; in gardens, with ample car parking
Food & drink breakfast, lunch, dinner; residential and restaurant licence
Prices B&B £37.50-£45; dinner from £17.75
Rooms 12 double, all with bath; all rooms have central heating, colour TV, phone
Facilities 2 sitting-rooms, dining-room, bar; tennis
Credit cards AE, DC, MC, V
Children accepted in small numbers
Disabled access possible – 2 ground-floor bedrooms
Pets accepted in small numbers **Closed** never
Proprietors Jamie and Felicity Robertson

West Cornwall

Town guest-house, Penzance

The Abbey

Jean and Michael Cox have taken a characterful house in the heart of old Penzance (it was built in the mid-17th century and given a Gothic façade in Regency times); they have decorated and furnished it with unstinting care, great flair and a considerable budget; and they have called it an hotel. But they run it much more as a private house, and visitors who expect to find hosts eager to satisfy their every whim are liable to be disappointed. If you poke your head into the kitchen in search of (say) a sandwich, you may or may not find someone able and willing to provide it.

For its fans, the absence of hovering flunkies is of course a key part of the appeal of The Abbey. But there are other attractions – the confident and original decor, with abundant antiques and bric-a-brac; the spacious, individual bedrooms (one with an enormous pine-panelled bathroom); the welcoming, flowery drawing-room and elegant dining-room (both with log fire burning "year-round"); the delightful walled garden behind the house and views of the harbour from the front windows; and, not least, the satisfying, straight-forward dinners (making good use of herbs from The Abbey's own garden).

Nearby Tregwainton Garden, 1.5 miles (2.5 km), St Michael's Mount, 3.5 miles (5.5 km); Land's End, 10 miles (16 km).

Abbey Street, Penzance, Cornwall TR18 4AR
Tel (0736) 66906
Location in middle of town, overlooking harbour; with private parking for 4 cars in courtyard
Food & drink breakfast, dinner; residential and restaurant licence
Prices B&B £27.50-£45; dinner £13.50
Rooms 6 double, 3 with bath, 3 with shower; all rooms have central heating, tea/coffee kit, colour TV
Facilities sitting-room, dining-room
Credit cards not accepted
Children welcome if well behaved **Disabled** access difficult **Pets** dogs allowed in bedrooms
Closed never
Proprietors Jean and Michael Cox

South Cornwall

Old Ferry Inn

"The Fowey estuary is a delightful part of Cornwall, and this is a marvellous place to see it from," says a reporter, summarizing much of the appeal of this 400-year-old inn. It is, in truth, not a place we would be likely to single out if it did not have such a privileged position. But it does. The cosily furnished public rooms give lovely views across the water, and there is much rewarding exploration to be done. Food is fresh, with an emphasis on local seafood. Rooms in the old part of the inn are preferable for charm, those in the modern extension better equipped.

Nearby Polperro, 5 miles (8 km); Looe, Mevagissey.

Bodinnick-by-Fowey, Cornwall PL23 1LY
Tel (072687) 237
Location 13 miles W of Liskeard; with terrace and ample car parking
Food & drink full breakfast, bar lunch, dinner; full licence
Prices B & B £22.50-£28.50; dinner £15
Rooms 12 double, 6 with bath, one with shower; one family room; 10 rooms have TV
Facilities sitting-room, TV room, 2 bars
Credit cards V
Children welcome; cots and high-chairs available
Disabled access difficult
Pets dogs welcome, but not allowed in public rooms
Closed B & B only Nov to Feb
Proprietors Mr K Farr and Mr and Mrs S Farr

Tregony House

The previous owners of this quiet village guest-house built up a considerable reputation for their hospitality and cooking, and for giving excellent value for money. The Marins are refugees from the rat race – he in financial services, she in public relations – who have moved to Tregony with the primary aim of indulging Mario's "flair and passion" for cooking. He has the right ideas – including regional dishes, local produce, herbs fresh from the walled garden – and reports on his four-course dinners, served in the pretty country-style, stone-floored dining-room, continue to be enthusiastic.

Nearby Trelissick Garden, 6 miles (10 km).

Tregony, Truro, Cornwall TR2 5RN
Tel (087253) 671
Location 7 miles (11 km) E of Truro on A3078; with gardens and private parking for 5 cars
Food & drink breakfast, dinner; residential and restaurant licence
Prices DB & B £21.50-£24; reductions for 7 nights or more
Rooms 5 double, one with bath, one with shower; one single
Facilities dining-room, sitting-room, bar
Credit cards not accepted
Children welcome over 7
Disabled access difficult
Pets guide dogs only
Closed Nov to Feb
Proprietors Mario and Verna Marin

South Cornwall

Country hotel, Calstock

Danescombe Valley Hotel

Martin Smith was a quantity surveyor until 1985 when he took over this ailing hotel with his Italian wife Anna; within a couple of years their zeal had the place back on its feet, and they continue to go from strength to strength. The colonial-style house, with first-floor balcony on three sides, has a splendid wooded position overlooking a bend in the River Tamar. The Smiths have completed the process of upgrading the furnishings, sticking to antiques and traditional styles. From the start Anna has set high standards in the kitchen, producing adventurous and satisfying no-choice four-course dinners. The Smiths' involvement with their hotel is total – they reckon to be on first-name terms with 95 per cent of their guests.

Nearby Cotehele House; Morwelham Quay, 4 miles (6 km).

Lower Kelly, Calstock,
Cornwall PL18 9RY
Tel (0822) 832414
Location 0.5 mile (0.8 km)
W of Calstock; with private
parking for 3 cars and
further parking in quiet
lane
Food & drink breakfast,
dinner; residential and
restaurant licence
Prices DB&B £44–£64.50
Rooms 5 double, all with

bath and shower; all rooms
have central heating
Facilities sitting-room, bar,
dining-room
Credit cards not accepted
Children welcome over 12
Disabled access difficult
Pets accepted in grounds
and guests' cars
Closed Nov to Mar; Wed,
Thu
Proprietors Martin and
Anna Smith.

South Cornwall

Coombe Farm

Within two years of quitting the world of a Fleet Street photographer and picture editor in 1979, Alex Low and his wife Sally had transformed run-down Coombe Farm into an award-winning guest house. They offer a thoroughly comfortable house, a friendly welcome, country cooking, and spacious rooms at prices families can afford. But the ace in their hand is the setting of Coombe Farm; its 10 acres give young and old plenty of space to amuse themselves swimming, lounging, playing croquet or cricket, exploring the woods or admiring the ducks, goats and other livestock.

Nearby Looe, Liskeard and Plymouth.

Widegates, near Looe, Cornwall, PL13 1QN
Tel (05034) 223
Location 4 miles (6 km) NE of Looe, on B3253; parking for 12 cars
Food & drink breakfast, dinner; residential and restaurant licence
Prices B&B £14.50-£18.50; dinner £10.50; reductions for children sharing parents' room; reductions for more than 2 nights
Rooms 3 double, 5 family; all rooms have central heating, tea/coffee kit; 6 have colour TV
Facilities sitting-rooms, dining-room, games room; heated outdoor swimming-pool, croquet
Credit cards not accepted
Children welcome over age 5 if well-behaved **Disabled** access easy **Pets** not accepted
Closed Nov to Feb
Proprietor Alexander Low

Trelaske

Although long-established as a guest-house, Trelaske has only recently taken on its present form, through the addition to the original brick farmhouse of a bar and 50-seat restaurant. The former is cosily old-world, the latter more elegant. Bedrooms are spotlessly clean and modern, with duvets and harmonising colour schemes. An acre of the gardens is given over to vegetables for the restaurant, where a reasonable range of conventional dishes is served. The Rawlings' printed tariff does not include VAT.

Nearby Polperro, 3 miles (5 km).

Polperro Road, Looe, Cornwall PL13 2JS
Tel (05036) 2159
Location 2 miles (3 km) W of Looe by A387; in gardens with parking for 30 cars
Food & drink breakfast, dinner; residential and restaurant licence
Prices B&B £17.25-£23; dinner £14
Rooms 4 double, one with bath, 3 with shower; all rooms have TV, tea/coffee kit
Facilities sitting-room with bar, dining-room
Credit cards MC, V
Children welcome **Disabled** easy ramp access to dining-room only **Pets** not accepted
Closed never
Proprietors Roger and Sylvia Rawlings

South Cornwall

Country house hotel, Tregrehan

Boscundle Manor

It is over a decade now since the Flints swapped their metropolitan existence for the different challenge of running this largely 18th-century house, but they still exude enthusiasm, still attend as carefully as ever to the needs of guests, still find time to tend the large terraced garden themselves. Mary is the chef, and her daily changing menu of simple but imaginative dishes (with the emphasis on fish) is an important ingredient in the Boscundle recipe. The wine list is long and interesting, too.

The delight of the place is its happy informality – the house is the Flints' home, with assorted furniture (some luxurious modern, some stripped pine, some elegant antiques) rather than a consistently applied formula. There are pictures, flowers, books everywhere – the bar houses Mary's extensive picture postcard collection.

Nearby Fowey, 5 miles (8 km); Restormel Castle and Gardens, 6 miles (10 km); Lanhydrock House, 7 miles (11 km).

Tregrehan, St Austell, Cornwall PL25 3RL
Tel (072681) 3557
Location 2.5 miles (4 km) E of St Austell, close to A390; in 10-acre woodland gardens; ample car parking
Food & drink full breakfast, light lunches and snacks, dinner; residential licence
Prices B & B £35-£90; dinner £17.50; reductions for 3 nights or more
Rooms 9 double, 6 with bath (5 with spa bath), 3 with shower; 2 single, both with shower; all rooms have central heating, colour TV with Teletext, phone, radio/alarm
Facilities 2 sitting-rooms, bar, 2 dining-rooms, conservatory/breakfast room, exercise room, heated outdoor swimming- pool, croquet, practice golf holes
Credit cards AE, MC, V
Children welcome **Disabled** access difficult to house, but access easy to bungalow in grounds
Pets accepted by arrangement, but not allowed in public rooms
Closed mid-Oct to mid-Apr
Proprietors A. and M. Flint

North Cornwall

Reeds

Margaret Jackson runs this Edwardian house practically single-handed, so it is scarcely surprising that it is usually open to visitors only four nights a week. Mrs Jackson is a woman of rare charm and enthusiasm, and has created a captivating atmosphere in her house – beautifully and elegantly furnished, immaculately kept and yet warmly inviting. The big gardens are a delight, the meals (based on the finest ingredients) excellent.
Nearby Coastal walks.

Poughill, Bude, Cornwall
EX23 9EL
Tel (0288) 2841
Location one mile (1.5 km)
NE of Bude just off A39; in
4-acre garden with adequate
car parking
Food & drink full breakfast,
light lunch, dinner;
residential licence
Prices B & B £30-£35; dinner
£17.50
Rooms 3 double, all with
bath and shower; all rooms
have hairdrier, tea/coffee kit

Facilities sitting-room with
drinks cabinet, study with
TV, dining-room
Credit cards not accepted
Children not accepted
Disabled not suitable – steps
to front door and no ground-
floor bedrooms
Pets may sleep in car
Closed Tue to Fri each week,
Christmas Day
Proprietor Margaret
Jackson

Old Millfloor

A steep path is the only access to this converted mill, situated (naturally) by a stream amid gardens, orchards and paddocks. It has been in Janice Waddon-Martyn's family since the early 1960s, and her home since the 1970s. Janice runs the house with the help of her daughter, and succeeds admirably in giving her guests a relaxing 'away from it all' stay. She adores cooking for her guests, and likes nothing better than to be told of their preferences so that she can be sure her creations will be enjoyed. You are welcome – indeed, exhorted – to take your own wine. Bedrooms are neat and pretty, with high beamed ceilings. Families are welcome.
Nearby Tintagel Castle, 2 miles (3 km); Bodmin Moor.

Trebarwith Strand,
Tintagel, Cornwall PL34 0HA
Tel (0840) 770234
Location 2 miles (3 km) S of
Tintagel on B3263; in
10-acre grounds with ample
car parking
Food & drink full breakfast,
tea, dinner; no licence
Prices B & B £13.50; dinner
£9.50
Rooms 3 double; all rooms

have TV, hairdrier
Facilities sitting-room,
dining-room
Credit cards not accepted
Children welcome
Disabled access difficult
Pets welcome by prior
arrangement; not allowed on
beds
Closed Dec to Feb
Proprietor Janice Waddon-
Martyn

West Devon

Country house hotel, Clawton

Court Barn

Robert and Susan Wood are old hands at running small hotels, but fairly new to Court Barn, which is a four-square Victorian country house – the 'barn' is a corruption of 'baron'. The spacious house is handsomely furnished with a mixture of antiques and modern styles, and the Woods have set about redecorating the bedrooms in William Morris prints.

Nearby Bude, 10 miles (16 km); Dartmoor within reach.

Clawton, Holsworthy, Devon EX22 6PS
Tel (040927) 219
Location 3 miles (5 km) S of Holsworthy, close to A388; with ample car parking
Food & drink full breakfast, bar lunch, tea, dinner, full lunch on Sun; residential and restaurant licence
Prices B&B £23-£25; dinner £15; reductions for children sharing parents' room
Rooms 7 double, 5 with bath, 2 with shower; one single with bath; all rooms have central heating, TV, phone, radio, tea/coffee kit, hairdrier; trouser-press on request
Facilities 2 sitting-rooms, bar, dining-room, sun-lounges, games room, TV room; croquet, gymnasium, solarium, badminton, putting, chip and putt
Credit cards AE, DC, MC, V
Children welcome; cot available **Disabled** access easy to public rooms **Pets** dogs, but not in public rooms
Closed 2 weeks in Jan
Proprietors S. and R. Wood

Restaurant with rooms, Gulworthy

Horn of Plenty

Until 1985 satisfied diners who, like Sonia Stevenson herself, 'do not like 'nouvelle cuisine', had to stagger elsewhere to recover from her sumptuous meals. The rooms which were added then can scarcely be called luxurious or even stylish, but they are bright and comfortable. The terrace (with some dining tables) and garden are a delight, with long views.

Nearby Cotehele House, 3 miles (5 km); Dartmoor.

Gulworthy, Tavistock, Devon PL19 8JD
Tel (0822) 832528
Location 3 miles (2 km) W of Tavistock on A390; ample car parking
Food & drink breakfast, lunch (except Thu, Fri), dinner; residential and restaurant licence
Prices B&B £31-£57.50; dinner £21-£32.50
Rooms 6 double, 4 with bath, 2 with shower; all rooms have central heating, phone, radio, TV, minibar, hairdrier, tea kit
Facilities conference room, dining-room
Credit cards AE, MC, V
Children welcome by arrangement
Disabled access easy – one bedroom for wheelchair, 4 ground-floor bedrooms
Pets accepted by arrangement
Closed Christmas Day, Boxing Day
Proprietors Sonia and Patrick Stevenson

South Devon

Manor house hotel, Dittisham

Fingals

Richard Johnston was already running a successful restaurant called Fingals (in London's Fulham Road) when he took on the restoration of this farm manor house in a secluded valley close to the River Dart. He styles it as a "hotel and restaurant", but anyone expecting a conventional example of either animal would be in for a surprise – in practice, Fingals comes much closer to the 'country house party' type of guest-house, where it is normal (though not necessary) for guests to share a big table at dinner, with any social ice melted by house wine.

The house – 17thC with Queen Anne front additions – has plenty of charm, and has been stylishly done out with a successful blend of new and old furniture, pine and mahogany. In 1988 it was sympathetically extended, adding 5 bedrooms. It is an exceptionally relaxed place – you pour your own drinks, eat breakfast whenever you like – and those who insist on everything being just so are likely to be disappointed. The four-course dinners chosen from a short menu are modern in style, competent in execution, and ample in quantity.

Nearby Dartmouth Castle, 3 miles (5 km).

Old Coombe Manor Farm, Dittisham, near Dartmouth, Devon TQ6 0JA
Tel (080422) 398
Location 4 miles (6 km) N of Dartmouth, one mile (1.5 km) from village; with garden and ample car parking
Food & drink breakfast, snack lunch, dinner; residential and restaurant licence
Prices B&B £27-£32; dinner £16; reductions for 3 nights or more **Rooms** 10 double, 9 with bath, one with shower; one family room, with bath; all rooms have central heating, phone, radio/alarm, tea/coffee kit; TV on request
Facilities dining-room, bar, library, TV room; swimming-pool, jacuzzi, snooker, croquet, tennis, wind-surfing **Credit cards** DC, MC, V
Children welcome if well behaved **Disabled** access difficult **Pets** accepted if well behaved, but not allowed in public rooms
Closed New Year to Easter
Proprietor Richard Johnston

Dartmoor

Bed and breakfast guest-house, Bovey Tracey

Willmead Farm

You might expect to see rabbits wearing aprons outside this idyllic thatched stone farmhouse, set in a quiet green valley on the eastern fringes of Dartmoor. But the human welcome is warm enough from Hilary Roberts, who has been running Willmead as a far-above-average bed-and-breakfast place for more than a decade. The 14thC building has been beautifully restored, to reveal a wealth of oak beams and vast open fireplaces, and there is antique furniture to match. For dinner, visitors are sent by private woodland footpath to the pretty village of Lustleigh, or to one of the nearby hotels – but you will find home-made breads and preserves on the breakfast table. The dining-room is something of a knock-out.

Nearby Lustleigh; Newton Abbot, 5 miles (8 km); Dartmoor.

Bovey Tracey, near Newton Abbot, Devon TQ13 9NP
Tel (06477) 214
Location 2 miles (3 km) NW of Bovey Tracey, off A382
Food & drink full breakfast
Prices B&B £17
Rooms 3 double, one with bath; all rooms have central heating
Facilities sitting-room, dining-room
Credit cards not accepted
Children accepted over 10
Disabled not suitable
Pets must sleep in cars
Closed Christmas, New Year
Proprietor Mrs H Roberts

Inn, Doddiscombsleigh

Nobody Inn

What marks this out from other charming Devon country inns is its consistently impressive hospitality – excellent snacks, including many local cheeses, served quickly and cheerfully in the cosy bars (along with a range of real ales and 200 whiskies), wholesome fresh-cooked meals and a staggering choice of wines in the traditional dining-room. The Nobody has freshly decorated cottagey bedrooms above – with much bigger rooms available in the Town Barton, a Georgian-style manor house in the same ownership, 150 yards away.

Nearby Dartmoor, south Devon coast.

Doddiscombsleigh, near Exeter, Devon EX6 7PS
Tel (0647) 52394
Location 6 miles (10 km) SW of Exeter, close to B3193; in 8-acre grounds with parking for 50 cars
Food & drink breakfast, bar lunch, bar supper, dinner (except Sun and Mon); full licence
Prices B&B £11-£25; dinner £10; reduction for 4 nights or more
Rooms 6 double, 2 with bath and shower, 4 with shower only; one single; all rooms have phone, tea/coffee kit; TV on request
Facilities sitting-room, bar, restaurant
Credit cards MC, V
Children not accepted
Disabled access fairly easy – only one step to entrance and one ground-floor bedroom
Pets not accepted
Closed never
Proprietor N F Borst-Smith

Dartmoor

Gidleigh Park

The Hendersons, Americans with no previous experience of running hotels, aim to provide nothing but the best; and over the years they have polished the interior of this Edwardian mock-Tudor house, in a privileged wooded setting, to the point where its combination of comfort and informal elegance is more-or-less unmatched. Service is meant to be 'always friendly and enthusiastic, sometimes efficient', and it works. The eclectic food, naturally, is wonderful, wines run to 400 bins plus 250 bin-ends.

Nearby Castle Drogo, 3 miles (5 km); Dartmoor.

Chagford, Devon TQ13 8HH	TV, radio, hairdrier
Tel (06473) 2367	**Facilities** sitting-room, bar
Location 2 miles (3 km) NW	and loggia, 2 dining-rooms;
of Chagford, in 40 acre	croquet, fishing, tennis
grounds with ample car	**Credit cards** MC, V
parking	**Children** welcome only if
Food & drink breakfast,	adult in behaviour
lunch, dinner; restaurant	**Disabled** no special facilities
and residential licence	**Pets** welcome
Prices DB&B £62.50-£190	**Closed** never
Rooms 14 double, all with	**Proprietors** Paul and Kay
bath, 10 also with shower; all	Henderson
rooms have central heating,	

Oxenham Arms

This granite inn has been serving the needs of the visitor since at least the 15thC. Plumbing and wiring apart, the building has changed little since Tudor times, with its wealth of mullions, flagstones, dark panelling and oak beams. The Henrys, who have been here since the early 1970s, have kept the inn well furnished, in keeping with its age, and take pride in offering a wide range of fresh local produce including trout, salmon, pheasant and venison. There is a pretty half-acre garden at the back.

Nearby Okehampton Castle; Dartmoor.

South Zeal, near	**Rooms** 8 double, 6 with bath,
Okehampton,	3 also with shower; all rooms
Devon EX20 2JT	have colour TV, telephone,
Tel (0837) 840244	tea/coffee kit
Location 4 miles (6 km) E of	**Facilities** bar with family
Okehampton, just off A30,	room, dining-room, sitting-
in middle of village; with	room
garden at rear, and adequate	**Credit cards** AE, DC, MC, V
car parking in forecourt	**Children** welcome **Disabled**
Food & drink breakfast,	access difficult **Pets** welcome
lunch, tea, dinner; full	**Closed** never
licence	**Proprietors** Mr and Mrs
Prices B&B £18-£34.50;	James H Henry
dinner from £11.50	

Dartmoor

Country house hotel, Chagford

Teignworthy

The Newells don't rely for custom only on the privileged outlook of their solid, Lutyens-style house – across a lush valley to the rolling edge of Dartmoor. They give it a warm, welcoming aura, with log fires in the hall and in the friendly sitting-room. Bedrooms are prettily and comfortably furnished (three of them across the courtyard in the Hayloft). In good weather the terrace and sloping garden are delightful places to idle away time, and the grass tennis court is well maintained; in case of rain, there are abundant books to browse through (there are also classical and jazz records).

Even former weak spots have reportedly been put right – the bar and dining-room have been refurbished in a fresh scheme of willow green and apple white.

Food is a strong point. John Newell shares the kitchen with David Woolfall, and the team produces impressive results in ambitious, modern French style (though plainer dishes are available if you prefer). Breakfast can now be had on the terrace, and the orange juice is fresh.

Nearby Castle Drogo, 4 miles (6.5 km); Dartmoor; Exeter and Newton Abbot within easy reach.

Frenchbeer, Chagford, Devon TQ13 8EX
Tel (06473) 3355
Location 3 miles (5 km) SW of Chagford; in 14-acre gardens and woodland, with ample car parking
Food & drink breakfast, lunch, dinner; restaurant and residential licence
Prices B&B £39-£45; DB&B £63.50-£69.50; bargain breaks
Rooms 9 double, 6 with bath, 3 with sunken bath; 2 rooms share a sitting-room; all rooms have central heating, colour TV, phone, radio; tea/coffee kit on request
Facilities dining-room, bar, sitting-room; sauna, solarium, tennis, croquet; helipad
Credit cards MC, V
Children welcome over 12; under 12 by arrangement
Disabled access not easy, but staircase is gradual
Pets dogs must stay in cars; kennels can be arranged
Closed never
Proprietors John and Gillian Newell

East Devon

Huntsham Court

This isn't the only place in these pages where all the guests eat at one table; but it is the only one where as many as 24 guests do so. It is also the only hotel in which the one piece of equipment in every bedroom is a pre-war wireless; or which has a music room where guests have the run of 3,000 recordings. It is not an ordinary hotel.

Mogens and Andrea Bolwig (he Danish, she Greek-Australian) are not ordinary people. Mogens bought the imposing Victorian Gothic house in 1978 when it was verging on ruin. The two of them subsequently invested all they possessed in its restoration, going out of their way to preserve the period feel of the house while building in modern comforts – the grandest bathroom does not have a jacuzzi but two freestanding Victorian tubs.

Huntsham Court is enormously enjoyable if its slightly eccentric flavour appeals to you. But it won't suit perfectionists, nor those who expect to be waited on hand and foot – you serve your own drinks, writing down your consumption as you go. It may be that parties who take over the whole place get the best out of it. Food is entirely in character – traditional English, with no choice.

Nearby Knightshayes Court, 3 miles (5 km), Tiverton Castle, 5 miles (8 km); Exmoor; Exe valley.

Huntsham, near Bampton, Devon EX16 7NA
Tel (03986) 210
Location 5 miles (8 km) NE of Tiverton, in middle of village; with car parking
Food & drink full breakfast, dinner; children's meal served in butler's pantry; residential licence
Prices B&B £37-£65; dinner £20
Rooms 15 double, all with bath and shower; all rooms have central heating, radio
Facilities dining-room, sitting-room, library, music room, bar, Great Hall; sauna, mini-gym, table-tennis, croquet, billiards, tennis, shooting, riding, fishing
Credit cards AE, V
Children welcome by arrangement **Disabled** access difficult **Pets** not accepted
Closed never
Proprietors M. and A. Bolwig

East Devon

Manor house hotel, Gittisham

Combe House

When they came here in 1970, John Boswell (direct descendant of 'the' Boswell) and his wife Thérèse faced the massive task of refurbishing the imposing Elizabethan manor from scratch. They have made it an exceptionally comfortable, quiet and spacious hotel in the grand maner, with moulded ceilings, panelled walls and Chippendale furniture. Thérèse oversees the young and enthusiastic chefs with a trained eye – and is also responsible for the murals which grace some of the public rooms.
Nearby Cadhay House, 4 miles (6 km); south Devon coast.

Gittisham, near Honiton, Devon EX14 0AD **Tel** (0404) 42756 **Location** one mile (1.5 km) SW of Honiton off A30; ample car parking **Food & drink** full breakfast, bar lunch, tea, dinner, full lunch Sun; restaurant & residential licence **Prices** B&B £36.50-£75; dinner from £17.50; reductions for children sharing parents' room; winter breaks Nov to Mar	**Rooms** 12 double, all with bath; all rooms have central heating, colour TV, phone **Facilities** bar, sitting-rooms, 2 dining-rooms; fishing **Credit cards** AE, DC, MC, V **Children** welcome; special supper facilities **Disabled** access easy to ground floor only **Pets** welcome, but not allowed in public rooms **Closed** 2nd week Jan to end Feb **Proprietors** John and Thérèse Boswell

Country house hotel, Whimple

Woodhayes

Antiques, oil paintings, prints and fabrics of high quality characterize the public rooms of this gracious Georgian house, while the bedrooms (some of them exceptionally large) are individually decorated, mainly in Victorian or Edwardian style, and equipped with every conceivable extra. A professional chef cooks delectable dishes to order, using home-grown herbs and vegetables. Prices are quite high now, and one of our reporters wishes for less hush and more hubbub in the dining-room – but that has not stopped her going back.
Nearby Cadhay House, 3 miles (5 km); Exe valley.

Whimple, near Exeter, Devon EX5 2TD **Tel** (0404) 822237 **Location** 9 miles (14.5 km) NE of Exeter, close to A30; in 3-acre grounds with parking for 20 cars **Food & drink** breakfast, dinner; lunch by arrangement; residential and restaurant licence **Prices** B&B £35-£55; dinner £19; reduced DB&B rates	for 3 nights or more **Rooms** 7 double, all with bath; all rooms have central heating, TV, phone, radio **Facilities** 2 sitting-rooms, dining-room; croquet, tennis **Credit cards** AE, DC, MC, V **Children** welcome over 12 **Disabled** access difficult **Pets** not accepted **Closed** Jan **Proprietors** Katherine and Frank Rendle

West Dorset

Country house hotel, Evershot

Summer Lodge

The Corbetts are the living evidence that not all 'professional' hoteliers are mediocre; we don't know what contribution they made to guests' happiness when they were at the Savoy, but the dedication and talent they have applied to that cause since they escaped to Dorset is remarkable indeed.

For many visitors, Summer Lodge is all that a country house hotel should be. The Georgian/Victorian building is on just the right scale to give a sense of slight extravagance without being intimidating, and the Corbetts are masters at making guests feel instantly at home in it. French windows lead from the public rooms (William Morris fabrics, open fires) to the beautiful flowery garden – and Margaret's professional flower arrangements are a special feature of the charming bedrooms.

Margaret Corbett now has assistance in the preparation of her four-course dinners, mainly traditional Anglo-French in style, highly successful in execution, no choice except of dessert.

Nearby Minterne Gardens, 6 miles (10 km), Mapperton Gardens, 6 miles (10 km), Parnham House, 6 miles (10 km).

Summer Lane, Evershot, Dorset DT2 0JR
Tel (0935) 83424
Location 8 miles (13 km) S of Yeovil, off A37 on edge of village; with ample car parking
Food & drink full breakfast, lunch, dinner; residential and restaurant licence
Prices B&B £40-£60; DB&B £60-£85; reductions for 2 nights or more and for children sharing parents' room
Rooms 8 double, 3 single, one family room, 6 suites, all with bath; all rooms have central heating, phone, tea/coffee kit, hairdrier; all suites have TV
Facilities dining-room, sitting-room, bar, TV room; croquet, outdoor heated swimming-pool, tennis
Credit cards MC, V
Children welcome over 8
Disabled access good to ground-floor bedrooms
Pets dogs welcome by arrangement
Closed first 2 weeks Jan
Proprietors Nigel and Margaret Corbett

West Dorset

Hams Plot

Hams Plot, a Regency villa with a strong French influence in its architecture, is Giles Dearlove's family home, to which he and Judy moved back in 1980. For fine days there are large, secluded grounds with a swimming-pool – and a sunny veranda for tea or pre-dinner drinks. For the not-so-fine days, a comfortable library, with books and maps of the area, as well as an airy sitting-room, dotted with antiques and water colours.

Nearby Parnham House, Mapperton Gardens, 1.5 miles (2.5 km); Kingcombe Meadows, 3 miles (5 km).

Beaminster, Dorset DT8 3LU
Tel (0308) 862979
Location on S edge of Beaminster just off A3066; ample car parking
Food & drink full breakfast, dinner by arrangement 4 days a week; residential licence
Prices B&B £18-£26; dinner £13.50; 5% reduction for 3 nights or more, 10% for a week or more

Rooms 5 double, 3 with bath, 2 with shower; all rooms have central heating, tea/coffee kit
Facilities sitting-room, library, bar; swimming-pool, tennis, croquet
Credit cards not accepted
Children welcome over 10
Disabled access not easy
Pets not accepted
Closed Nov to Mar, except Christmas
Proprietors J and G Dearlove

The Manor Hotel

Unlike the proprietors of most other Manors, Richard and Jayne Childs have not striven for elegance or richness in their decorations; in character with the farmhouse-style of this inn-cum-hotel-cum-restaurant (which dates from the 15th and 16th centuries but is partly Victorian) they have aimed for the warmth of a private home. Bedrooms are neat and bright, and the dining-room retains its stone-flagged floor. The 'cellar' bar is actually on a lower-ground floor, opening on to the big garden (via a new 'Victorian' conservatory) with children's play area.

Nearby Abbotsbury Gardens, 2.5 miles (4 km).

West Bexington, Dorchester, Dorset DT2 9DF
Tel (0308) 897616
Location 5.5 miles (9 km) SE of Bridport, close to B3157; in 3.5-acre grounds with ample car parking
Food & drink breakfast, lunch, dinner, bar snacks; full licence
Prices B&B £23.50-£31.95; dinner £14.95
Rooms 10 double, 6 with bath, 4 with shower; all

rooms have central heating, colour TV, tea/coffee kit
Facilities sitting-room, bar, dining-room, skittle alley, conference room, function room
Credit cards AE, MC, V
Children welcome
Disabled access difficult
Pets not accepted
Closed Christmas
Proprietors Richard and Jayne Childs

West Dorset

Country house hotel, Maiden Newton

Maiden Newton House

'Breakfast served when you are ready,' is the rule here, summing up the approach that Bryan and Elizabeth Ferriss take to their guests – which is to attend personally and carefully to your every need. They opened their doors only in 1985, but settled immediately into their stride.

Maiden Newton House is very firmly a non-hotel. You are entertained as friends visiting a private house: guests foregather in the library for pre-prandial drinks, and proceed to dine at one table with the Ferrisses on the stroke of 8pm. Elizabeth's eclectic menus offer no choice until the pudding, but adjustments can be made if necessary; you are not obliged to take dinner, and there are good restaurants within driving distance.

The house is a Victorian reconstruction of a much older dwelling, and has a distinctly medieval look. It is richly and tastefully furnished, with abundant antiques, and each of the inviting bedrooms decorated in an individual style. The only distractions are the sounds of agriculture and worship – the village church is next door.

Nearby Cerne Abbas, 5 miles (8 km), Mapperton Gardens, 6 miles (10 km), Minterne Gardens, 6 miles (10 km), Dorchester, 7 miles (11 km).

Maiden Newton, near Dorchester, Dorset DT2 0AA
Tel (0300) 20336
Location 7 miles (11 km) NW of Dorchester, close to A356; in 2-acre garden and 9 acres of parkland, with ample car parking
Food & drink full breakfast, tea, dinner; full licence
Prices B&B £35-£70; dinner £20
Rooms 5 double, all with bath; all rooms have central heating, TV, hairdrier, trouser-press
Facilities library with TV/video, sitting-room, dining-room; fishing, croquet
Credit cards MC, V
Children accepted, but under 12 not allowed at dinner **Disabled** access easy to ground floor, but no ground-floor bedrooms
Pets accepted, but not allowed in public rooms
Closed mid-Dec to mid-Feb
Proprietors Bryan and Elizabeth Ferriss

East Dorset

Country house hotel, Gillingham

Stock Hill House

This restored Victorian manor house, reached up a long drive through wooded grounds, has been beautifully furnished and decorated, with many of the Hausers' personal possessions in evidence. Sanderson and Baker designs abound, although each of the luxurious bedrooms is individual in style. The public rooms, too, are full of character and charm.

But your lasting memory of Stock Hill House is more likely to be of the Hausers' boundless enthusiasm and obvious delight in their work. Peter does all the cooking and produces superb results. His Austrian roots are reflected in the menu, which changes daily. Fruit and vegetables come from Peter's own immaculate walled kitchen garden. While he works away in the kitchen, guests pop in for a chat or to see what he is planning for dinner that evening. Before the evening meal, Chef Hauser draws his guests together before the grand fireplace in the entrance hall by playing his zither: thus begins an evening of good food and wine, hosted by a charming couple. Ties must be worn at dinner.

Nearby Shaftesbury, 5 miles (8 km), Stourhead House and gardens, 6 miles (10 km); Salisbury, Longleat within reach.

Wyke, Gillingham, Dorset SP8 5NR
Tel (0747) 823626
Location 5 miles (8 km) NW of Shaftesbury on B3081; in 10-acre grounds with ample car parking
Food & drink breakfast, lunch, dinner; restaurant licence
Prices DB&B £55-£90
Rooms 5 double, 4 with bath (2 also with shower), one with shower; 2 singles, one with bath, one with shower; all rooms have central heating, radio, colour TV, phone, alarm clock, hairdrier, trouser-press
Facilities sitting-room, dining-room, breakfast room; indoor swimming-pool, croquet (all Easter to Oct)
Credit cards MC, V
Children welcome over 5 if well behaved **Disabled** access difficult, no ground-floor bedrooms
Pets not accepted
Closed middle two weeks Nov
Proprietors Peter and Nita Hauser

East Dorset

Plumber Manor

This Jacobean manor house, 'modernized' earlier this century, has been in the Prideaux-Brune family for well over 300 years. Since 1973 they have been running it as a restaurant with rooms, with six comfortable bedrooms; and in 1982 the conversion of a stone barn 100 yds away provided a further six, even more spacious rooms. The owner's brother Brian produces highly regarded food. Casual dress and house-keeping have disappointed some reporters in the past.

Nearby Purse Caundle Manor, 6 miles (10 km).

Hazelbury Bryan Road, Sturminster Newton, Dorset DT10 2AF
Tel (0258) 72507
Location 2 miles (3 km) SW of Sturminster Newton; private car parking
Food & drink full breakfast, dinner; full licence
Prices B&B £30-£60; dinner £17-£20; 10% reduction for 7 nights or more
Rooms 10 double, one with bath, 9 with bath and shower; 2 single, both with bath and shower; all rooms have central heating, TV, phone, tea/coffee kit
Facilities dining-room, sitting-room, bar; croquet, tennis
Credit cards MC, V
Children welcome over 12
Disabled easy access to stable-block bedrooms and dining-room **Pets** not accepted
Closed first 2 weeks Feb
Proprietor Richard Prideaux-Brune

Kemps

Though the bedrooms of this solid Victorian rectory are prettily decorated and spacious (and those in the converted coach house quiet), and there are attractive sitting-rooms, the popularity of the dining-room gives the place a restaurant-with-rooms feel. The limited-choice dinner menu changes daily and is competently executed, and there is a richly French 'carte' at lunch and dinner too. A regular visitor sums it up: 'excellent food, helpful staff, remarkable value for money'.

Nearby Corfe Castle, 5.5 miles (9 km); Isle of Purbeck.

East Stoke, Wareham, Dorset BH20 6AL
Tel (0929) 462563
Location 2.5 miles (4 km) W of Wareham on A352; in 1.5-acre gardens with ample car parking
Food & drink full breakfast, lunch, dinner; restaurant and residential licence
Prices B&B £28.50-£35; DB&B £38.50-£45; dinner from £12; bargain breaks
Rooms 4 double, 3 with bath, one with shower; one single; 4 family rooms 2 with bath, 2 with shower; all rooms have central heating, colour TV, phone, tea/coffee kit
Facilities 2 sitting-rooms, bar, dining-room
Credit cards AE, DC, MC, V
Children welcome
Disabled access reasonable – ground-floor bedrooms, wide doorways
Pets not accepted
Closed Dec 10 to Jan 10
Proprietors Paul and Gill Warren

North Devon

Whitechapel Manor

Whitechapel is a new hotel (opened at the end of 1897), but one which could have been going for years, so sure is its style. The secret is that until they bought the house in 1984, the Shaplands took guests in their farmhouse at nearby Kerscott. They have brought to this much grander Elizabethan manor house the qualities of the British guest-house at its best – the emphasis is on comfort and hospitality, not on appearances and ceremony. Which is not to say that the house lacks visual style – on the contrary, it is richly furnished with great taste (and at great expense). Food is 'modern French', professionally prepared.
Nearby Exmoor.

South Molton, Devon
EX36 3EG
Tel (07695) 3377
Location 3 miles (5 km) E of South Molton, one mile from A361; with car parking
Food & drink full breakfast, lunch, dinner; restaurant licence
Prices B&B £33.75-£93.75; dinner £22.50
Rooms 9 double, one single; all with bath and shower; all rooms have central heating, colour TV, radio, hairdrier
Facilities sitting-room, bar, dining-room; croquet
Credit cards MC, V
Children accepted by arrangement **Disabled** access difficult **Pets** accepted on lead in grounds only
Closed never **Proprietors** John and Patricia Shapland

The Whiteleaf

The Wallingtons built a high reputation for themselves as pro-prietors of the Rhydspence Inn at Whitney-on-Wye (see page 105), which they left in 1986 to revamp this unremarkable but pleasant and spacious 1930s guest-house. Sticklers may find it thin on charm, but there is no shortage of comfort or of hospitality. The garden is a peaceful retreat from the lively seaside village of Croyde (which has an excellent beach). What's more, David's cooking goes from strength to strength – English/Continental, some original dishes, regularly changing menus.
Nearby Exmoor, Lundy Island.

Croyde, Nr Braunton, Devon EX33 1PN
Tel (0271) 890266
Location quarter of a mile (400m) SW of village, on B3231; with car parking
Food & drink breakfast, dinner; residential licence
Prices B&B £19.50-£27; DB&B £29-£42
Rooms 4 double, 3 with bath, 4 with shower; one family room with bath and shower; all rooms have central heating, TV, radio, alarm, hairdrier, tea/coffee kit, minibar
Facilities bar, sitting-room, dining-room
Credit cards MC, V
Children welcome – but not special meals
Disabled not suitable
Pets welcome
Closed never
Proprietors David and Flo Wallington

North Devon

Country house hotel, Bishop's Tawton

Downrew House

Desmond and Aleta Ainsworth were ahead of their time when, in the mid-1960s, they left London to create Downrew, and if the hotel has a flaw it is the rather dated look of some of its furnishings. But the new owners have already carried out extensive refurbishment (more improvements are planned for the bedrooms), and for many regular visitors this much-modified 17thC house approaches the ideal as a relaxing holiday hotel – spacious rooms both private and public (a grand piano in the library, off the sitting-room), lush secluded gardens, a range of sports facilities (the pool is particularly attractive – and warm), excellent 'cordon bleu'-style cooking.

Nearby Tapeley Park House and Gardens, 5 miles (8 km); Exmoor.

Bishop's Tawton, Devon
EX32 0DY
Tel (0271) 42497
Location 1.5 miles (2.5 km) SE of Barnstaple off A377; in 12 -acre grounds with ample car parking
Food & drink full breakfast, light or packed lunch, dinner; residential and restaurant licence
Prices DB&B £47-£65; reductions for 2 nights or more
Rooms 12 double, 2 family rooms; all with bath and shower; all rooms have central heating, colour TV,

radio, phone
Facilities sitting-room, bar, billiard room, card room, games room; solarium, outdoor heated swimming-pool, tennis, croquet, 15-hole golf 'approach' course
Credit cards MC, V
Children accepted from 7
Disabled reasonable access – 3 ground-floor bedrooms, wheel-chairs difficult but possible **Pets** accepted by arrangement
Closed Jan
Proprietors J and M Spencer, A and S Middleton

North Devon

Country house hotel, Combe Martin

Coulsworthy

The Anthony family, consisting of Mr and Mrs Anthony, their daughter and her husband aim 'to provide the relaxed and welcoming atmosphere of a friendly house party' in their largely Georgian house, high on the western extremity of Exmoor with fine views down to the sea. They hit the target convincingly and enjoy many return visits from well-satisfied guests. Alison Osmond is in charge of the kitchen, and plans her satisfying menus around locally bought ingredients.

Nearby Arlington Court, 3 miles (5 km).

Combe Martin, Devon, EX34 0PD
Tel (027188) 2463
Location 2.5 miles (4 km) SE of Combe Martin, close to A399; parking for 15 cars
Food & drink breakfast, dinner, residential and restaurant licence
Prices B&B £26-£35; DB&B £31-£52; reductions for children
Rooms 8 double, 5 with bath, 2 with shower, one single; one family room with bath, all rooms have central heating
Facilities sitting-room, bar, restaurant, heated swimming-pool, croquet, tennis
Credit cards MC, V
Children welcome
Disabled access difficult
Pets dogs accepted
Closed mid-Dec to early Feb
Managers Anthony family

Country hotel, Ilfracombe

Langleigh

This 400-year old house in lush gardens, taken over by the Crawfords only a couple of years ago, offers a relaxing and civilized oasis, only a short walk from Ilfracombe seafront, and with its large bedrooms successfully meets the needs of the families who are its obvious market. The emphasis in the kitchen is on quality ingredients simply cooked; vegetarians, vegans and other special diets are catered for.

Nearby Chambercombe Manor, 0.75 miles (one km); Exmoor.

Langleigh Road, Ilfracombe, Devon EX34 8EA
Tel (0271) 62629
Location on W side of town; in 3-acre gardens with off-street parking for 10 cars
Food & drink full breakfast, bar lunch, dinner; residential and restaurant licence
Prices B&B £15-£20; dinner £8.50; bargain breaks
Rooms 3 double, 2 with bath and shower, one with shower; one single, with shower; 2 family rooms, both with bath and shower; 2 cottage suites, both with bath and shower; all rooms have central heating, colour TV, radio, tea/coffee kit
Facilities sitting-room, dining-room, bar, games room, playroom; solarium, croquet, tennis practice
Credit cards MC, V
Children welcome; baby-listening, cots, high-chairs available **Disabled** access difficult **Pets** dogs welcome, but not in public rooms
Closed never
Proprietors Ann and Ken Crawford

Exmoor

Ashwick House

The Sherwoods, mother and son, are considerate hosts who manage to run Ashwick House with an admirable mixture of efficiency and flexibility – it is immaculately kept in the best British hotel-keeping tradition, but there is no hint of regimentation (the rooms are not numbered, but named after trees).

Their fine Edwardian house has more than a hint of Lutyens about it, with a heavy-looking, low roof and 'baronial' hall. It has a grand setting, looking south over the enchanting wooded valley of the Barle.

Inside, it is furnished with a confident touch which banishes any trace of the gloom which sometimes afflicts houses of this vintage – colonial-style cane in the library, light fabrics in the airily spacious bedrooms, William Morris in the hall.

The dining-room (which can accommodate a few non-residents) opens on to a terrace where you can have breakfast when the weather allows. At dinner there is a small choice of interesting dishes. The daily changing menu has diners' names inscribed at the top, so it is not a place for illicit assignations.

Nearby Tarr Steps, and the rest of Exmoor; Taunton within reach.

Near Dulverton, Somerset
TA22 9QD
Tel (0398) 23868
Location 3 miles (5 km) NW
of Dulverton, close to B3223;
in 6-acre grounds with ample
car parking
Food & drink breakfast,
lunch, dinner; residential
and restaurant licence
Prices B&B £28-£33.50;
DB&B £36-£49; special 2- or
5-night reductions all year
Rooms 6 double, all with
bath; all rooms have central
heating, colour TV, radio,
cassette player, hairdrier,
trouser-press
Facilities bar, sitting-room,
library, baronial hall,
restaurant, solarium
Credit cards not accepted
Children accepted over 8
Disabled access difficult
Pets allowed in grounds, but
not in hotel
Closed a few weeks after
Christmas
Proprietor P E Sherwood

Exmoor

Country house hotel, Hawkridge

Tarr Steps Hotel

This long, low whitewashed building, originally a Georgian rectory, has just enough of the surrounding woods cleared to give most rooms a delectable view. Desmond Keane has taken great care to keep the character of a private house, with fine antiques in the relaxed, comfortable public rooms, and a menu which emphasizes fresh produce and home cooking.

Nearby Tarr Steps bridge; Exmoor.

Hawkridge, near Dulverton, Somerset TA22 9PY
Tel (064385) 293
Location 7 miles (11 km) NW of Fulverton, W of B3223, in countryside; in 8-acre grounds with parking for 20 cars
Food & drink full breakfast, lunch, tea, dinner; residential and restaurant licence
Prices DB&B £39.50-£42.50; reductions mid-week and for children sharing parents' room
Rooms 12 double, 8 with bath; 3 single; all rooms have central heating
Facilities bar, sitting-room, 2 dining-rooms; stables; clay pigeon shooting, rough shooting, fishing
Credit cards AE, MC, V
Children welcome if well behaved **Disabled** access good to all public rooms and one ground-floor bedroom
Pets dogs accepted if well behaved, but not in public rooms; kennels available
Closed Jan to Mar
Proprietor Desmond Keane

Inn, Winsford

Royal Oak

An ancient, remarkably picturesque inn, thatched and cream-painted. Inside, the cosy and well furnished part-panelled lounge bar, with its huge stone hearth, does not disappoint. The Stevenses, who have been here since the early 1970s, have a firm eye on standards, which are as well maintained in the food – both bar and restaurant – as in the surroundings. Roughly half the bedrooms are in the relatively new (and newly refurbished) courtyard annexe.

Nearby Winsford Hill; Exmoor, Brendon Hills.

Winsford, near Minehead, Somerset TA24 7JE
Tel (064385) 455
Location 10 miles (16 km) SW of Minehead, 1.5 miles (2.5 km) W of A396; in middle of village, with ample car parking
Food & drink full breakfast, lunch, bar meals, dinner; full licence
Prices B&B £33-£58; dinner £17; off-season breaks
Rooms 13 double, 12 with bath; one single, with bath; one family room, with bath; all rooms have central heating, TV, phone; radio/alarm, hairdrier on request
Facilities 3 sitting-rooms, 2 bars, dining-room; fishing
Credit cards AE, DC, MC, V
Children welcome
Disabled access easy to public rooms and annex bedrooms
Pets welcome
Closed never
Proprietors Charles and Sheila Steven

Exmoor

Country house hotel, Simonsbath

Simonsbath House

The first house on Exmoor when it was built in 1654, this long, low whitewashed stone building still presides over an isolated stretch of the moor, well placed for exploring (either by car or on foot) all the corners of the splendidly varied National Park. But the hotel itself is anything but desolate – Mike and Sue Burns, fairly recent arrivals here, have carried on their predecessors' policy of providing unstinting comfort, generous and interesting food and a warm welcome in almost wickedly luxurious surroundings. Original features abound – wood panelling and large open fires in the sitting-room and bar/library, four posters in some of the bedrooms – and great efforts have been made to keep the furnishings and decorations in harmony with the antiquity of the building. There is a modest but relaxing lawned garden.

A recent view from one of our most widely travelled reporters sums up Simonsbath: "Very suave and comfortable; I'd love to go again, but it would have to be at someone else's expense."

Nearby Lynton, 10 miles (16 km); Exmoor.

Simonsbath, Exmoor,
Somerset TA24 7SH
Tel (064383) 259
Location 10 miles (16 km) S
of Lynton, on B3223, in
village; in one-acre grounds,
with two lock-up garages and
ample car parking
Food & drink breakfast,
lunch, dinner; residential
and restaurant licence
Prices B&B £36-£38; dinner
£15; reductions for 2 nights
or more
Rooms 7 double, all with
bath, 4 also with shower; all
rooms have central heating,
colour TV, phone, radio,
hairdrier
Facilities library with bar,
sitting-room, dining-room
Credit cards AE, DC, MC, V
Children welcome over 10
Disabled access difficult –
steps to entrance
Pets not allowed in house
Closed Dec to Jan
Proprietors Mike and Sue
Burns

West Somerset

Country hotel, Kilve

Meadow House

The amiable white-painted house, a mainly Georgian rectory in a beautifully peaceful setting between the Quantocks and the sea, is furnished with real taste, and immaculately cared for; the bedrooms (and bathrooms) are large, the public rooms warm and inviting. The Samsons took over recently from the MacAuslans, but are committed to the same high standards. Cooking is based on local and seasonal produce.

Nearby Dunster Castle, 10 miles (16 km); Quantock Hills.

Sea Lane, Kilve, Somerset TA5 1EG
Tel (027874) 546
Location 5 miles (8 km) E of Williton, just off A39; in 8-acre grounds with ample car parking
Food & drink full breakfast, dinner; retail, residential and restaurant licence
Prices B&B £29-£34, suite £38; dinner £17; reductions for 3 nights or more
Rooms 5 double, all with bath, 2 also with shower; family suite in cottages; all rooms have central heating, colour TV, radio/ alarm, tea/coffee kit, hairdrier
Facilities dining-room, sitting-room, study, bar, snooker; croquet
Credit cards MC, V
Children welcome over 9 in house, any age in family suite
Disabled access difficult
Pets not accepted
Closed Christmas and New Year
Proprietors A & T Samson

Country hotel, Williton

White House

Dick and Kay Smith have been at Williton for more than 20 years now, and show no sign of flagging. The mostly Georgian house remains immaculately decorated, with pretty co-ordinated fabrics in the comfortable bedrooms and a relaxed mix of furniture downstairs. The Smiths' passionate interest in food and wine ensures that the daily-changing menus are appetizing, and the wine cellar is one of the best in the west.

Nearby Cleeve Abbey, 1.5 miles (2.5 km); Quantock Hills.

11 Long Street, Williton, Somerset TA4 4QW
Tel (0984) 32306
Location 9 miles (14.5 km) SE of Minehead, in middle of village set back from A39; ample car parking
Food & drink full breakfast, dinner; residential and restaurant licence
Prices B&B £23-£34; DB&B £41-£52; reductions for children sharing parents' room
Rooms 11 double, 9 with bath, 3 also with shower; one single; one family room, with bath; eight rooms have central heating
Facilities sitting-room, bar, dining-room
Credit cards not accepted
Children welcome if well behaved; cots and high-chairs available **Disabled** access good; ground-floor bedrooms **Pets** dogs accepted if well behaved, but not in dining-room
Closed Dec to mid-May
Proprietors Dick and Kay Smith

Country house hotel, Wiveliscombe

Langley House

This is the first hotel the Wilsons can call their own, but they are hardly beginners in the business: Peter, who cooks, comes to it via the Lygon Arms at Broadway and then Ston Easton Park (in their different ways, both excellent hotels, and excluded from this guide only because they fall outside our price and size limits); and Anne, who fronts, used to run the British Tourist Authority's Commendation Scheme – gamekeeper turned poacher, as it were. Between them, they ought to know what they are about.

The house is a modest building with an amiable, rambling garden in delectable, rolling Somerset countryside which is neglected by most visitors to the West Country. (Anne Wilson is happy to advise guests on where to go touring during the day and provides them with maps.) It is not ideally furnished – less elegance, more informality would be our prescription both for the sitting-rooms and some of the bedrooms – but the Wilsons' warmth of welcome overcomes such reservations. Peter's five-course dinners help too. They are entirely fixed until the dessert, when there is an explosion of choice. His style is light and unconventional, lovingly presented, in the best modern British manner and elicits plenty of praise from his guests.

Nearby Gaulden Manor, 2.5 miles (4 km); Exmoor; Quantock Hills; Taunton within reach.

Langley Marsh,
Wiveliscombe, Somerset
TA4 2UF
Tel (0984) 23318
Location one mile (1.5 km)
NW of Wiveliscombe, off
A361; in 4-acre gardens with
ample car parking
Food & drink breakfast,
lunch, dinner; residential
and restaurant licence
Prices B & B £28.50-£50;
dinner £17.50-£19.75;
reductions for 2 nights or
more
Rooms 7 double, 5 with bath,
2 with shower; 2 single, both
with bath; one family room,
with bath; all rooms have
central heating, TV, phone,
radio, hairdrier
Facilities bar, 2 sitting-
rooms, restaurant; croquet
Credit cards AE, MC
Children welcome over 7,
under 7 only by
arrangement
Disabled access to ground
floor easy but no lift to
bedrooms **Pets** accepted
Closed never
Proprietors Peter and Anne
Wilson

West Somerset

Converted watermill, Williton

Curdon Mill

The Criddles specialized in outside catering for many years before opening the doors of their carefully converted watermill in 1985. Hence, perhaps, their novel approach to catering for guests: dinner is essentially a no-choice affair, but you can order dishes in advance from a long menu, sent when you book. Other attractions are more conventional: chintzy chairs and antiques in the public rooms, pretty decorations in the bedrooms (which vary widely in size), a secluded farmland setting.

Nearby Cleeve Abbey, 3 miles (5 km); Quantock Hills, Exmoor.

Lower Vellow, Williton, Taunton, Somerset TA4 4LS
Tel (0984) 56522
Location in countryside 2 miles (3 km) SE of Williton, one mile off A358; with ample car parking
Food & drink breakfast, dinner; restaurant licence
Prices B&B £16.50-£25; DB&B £28.50-£37
Rooms 6 double, one with bath, 5 with shower; all rooms have central heating, TV, tea/coffee kit
Facilities sitting-room, dining-room with bar; heated swimming-pool, croquet, fishing
Credit cards not encouraged
Children not accepted
Disabled access difficult
Pets accepted in grounds only **Closed** never
Proprietors Richard and Daphne Criddle

Country guest-house, West Bagborough

Higher House

William and Jo Beaumont have gradually built up their guest-house business during the 1980s. The house (17thC, extended 19thC and 20thC) has a splendid setting on the south slopes of the Quantock hills, with walking for the energetic and views for the rest of us. It is above all a comfortable, home-like place, with easy chairs and books in the bedrooms, and a mix of antique and less distinquished furniture. Jo cooks English 'dinner party' food.

Nearby Gaulden Manor, 4 miles (6.5 km); Quantocks, Exmoor.

West Bagborough, Taunton, Somerset TA4 3EF
Tel (0823) 432996
Location on outskirts of village, 2.5 miles (4 km) NE of Bishops Lydeard; with parking for 13 cars
Food & drink breakfast, dinner; children's tea; restaurant licence
Prices B&B £16-£25; dinner £10
Rooms 5 double, 2 with bath, one with shower; one two-room suite with bath; all rooms have central heating, colour TV, phone, alarm, tea/coffee kit
Facilities sitting-room, dining-room, morning-room with TV, hall with bar; snooker, outdoor heated pool
Credit cards MC, V
Children welcome; cot, small beds, high chairs, children's tea provided **Disabled** access difficult – many steps
Pets welcome if well-behaved, but not allowed in dining-room
Closed Christmas week
Proprietors W and J Beaumont

South Somerset

Farm guest-house, Beercrocombe

Frog Street Farm

Veronica Cole's plain-looking but flower-bedecked Somerset 'longhouse' is hidden deep in the countryside.

When you eventually find Frog Street Farm, you can be sure of a warm welcome from Mrs Cole and her two daughters, who have been looking after guests with care and generosity since 1981. Inside, the house has great character and warmth, with a handsome oak-beamed inglenook in one sitting-room and some very antique panelling. The guests share two tables at dinner – a carefully prepared set meal of English food, employing vegetables and dairy produce fresh from the farm, with a choice of delicious puddings. Mrs Cole is pleased to cater for special diets, and you are welcome to take your own wine.

Nearby Barrington Court, 5 miles (8 km); Vale of Taunton.

Beercrocombe, Taunton, Somerset TA3 6AF
Tel (0823) 480430
Location 6 miles (10 km) SE of Taunton, one mile (1.5 km) from A358; car parking
Food & drink full breakfast, dinner; no licence
Prices B&B £14-£20; dinner £12; reductions for weekly stays
Rooms 3 double, one with bath, one with shower; 2 single; all rooms have central heating, tea/coffee kit
Facilities 2 sitting-rooms; outdoor heated swimming-pool
Credit cards not accepted
Children welcome over 11
Disabled access difficult
Pets not accepted
Closed Christmas/New Year
Proprietor Veronica Cole

Country guest-house, Yeovil

Little Barwick House

The great appeal of this white-painted listed Georgian dower house is its friendly informality – it is first and foremost the family home of the Colleys, with no sign of hotel rules or regulations. The bedrooms are comfortable, but simply furnished – don't expect four-star luxury – and the public rooms are lived-in, not smart. Veronica has gained an enviable reputation for her cooking, with local game a speciality. Christopher tends to the restaurant and cellar bar – the latter the original kitchen of the house, with an interesting old bread oven.

Nearby Brympton d'Evercy, 2.5 miles (4 km), Montacute House, 5 miles (8 km).

Barwick, near Yeovil, Somerset BA22 9TD
Tel (0935) 23902
Location 2 miles (3 km) S of Yeovil off A37; car parking
Food & drink breakfast, dinner; residential and restaurant licence
Prices B&B £30-£38; DB&B £44.50-£52.50
Rooms 6 double, 4 with bath, 2 with shower; all rooms have central heating, colour TV, tea/coffee kit
Facilities sitting-room, bar, dining-room
Credit cards AE, DC, MC, V
Children welcome if well behaved **Disabled** access difficult **Pets** dogs welcome
Closed Christmas **Proprietors** Christopher & Veronica Colley

North Somerset

Number 3

Although this listed Georgian town house is well established as a good restaurant, the Tynans have been running it for only a couple of years. Ann does the cooking – a short menu of sensitively executed dishes employing highly original combinations of flavours. Everything is freshly made, from the cheese straws served with pre-dinner drinks to the exquisite sorbets.

The dining-room is over-richly decorated, with oil paintings on red felt walls and colourful patterned tablecloths, and the bar furniture is more interesting than comfortable. But there is a welcoming residents' sitting-room on the first floor, and the bedrooms are large and comfortable.

Nearby Abbey, Tor; Wells Cathedral, 5 miles (8 km).

3 Magdalene Street,
Glastonbury, Somerset
BA6 9EW
Tel (0458) 32129
Location in middle of town;
with garden and parking for
8 cars
Food & drink breakfast,
lunch by arrangement (Tue-
Sun), dinner; restaurant
licence
Prices B&B £22.50-£35;
dinner £21

Rooms 3 double, one family
room; all with bath; all rooms
have central heating, tea/
coffee kit, TV, phone
Facilities bar, sitting-room
Credit cards AE, V
Children welcome **Disabled**
access difficult – two steps to
front entrance **Pets** not
accepted
Closed first three weeks Jan
Proprietors John and Ann
Tynan

Model Farm

No longer a model farm in practice, but in some ways a model guest-house: for example, the owners (refugees from the City) never take more than eight guests, so that they are never over-stretched. The house was the local manor, extended in Victorian times; its character was carefully preserved when it fully refurbished before opening as a hotel in 1988.

Nearby Barford Park, 2.5 miles (4 km); Hestercombe Gardens 6 miles (10 km).

Perry Green, Wembdon,
Nr Bridgewater, Somerset
TA5 2BA
Tel (0278) 423870
Location in countryside
3.5 miles (5.5 km) NW of
Bridgewater, off A39;
with ample car parking
Food & drink breakfast;
lunch, tea, dinner by
arrangement; no licence, but
drinks provided
Prices B&B £12-£22; lunch
from £2.50; dinner £8.50

Rooms 3 double, 2 with
shower; 2 family rooms, one
with shower; all rooms have
central heating, TV, tea/
coffee kit **Facilities** sitting-
room, dining-room
Credit cards not accepted
Children accepted over 12,
younger by arrangement
Disabled access difficult
Pets not accepted
Closed never
Proprietors Peter Rees-
Jones and Eric Holliday

North Somerset

Restaurant with rooms, Shepton Mallet

Bowlish House

Bowlish House developed an enviable reputation for quality and value under its previous owner, Brian Jordan, who over a decade transformed it from a 10-bedroom hotel into what he called "a 5-bedroom restaurant with rooms, with wine-list attached" – a reference to the size and general wonderfulness of the list. Bob and Linda Morley seem set to carry on in the same fashion; the list still embraces 250 bins, and Linda brings 20 years' experience to the kitchen and the seasonally changing menus. Like their predecessor, they aim to offer 'more than you'd expect for less than you'd think'.

The house itself is a grand Palladian affair, built in the early 18th century. As well as comfortable, individually furnished bedrooms – elegant ones on the first floor, cosier ones in the roof on the second – there is a welcoming sitting-room, a panelled bar and a stylish new conservatory where you can take coffee after dinner. The furnishings are a mix of antiques and good reproductions, and the Morleys have introduced displays of china and hung family portraits on the walls. Behind the house is an enclosed garden for the use of guests – you can play croquet in summer.

Nearby Wells Cathedral, 4 miles (6 km), Glastonbury, 7 miles (11 km); Mendip Hills; Bath within reach.

Wells Road, Shepton Mallet, Somerset BA4 5JD
Tel (0749) 2022
Location 0.75 miles (one km) W of Shepton Mallet on A371; with walled garden and parking for 15 cars
Food & drink breakfast, dinner; full licence
Prices B&B £21; dinner £15
Rooms 5 double, all with bath; all rooms have central heating, TV, radio/alarm, tea/coffee kit
Facilities dining-room, bar, sitting-room, conservatory; croquet
Credit cards not accepted
Children welcome
Disabled access difficult – 5 steps to front door
Pets welcome in bedrooms, at owner's risk
Closed 24 to 27 Dec
Proprietors Bob and Linda Morley

Avon

Number Nine

Provided you are not overburdened with luggage, the position of Number Nine, on a pedestrian alley in the heart of Bath, is ideal – sights in every direction, two of the city's best restaurants within easy walking distance. The Haywards – ex-teachers, who lived here for many years before taking guests – have furnished their house comfortably and richly (the bedrooms, with their four-posters and canopies, are too rich for some tastes). The sitting-room is cosy, the dining-room more gracious than is usual in a B&B place. The pretty enclosed garden makes a peaceful retreat.

Nearby Museum of Costume, Assembly Rooms.

Miles Buildings, Bath, Avon BA1 2QS
Tel (0225) 25462
Location off George Street, in middle of town; with walled garden, and car parking arranged by hotel where possible
Food & drink full breakfast, snacks, tea; residential licence
Prices B&B £32.50-£60
Rooms 9 double, 3 with bath, 6 with shower; all rooms have central heating, colour TV, phone, tea/coffee kit
Facilities sitting-room, dining-room; use of health club facilities
Credit cards AE, DC, MC, V
Children not accepted
Disabled one room suitable
Pets not accepted
Closed never
Proprietors Paul and Sue Hayward

Paradise House

The Cuttings' handsome Georgian house was sadly neglected before they took it over in the 1970s; they now take pride in showing it to hotel guide inspectors, so confident are they in what they have achieved. The house is a steep walk or a winding drive up the wooded hill to the south of the city. This accounts for one of the guest house's main attractions – the fine views shared by the secluded, rear garden and several of the spacious, prettily decorated rooms.

Nearby Abbey, Roman Baths and Pump Room, Holburne Museum, Victoria Art Gallery (all in Bath).

86 Holloway, Bath, Avon BA2 4PX
Tel (0225) 317723
Location on S side of city off A367; in 0.5-acre gardens with three locking garages and ample car parking
Food & drink full breakfast; no licence
Prices B&B £17-£45; 10% reduction for 5 nights or more
Rooms 7 double, 5 with bath, 1 with shower; one family room, with bath and shower; all rooms have central heating, colour TV, phone, tea/coffee kit
Facilities breakfast room, sitting-room
Credit cards MC, V
Children welcome **Disabled** access easy **Pets** not accepted
Closed Dec and Jan
Proprietors Janet and David Cutting

Avon

Town apartments, Bath

Fountain House

Fountain House offers an unusual formula in a provincial British city, but one which seems to be gaining popularity: serviced apartments, with the convenience of living and cooking space but the services of a bed-and-breakfast hotel. The building is a fine old Georgian townhouse, once split into two but recently re-united and renovated. The sites vary widely in size, shape and style – some essentially open-plan, others divided into several separate rooms. Furnishings are smartly luxurious, in a variety of modern and reproduction styles. Guests have signing facilities at the nearby Hole in the Wall restaurant – though it does not enjoy such a high reputation as it once did.

Nearby Assembly Rooms, Museum of Costume.

9 Fountain Buildings,
Lansdown Road, Bath, Avon
BA1 5DV
Tel (0225) 338622
Location in middle of city,
close to main shopping area;
lock-up garages available
Food & drink breakfast
Prices B&B £39-£63
Rooms 14 suites, sleeping 2
to 5 people, all with one or 2
baths; all suites have kitchen,
central heating, colour TV,
phone, hairdrier, entry-phone
Facilities suites are serviced
daily, as in a hotel
Credit cards AE, DC, MC, V
Children welcome
Disabled access possible;
lift/elevator **Pets** accepted
Closed never **Proprietors**
Susan and Robin Bryan

Town guest-house, Bath

The Queensberry Hotel

This new Bath hotel is slightly large for our purposes, but cannot be allowed to escape the net. The hotel is an offshoot of the justly famous country hotel Homewood Park (see page 50); and, predictably, the Rosses have transformed its three Georgian terraced houses into one of the most relaxing, stylish and personal places to stay in the city. The sitting-room, beautifully furnished in muted blue, green and cream, is small – but the bedrooms are spacious and equipped with easy chairs as well as breakfast tables. Furnishings are a tasteful mix of antiques and reproductions, with appropriately sumptuous fabrics throughout. Chauffeured car to Homewood Park for dinner is free.

Nearby Assembly Rooms, Museum of Costume, The Circus.

Russel Street, Bath, Avon
BA1 2QT
Tel (0225) 447928
Location in middle of city,
close to main shopping area;
paved gardens behind;
daytime car parking
restricted
Food & drink breakfast,
snacks; residential licence
Prices B&B £35-£70
Rooms 26 double, all with
bath; all rooms have central
heating, phone, colour TV
Facilities sitting-room
Credit cards AE, DC, MC, V
Children welcome; cots
available
Disabled access possible;
lift/elevator
Pets not accepted
Closed 2 weeks Christmas/
New Year
Proprietor Stephen Ross

Avon

Bed and breakfast guest-house, Bath

Holly Lodge

Carrolle Sellick is well established on the Bath bed-and-breakfast scene, having run the highly regarded Haydon House for several years. She opened up in this larger Victorian house in 1986 having rescued it from dereliction, and has again produced a base for tired sightseers which is pretty and restful as well as thoroughly comfortable. There are grand views of Bath from the garden as well as the breakfast and some of the bedrooms, which are large and carefully furnished. The sitting-room too is spacious, with comfy sofas, antiques and fresh flowers. Breakfast is impressive, with home-made croissants and exotic-fruit platters as an alternative to the full English treatment.

Nearby sights of central Bath.

8 Upper Oldfield Park, Bath, Avon BA2 3JZ
Tel (0225) 339187
Location in residential area, half a mile (one km) SW on city centre off A367; in garden, with car parking
Food & drink full English breakfast
Prices B&B £25-£50
Rooms 5 double, 4 with bath, one with shower one single with shower; all rooms have central heating, colour TV, phone, tea/coffee kit; most have trouser-press, hairdrier
Facilities sitting-room
Credit cards DC, MC, V
Children accepted over age 10
Disabled access difficult
Pets not accepted **Closed** never
Proprietor Carrolle Sellick

Town guest-house, Bath

Somerset House

The Seymours took the name of their established guest-house with them when they moved further up steep Bathwick Hill in 1985, and with it the formula for which they had become known: caring, personal service (not for those who seek anonymity), harmoniously furnished rooms and thoroughly good food – mainly traditional English in style, but with occasional excursions into foreign territory – at impressively modest prices. The Regency character of the building has been carefully preserved; it is a strictly no-smoking house.

Nearby Holburne Museum and other sights of Bath.

35 Bathwick Hill, Bath, Avon BA2 6LD
Tel (0225) 66451 & 63471
Location on SE side of city; private car parking
Food & drink breakfast, dinner, lunch on Sun only; restaurant licence
Prices DB&B £32.25-£42.25; reduction for 5 nights or more and for children aged 10-13 sharing parents' room
Rooms 4 double, all with bath and shower; one single, with shower; 4 family rooms, all with bath and shower; all rooms have central heating, phone
Facilities 2 sitting-rooms (one with bar), dining-room
Credit cards AE, MC, V
Children welcome over 10
Disabled not suitable for severe disabilities **Pets** small dogs only welcome
Closed 2 weeks mid-Jan
Proprietors J. and M. Seymour and family

Avon

Country guest-house, Bathford

Eagle House

No sign is displayed outside Eagle House, standing behind a stone wall and dignified wrought-iron gates, to suggest it is anything other than a fine, privately-owned, listed Georgian mansion. Inside, too, there is little to dispel that impression, particularly when sitting in the superb drawing-room which overlooks landscaped grounds and commands beautiful views across the Avon Valley. Owners John and Rosamund Napier are skilled hosts, combining professional service (John Napier trained at the Savoy and managed the Priory in Bath before moving here) with commendable informality. Guests are trusted; the first drinks of the evening are served by John Napier from the sideboard and thereafter guests can help themselves ("I just look at the bottle in the morning"). The house is decorated without pomp – it is after all a guest-house rather than a full-blown hotel; the spacious bedrooms and adjoining bathrooms display simple wallpapers and an eclectic mix of furniture, ranging from the grand to the straightforward. Children are welcomed unreservedly.

Nearby Bath; American Museum, 2.5 miles (4 km).

Church Street, Bathford, Bath, Avon BA1 7RS
Tel (0225) 859946
Location 2.5 miles (4 km) E of Bath, off A363, in village; in 2-acre gardens, with ample car parking
Food & drink breakfast; residential licence
Prices B&B £17-£28; £1.95 extra for full breakfast; children sharing parents' room charged only for breakfast
Rooms 3 double with bath, 2 with shower; one single with shower; 2 family rooms with bath, one also with shower; all rooms have central heating, colour TV, phone, tea/coffee kit, hairdrier
Facilities sitting-room, dining-room; croquet
Credit cards not accepted
Children welcome; cots, baby-sitting available
Disabled access difficult
Pets dogs accepted
Closed 10 days over Christmas
Proprietors John and Rosamund Napier

Avon

Town guest house, Bath

Sydney Gardens

Off the main tourist track in a quiet residential area of Bath overlooking a small park, Sydney Gardens is nevertheless conveniently close to Bath's popular sights. The large Italianate Victorian house has been completely renovated by the Smithsons, and Stanley's own paintings adorn the walls. Bedrooms are individually and freshly decorated in well co-ordinated colours – and even those right at the top of the house have enough space for easy chairs. The breakfast room and sitting-room are light and gracious, and the smoking ban (in the whole house) ensures that non-smokers will enjoy their coffee and croissants.

Nearby Holburne Museum, canal towpath walk.

Sydney Road, Bath, Avon, BA2 6NT
Tel (0225) 64818
Location close to middle of town; in small garden with some private car parking and more on street
Food & drink full breakfast; no licence
Prices B&B £25-£45; winter breaks
Rooms 6 double, all with bath; all rooms have central heating, phone, colour TV, tea/coffee kit, hairdrier, radio alarm, phone
Facilities sitting-room, breakfast room
Credit cards MC, V
Children welcome over 4
Disabled access difficult
Pets small dogs only by arrangement; must be kept in bedrooms
Closed Christmas and Jan
Proprietors Stanley and Diane Smithson

Country guest-house, Bathford

The Orchard

Bath itself is not short of well-run mid-priced guest-houses, but few can match the style and refinement of this detached Georgian house, in the middle of the attractive outlying village of Bathford, which the Londons have been running since the early 1980s. The bedrooms are large and uncluttered, with pleasant views over the secluded garden (which has an exceptional range of fine trees), and the spacious sitting-room is dotted with antiques. A log fire burns in cool weather, and there are plenty of books, magazines and games on hand.

Nearby Bath; American Museum, 2.5 miles (4 km).

80 High Street, Bathford, Bath, Avon BA1 7TG
Tel (0225) 858765
Location 3 miles (5 km) E of Bath, close to A363, in village; 1.5-acre grounds with ample car parking
Food & drink breakfast, no licence
Prices B&B £21.75
Rooms 4 double, all with bath and shower; all rooms have central heating, colour TV
Facilities sitting-room, dining-room
Credit cards not accepted
Children welcome over 11
Disabled access difficult
Pets not accepted
Closed Nov to Feb
Proprietors John and Olga London

Avon

Homewood Park

The practice of promoting the new edition of a hotel guide by picking out a few places for special awards is harmless enough (perhaps even the *Charming Small Hotel Guides* will be driven to it in due course) provided readers don't attach too much import-ance to the choice of hotels. But what does it mean when guides as widely different in spirit and method as *Egon Ronay* and *The Good Hotel Guide* single out the same hotel in succeeding years? In the case of Homewood Park it simply means that Stephen and Penny Ross have got together an act which is about the most successful combination of professional skill and amateur thoughtfulness you could hope to find.

Homewood Park's secret is not that it sets new standards in any one respect; it is that it scores consistently high in all respects, leaving only the slightest room for dissatisfaction. One of our inspectors prescribes more reading matter in the warmly refined sitting-room; another observes that the lawned garden in front of the house feels slightly too exposed for complete comfort. They are clutching at straws. Most visitors are content to drown in a sea of modest elegance, deep comfort, friendly but solicitous service and first-rate, imaginative cooking. Before you rush to book, note that the prices are about as high as any in these pages.

Nearby American Museum, 4 miles (6 km), Bath, 5 miles (8 km).

Hinton Charterhouse, Bath, Avon BA3 6BB
Tel (022122) 3731
Location 5 miles (8 km) S of Bath, close to A36; in 10-acre grounds with parking for 35 cars
Food & drink breakfast, lunch, dinner; restaurant licence
Prices B&B £42.50-£100; dinner £21.50-£25
Rooms 15 double, all with bath and shower; all rooms have central heating, colour TV, phone, radio, hairdrier
Facilities sitting-room, bar, 3 dining-rooms; tennis
Credit cards AE, DC, MC, V
Children welcome **Disabled** access easy – entrance and public rooms on one level and 2 ground- floor bedrooms
Pets not accepted
Closed 24 Dec to 7 Jan
Proprietor Stephen Ross

Avon

Country Ways

'Hotel keeping is above all about hospitality and not about putting hairdriers and trouser presses in bedrooms,' says Desmond Pow. Exactly. The Pows practise what they preach, in their cottagey country house between Bristol and Wells; the public rooms are cosily furnished, with open fires, and the bedrooms are all in their different ways equally welcoming. Susan's cooking sticks to similar principles – honest, fresh ingredients prepared with care.
Nearby Wells 9 miles (14.5 km); Bath 10 miles (16 km).

Marsh Lane, Farrington Gurney, Bristol, Avon, BS18 5TT
Tel (0761) 52449
Location 10 miles (16 km) SW of Bath, close to A39; ample car parking
Food & drink full breakfast, dinner; restaurant licence
Prices B&B £23.75-£42.75; dinner from £12.50
Rooms 5 double, all with bath; one single, with shower; –
all rooms have central heating, colour TV, phone, radio/alarm
Facilities bar sitting-room, dining-room, garden room
Credit cards AE, DC, MC, V
Children welcome over 8
Disabled access difficult, many different levels
Pets not accepted
Closed 2 weeks Christmas, 2 weeks Feb
Proprietors Desmond and Susan Pow

Green Lane House

The Baxters spent five years gently but thoroughly renovating this handsome Georgian house before they opened for visitors in 1987. Antique and reproduction furniture and pleasing country fabrics complement the muted decorations, exposed beams and comforting open log fires. Two of the four prettily decorated bedrooms now have private bathrooms, so there are no more queues. The position of the house, next to the shabby village garage, could hardly be considered ideal; but guests have use of the south-facing rear garden – and prices are modest, considering the ample breakfast.
Nearby Westwood Manor, 2.5 miles (4 km); American Museum, 6 miles (10 km); Bath, 6 miles (10 km).

1 Green Lane, Hinton Charterhouse, Bath, Avon BA3 6BL
Tel (0225) 723631
Location 6 miles (10 km) S of Bath off B3110; with garden and parking for 4 cars
Food & drink full breakfast; packed lunch arrangement; no licence
Prices B&B £12-£26.50; 50% reduction for children under 14 sharing parents' room and for 5 nights or more
Rooms 4 double, 2 with bath; all rooms have central heating, hairdrier
Facilities sitting-room, dining-room
Credit cards MC, V
Children welcome; high tea and baby-sitting by arrangement
Disabled access easy to public rooms only
Pets not accepted
Closed Christmas and Jan
Proprietors J and L Baxter

West Wiltshire

Country house hotel, Beanacre

Beechfield House

There is much to admire about this country house on the fringes of Bath. The Victorian building strikes a fine balance between grandeur and intimacy; it has been decorated and furnished with great taste and at considerable expense – walls have special decorated paint finishes, or are delicately patterned, furniture is antique; the extensive grounds are delightful; the food is ambitious and generally successful. Some visitors have had reservations in the past about both the service and the arrangement of the sitting-rooms, but the new owners, Hidden Hotels, have done much to improve matters.

The bedrooms vary quite widely but all are carefully furnished and amply supplied with thoughtful little extras. Some are in the adjacent converted coach house – another splendid building, backing on to the pretty pool area.

Nearby Lacock 1.5 miles (2.5 km); Great Chalfield Manor, 3 miles (5 km); Bowood House, 5 miles (8 km); Bradford-on-Avon, 6 miles (10 km); Bath, 9 miles (14.5 km).

Beanacre, Melksham, Wiltshire SN12 7PU
Tel (0225) 703700
Location one mile (1.5 km) N of Melksham on A350; in 8-acre grounds with ample car parking
Food & drink full breakfast, lunch, dinner; residential and restaurant licence
Prices B&B £60-£90; dinner from £25
Rooms 24 double, all with bath; all rooms have central heating, TV, radio, phone, hairdrier, trouser-press
Facilities sitting-room, 2 dining-rooms; croquet, tennis, heated outdoor swimming-pool; helipad
Credit cards AE, DC, MC, V
Children welcome if well behaved
Disabled access easy and 4 ground-floor bedrooms
Pets not accepted
Closed one week after Christmas
Manager Robert Smith

West Wiltshire

Priory Steps

Very much in harmony with the mellow old weaving town of Bradford, this is an amalgamation of a whole row of weavers' cottages, built in the late 17thC and sympathetically decorated and furnished by Diana and Carey Chapman when they moved here from London in 1985. Diana is a trained cook, and her three-course dinners (no choice, but any requirements happily met given notice) can be served either in the elegantly rustic dining-room or on the terrace overlooking the town.

Nearby Barton Tithe Barn; Bath, 5.5 miles (9 km).

Newtown, Bradford-on-Avon, Wiltshire BA15 1NQ
Tel (02216) 2230
Location close to middle of town, on N side; with limited private parking
Food & drink full breakfast, dinner; residential licence
Prices B&B £22-£32; dinner £12
Rooms 5 double, all with bath; all rooms have central heating, colour TV, tea/coffee kit

Facilities sitting-room, dining-room
Credit cards MC, V
Children accepted
Disabled access easy to one ground-floor bedroom, but dining-room on lower ground floor
Pets not encouraged
Closed never
Proprietors Carey and Diana Chapman

Bradford Old Windmill

Although it functioned only briefly, the Robertses' extraordinary guest-house was built in 1807 as a windmill. The sitting-room and the principal bedrooms each occupy a whole floor of the old tower; all the rooms are charmingly furnished, with stripped pine furniture and odds and ends from around the world.

You are very much guests in the Robertses' home, and the vegetarian feasts they offer reflect their own interests and travels – dinners ranging from Mexican to Thai, and a choice of Continental, English, Healthy and American breakfasts. Smoking is not allowed.

Nearby Barton Tithe Barn; Bath, 5.5 miles (9 km).

Masons Lane, Bradford-on-Avon, Wiltshire BA15 1QN
Tel (02216) 6842
Location just N of town centre; with cottage garden and parking for 5 cars
Food & drink full breakfast, dinner; residential licence
Prices B&B £15-£25; dinner £12; reduction for children sharing parents' room
Rooms 3 double, 2 with bath; one single; one family room

with bath; all rooms have central heating, colour TV, tea/coffee kit, alarm
Facilities sitting-room, dining-room
Credit cards V
Children welcome if well behaved
Disabled access difficult
Pets not accepted
Closed Christmas
Proprietors Peter and Priscilla Roberts

West Wiltshire

Inn. Lacock

At the Sign of the Angel

Lacock and The Sign of the Angel go hand-in-hand: the 'perfect' English village (almost entirely in the preserving hands of the National Trust) and the epitome of the medieval English inn – half-timbered without, great log fires, oak panelling, beamed ceilings and polished antique tables within.

There are many such inns sprinkled around middle England, but most are better enjoyed over a beer or two or a meal than overnight. Even here, the rooms vary in comfort and none could be called spacious. But they are all cosy and charming nonetheless; and the Angel is emphatically run as a small hotel rather than a pub – tellingly, there are no bars, and the residents' sitting-room on the first floor is quiet.

The Angel has been run by the Levis family for over 35 years, and another way in which they have managed to distinguish it from the run-of-the-mill 'olde inne' is by taking care to serve good English food – traditional roasts which are complemented by fresh locally grown vegetables. Part of the garden behind the hotel, which stretches along the banks of little Byde Brook, is populated by ducks and hens which produce more fresh ingredients for the Angel's table.

Nearby Lacock Abbey; Bowood House, 3 miles (5 km), Corsham Court, 3 miles (5 km), Sheldon Manor, 5 miles (8 km).

6 Church Street, Lacock, near Chippenham, Wiltshire SN15 2LA
Tel (024973) 230
Location 3 miles (5 km) S of Chippenham off A350, in middle of village; with gardens, but car parking on street
Food & drink full breakfast, lunch, dinner Mon-Sat; cold supper on Sun; full licence
Prices B & B £35-£45; dinner from £20; bargain breaks

Rooms 8 double, all with bath; all rooms have central heating, phone, tea/coffee kit
Facilities 2 dining-rooms, sitting-room
Credit cards MC, V
Children welcome over 12
Disabled access difficult
Pets dogs accepted, but not allowed in public rooms
Closed 22 Dec to 1 Jan
Proprietor J S Levis

Isle of Wight

Seaview Hotel

We wish there were more seaside hotels like this, catering for families but not compromising on standards of housekeeping and hospitality and (particularly) food and wine, for which Nicola Hayward (a former professional wine taster) has built a high reputation. The Seaview is also the central pub of the village, making it all the more attractive for most visitors. It is a mainly Edwardian/Victorian building.

Nearby Flamingo Park, one mile (1.5 km); Bembridge Maritime Museum, 4 miles (6 km).

High Street, Seaview, Isle of Wight PO34 5EX
Tel (0983) 612711
Location near the beach in seaside village 3 miles (5 km) E of Ryde; with car parking
Food & drink breakfast, lunch, dinner; pub meals; full licence
Prices B & B £25-£36; dinner from £14
Rooms 14 double, 12 with bath and 2 with shower; 2 suites, both with bath; all rooms have central heating,

TV, radio, baby listening
Facilities 2 sitting-rooms (one non-smoking), dining-room, bar, public bar
Credit cards AE, MC, V
Children very welcome – special meals and rooms provided
Disabled 2 ground-floor bedrooms, but doors too narrow for wheelchairs
Pets welcome if well behaved, except in public rooms
Closed never **Proprietors** N and N Hayward

Clarendon Hotel/Wight Mouse Inn

Staying at the Clarendon gives you the best of two worlds. The hotel itself is a listed Georgian building, sympathetically and comfortably furnished, and imbued with the jolly country-pub atmosphere of the attached Wight Mouse pub, built with oak beams salvaged from a wrecked sailing ship; the pub has a notable collection of malt whiskies behind the bar, and carefully controlled entertainment every night. The Bradshaws go out of their way to create a happy holiday atmosphere.

Nearby Carisbrooke Castle, 6 miles (10 km), Arreton Manor, 6 miles (10 km); the Needles; St Catherine's Point.

Chale, Isle of Wight PO38 2HA
Tel (0983) 730431
Location 7 miles (11 km) S of Newport close to B3399, on N side of village; ample car parking
Food & drink breakfast, lunch, dinner; full licence
Prices B & B £17-£19; DB & B £26-£28; reductions for children sharing parents' room
Rooms 5 double, one with

bath; 8 family rooms, one with bath, 7 with shower; all rooms have central heating, colour TV, coffee/tea kit
Facilities sitting-room, dining-room, bar, children's indoor and outdoor play areas
Credit cards not accepted
Children welcome
Disabled very difficult
Pets welcome if well trained
Closed never **Proprietors** John and Jean Bradshaw

Hampshire

Country house hotel, Hurstbourne Tarrant

Esseborne Manor

Peter Birnie and his young crew had this gracious, mainly Victorian house for only a few years, but quickly won friends. The new owners are well qualified to keep them. Bedrooms are well equipped and prettily done up, the sitting-room spacious and relaxed, the sitting-room bar stylish, the dining-room elegant. The menus, changing daily, present modern variation on traditional dishes, tailored to the season.

Nearby Hawk Conservancy, Weyhill, 7.5 miles (12 km).

Hurstbourne Tarrant,
Andover, Hampshire
SP11 0ER
Tel (026476) 444
Location 7 miles (11 km)
N of Andover, on A343 1.5
miles (2.5 km) N of village; in
2.5-acre grounds with ample
car parking
Food & drink breakfast,
lunch, dinner; residential
and restaurant licence
Prices B & B £39-£65; dinner
about £23; reductions for 2
nights or more
Rooms 12 double, all with
bath and shower; all rooms
have central heating, TV,
phone, clock, radio
Facilities sitting-room, bar,
dining-room; tennis,
croquet, golf practice net
Credit cards AE, DC, MC, V
Children welcome over 12
Disabled access easy to
restaurant and one ground-
floor bedroom with wider
doors **Pets** not accepted
Closed 2 weeks Christmas
Managers Frieda Yeo and
son, Simon Richardson

Manor house hotel, Middle Wallop

Fifehead Manor

The dreary chairs in reception, the uninspired decorations of the beamed dining-room and the slightly routine bedroom furniture are more than offset by this hotel's attractions – charm of the venerable red-brick building and its mature garden, the comfort and spaciousness of the smartly decorated bedrooms (particularly the newer ones), the excellent modern cooking of Matthew Beard and the friendliness of the young staff.

Nearby Museum of Army Flying; Stonehenge, 10 miles (16 km); Salisbury and Winchester within reach.

Middle Wallop, Stockbridge,
Hampshire SO20 8EG
Tel (0264) 781565
Location 5 miles (8 km)
SW of Andover on A343; in
gardens with parking for 50
cars
Food & drink breakfast,
lunch, dinner; full licence
Prices B & B £32.50-£50;
dinner from £20; bargain
breaks; children sharing
parents' room £10 (under 5
free)
- **Rooms** 10 double, all with
bath, 5 also with shower; 6
single, one with bath, 5 with
shower; all rooms have
central heating, TV, phone;
4 rooms have radio
Facilities sitting-room, bar,
2 dining-rooms; croquet
Credit cards AE
Children welcome
Disabled access to 2 rooms
Pets welcome
Closed 2 weeks Christmas
Proprietor Mrs M van Veelen

Hampshire

Wykeham Arms

This unusual back-street pub takes its name from the founder of Winchester College, only yards away; the cathedral is also close by, making this a natural port of call for senior members of the choir. Graeme Jameson – a 'regular' here before taking over the pub in 1984 – has created an appealing ambience. The bedrooms are simply but freshly done out (with bathrooms and even a sauna squeezed into the most unlikely spaces). There is a pleasant breakfast room, and varied casual meals as well as real ales are served in the cheerful bars.

Nearby Cathedral, Venta Roman Museum, Winchester College.

75 Kingsgate Street,
Winchester, Hampshire
SO23 9PE
Tel (0962) 53834
Location in middle of city, between College and cathedral, on corner of Canon Street; small rear garden with some car parking
Food & drink breakfast, lunch Mon-Sat, dinner Tue-Sat; full licence
Prices B&B £19.75-£42.50; dinner about £12

Rooms 7 double, 5 with bath; one family room; all rooms have central heating, colour TV, tea/coffee kit, radio/alarm
Facilities sitting-room, 3 bars, sauna; patio
Credit cards not accepted
Children welcome over 14
Disabled access difficult
Pets welcome
Closed never
Proprietors Graeme and Anne Jameson

Langrish House

A secluded country house, rescued from ruin in 1980 by its present owners. The rambling, white stone building dates back to the 16thC, though it is the Victorian gothic extensions which predominate from the sweeping gravel drive. The cellars have been cleverly excavated to provide a cosy restaurant, breakfast room and sitting areas. The plain, smallish sitting-room is rather unimaginative, but everything is spotlessly kept.

Nearby South coast, South Downs and Winchester within reach.

Langrish, Petersfield,
Hampshire GU32 1RN
Tel (0730) 66941
Location 3 miles (5 km) W of Petersfield, off A272; in 13-acre grounds, with ample car parking
Food & drink breakfast, dinner (except Sun and bank holidays); residential and restaurant licence
Prices B&B £25-£30; dinner from £10
Rooms 13 double, 5 single; all with bath; all rooms have

central heating, TV, phone
Facilities 3 sitting-rooms, dining-room, 2 bars
Credit cards AE, DC, MC
Children accepted, but not encouraged
Disabled access easy for ground-floor bedrooms; difficult for dining-room
Pets accepted by prior arrangement only
Closed never
Proprietor Monique von Kospoth

Hampshire

Town hotel, Wickham

Old House

The Old House has just about everything that we have been looking for in compiling this guide: a lovely setting – at a corner of the main square of one of the finest villages in Hampshire; a superb building – Grade II listed early Georgian; a delightful secluded garden full of roses; an immaculately kept and interesting interior, with antiques and 'objets' arranged to the best possible effect; and a restaurant serving far-above-average food – French regional in style, making excellent use of fresh ingredients. And, not least, there are the proprietors, Richard and Annie Skipwith, who keep a relaxed but attentive eye on the needs of the guests.

Nothing is over-stated – except perhaps the generous arrangements of fresh flowers which adorn all the public rooms. Bedrooms vary considerably – some are palatial, one or two rather cramped – but again a mood of civilized comfort prevails. Note however that the bedrooms are closed on Saturdays and Sundays, the restaurant on Sundays – which suggests that it is the business market which is predominant.

Nearby Portsmouth, 9 miles (14.5 km); South Downs; Winchester, Chichester within reach.

The Square, Wickham, Hampshire PO17 5JG
Tel (0329) 833049
Location 2.5 miles (4 km) N of Fareham, on square in middle of village; car parking
Food & drink full breakfast, lunch, dinner; residential and restaurant licence
Prices B & B £40-£60; dinner from £18
Rooms 9 double, 3 single, one family room, all with bath; all rooms have central heating, colour TV, phone, trouser-press, hairdrier, radio/alarm
Facilities 2 sitting-rooms, dining-room, bar
Credit cards AE, DC, MC, V
Children very welcome; special meals provided
Disabled access easy to dining-room **Pets** not accepted
Closed Sat and Sun; 2 weeks Christmas, Easter and July/August
Proprietor R P Skipwith

West Sussex

Ghyll Manor

The gabled half-timbered buildings and vast, park-like garden of Ghyll Manor lie only four miles from the west end of Gatwick's main runway. You pay jetset prices, but you get value for your money, especially on a 'bargain break' – a sitting-room lined with fine linenfold panelling, a beamed and chicly furnished restaurant featuring locally caught game, and stylish, antique-laden bedrooms (many with four-posters). Many rooms have been added recently, but the hotel still feels small.

Nearby Nyman's Gardens, 6 miles (10 km).

High Street, Rusper, West Sussex RH12 4PX
Tel (0293) 871571
Location 4 miles (6 km) W of Crawley off A264
Food & drink breakfast, lunch, tea, dinner; full licence
Prices B&B £46.50-£79.60; dinner from £18; weekend breaks
Rooms 17 double, 6 single and 5 suites all with bath and shower; all rooms have central heating, colour TV, phone, hairdrier, trouser-press, radio/alarm
Facilities library, bar, dining-room, sitting-room, 2 conference rooms; outdoor heated swimming-pool, tennis, croquet, sauna, solarium
Credit cards AE, DC, MC, V
Children welcome, complimentary cots
Disabled access difficult
Pets accepted
Closed never
Proprietor Jim Souter

Springwells

Close to the shops in Steyning's quiet, pretty High Street, this Georgian house has welcoming individually decorated bedrooms (a couple have four-poster beds), and offers a refreshingly personal welcome. It keeps the feel of a town house, with a sitting-room and breakfast room at the front, and a friendly bar (complete with conservatory extension) at the back. The terraces to the rear are especially attractive, and there is even an outdoor swimming-pool. There is a reasonable choice of places to eat in the village and nearby.

Nearby Cissbury Ring, 3 miles (5 km).

9 High Street, Steyning, West Sussex BN4 3GG
Tel (0903) 812446
Location in middle of village, with large garden and parking for 5 cars
Food & drink full breakfast; residential licence
Prices B&B £25-£39
Rooms 8 double, 6 with bath; 2 single, one with bath; one suite/family room, with bath; all rooms have central heating, colour TV, phone, tea/coffee kit
Facilities sitting-room with TV, dining-room, bar and conservatory; sauna, swimming-pool
Credit cards AE, DC, MC, V
Children welcome; cot and baby-sitting available
Disabled access easy only to public rooms **Pets** accepted only by arrangement
Closed Christmas
Proprietors Jeanne Heselgrave

West Sussex

Mill House

Peter and Jan Bench took over here in the middle of 1988. Unlike their predecessors, they are old hands at the hotel business.

First appearances are not promising – the approach to the hotel is down a decidedly rutted track on the fringes of the scatter suburban village of Ashington, the middle of which is bisected by the whizzing traffic of the A24. All the more pleasant, then, to come to the rambling white-painted 17thC building, standing amid mature trees with a graceful and secluded lawned garden and terrace to one side. Inside, the atmosphere is home-like rather than grand, though the long, split-level sitting-room has some fine antiques and a splendid inglenook fireplace at one end. Great efforts have been made to make visitors comfortable, with fresh flowers, pictures, books and table-lamps much in evidence here and in the small, cosy bar. The dining-room has bare-brick walls and exposed beams, and the solid wooden tables are candle-lit at night. Bedrooms vary in size, shape and style, but most have until recently been quite simply furnished with a mixture of modern, reproduction and antique pieces. As the guide went to press, all the rooms were being refurbished.

Nearby Parham House, 5 miles (8 km), Cissbury Ring, 5 miles (8 km), Arundel Castle, 10 miles (16 km); South Downs.

Mill Lane, Ashington, West Sussex RH20 3BZ
Tel (0903) 892426
Location 8 miles (13 km) N of Worthing, close to A24, just S of Ashington; in one-acre garden with ample car parking
Food & drink full breakfast, lunch, dinner; residential and restaurant licence
Prices B&B £25-£35; dinner from £10.50
Rooms 8 double, 6 with bath, one with shower, one with separate bathroom; 3 single, one with bath, one with shower, one with separate bathroom; all rooms have electric heater, colour TV, phone, hair-drier, trouser-press, tea/coffee kit
Facilities 2 sitting-rooms, cocktail bar, dining-room
Credit cards AE, DC, MC, V
Children welcome; cot and high chair provided; early meals on request
Disabled access difficult
Pets welcome, but not allowed in public rooms
Closed never
Proprietors Peter and Jan Bench

West Sussex

Millstream Hotel

A modern extension takes this comfortable and relaxed hotel slightly over our usual size limit, but the place remains informal, centred on an airy and pleasant bar, sitting-room and restaurant. Sensible modern furnishings predominate, and the pretty bedrooms are decked out in natural pine and quality patterned fabrics.

Nearby Fishbourne Roman Palace, 1.5 miles (2.5 km), Chichester Cathedral, 4 miles (6.5 km); South Downs.

Bosham Lane, Bosham, Chichester, West Sussex PO18 8HL
Tel (0243) 573234
Location 4 miles (6 km) W of Chichester off A259; in secluded garden with parking for 40 cars
Food & drink full breakfast, lunch, tea, dinner; residential and restaurant licence
Prices B&B £28.50-£32; DB&B £37-£42; reductions for 2 nights or more
Rooms 24 double, 5 single, all with bath; all rooms have central heating, colour TV, radio, hairdrier, trouser-press, phone, tea/coffee kit
Facilities sitting-room, dining-room, bar
Credit cards AE, DC, MC, V
Children welcome **Disabled** easy access to public rooms on ground floor **Pets** welcome, but not in public rooms
Closed never
Manager Nicholas Barker

Bailiffscourt

An extraordinary architectural fantasy, in the form of a 'medieval' manor house put together in the 1930s, Lego-like, from beams, arches and stones scrounged from the west country and elsewhere. But the illusion is as good as the real thing, and Bailiffscourt makes for a thoroughly relaxing place to stay, its mellow stone buildings grouped around a neat terraced courtyard and surrounded by sweeping lawns. The spacious and lavishly equipped bedrooms vary in style.

Nearby Arundel Castle, 3 miles (5 km), Bognor Regis, 5 miles (8 km), Boxgrove Priory, 6 miles (10 km).

Climping, Littlehampton, West Sussex BN17 5RW
Tel (0903) 723511
Location 1.5 mile (2.5 km) W of Littlehampton, close to A259; in 23 acres with ample car parking
Food & drink full breakfast, lunch, dinner; full licence
Prices B&B £45-£77.50; dinner £22.95
Rooms 16 double, all with bath, one also with shower; 4 single, all with bath; all rooms have central heating, colour TV, phone, clock/radio, hairdrier
Facilities 2 sitting-rooms, bar, library, dining-room, music room, card room; tennis, croquet, swimming-pool; helipad
Credit cards AE, DC, MC, V
Children welcome over 8
Disabled 2 ground-floor bedrooms
Pets dogs welcome; baskets and food provided
Closed never
Manager Tim Lamming

West Sussex

Ockenden Manor

Ockenden Manor is not the sort of hotel to treat as a goal in itself – it is 'professionally' managed, with the usual insensitivity. But the bedrooms are spacious, comfortable and individual (as well as being crammed with giveaways), and the staff friendly and obliging. Cooking is ambitious – modern, innovative dishes complemented by 'Plain Dishes' – and Kerry Turner assures us that portions can no longer be described as 'miniscule'.

Nearby Nyman's Garden, 3 miles (5 km), Bluebell Railway, 5 miles (8 km), Sheffield Park gardens, 6 miles (10 km).

Ockenden Lane, Cuckfield, West Sussex RH17 5LD
Tel (0444) 416111
Location 2 miles (3 km) W of Hayward's Heath close to middle of village, off A272; in 9-acre grounds, with ample car parking
Food & drink breakfast, lunch, tea, dinner; residential licence
Prices B&B £35-£65; dinner from £18.50; half-price meals for children under 10; weekend breaks

Rooms 12 double, all with bath; 3 single, 2 with bath, one with shower; all rooms have central heating, colour TV, phone, radio, trouser-press, hairdrier
Facilities sitting-room, bar, dining-room
Credit cards AE, DC, MC, V
Children welcome **Disabled** access easy to restaurant **Pets** dogs accepted, but not allowed in public rooms
Closed never
Manager Mr Kerry Turner

Findon Manor

Hospitality and good humour are everywhere at this mellow stone-and-flint ex-rectory at the heart of a famous Sussex horse-racing village. Individually furnished bedrooms, a couple with four-posters, have names rather than numbers; fresh flowers are much in evidence in the light, airy dining-room and small, beamed sitting-room; and the brochure even promises you a glass of 'aquavit' and two raw eggs at six in the morning if that is your idea of the perfect breakfast.

Nearby Parham House, 5 miles (8 km); South Downs.

High Street, Findon, West Sussex BN14 0TA
Tel (090671) 2733
Location 4 miles (6 km) N of Worthing off A24, in middle of village; in garden with parking for 30 cars
Food & drink full breakfast, lunch, tea, dinner; full licence
Prices B&B from £45; dinner from £12
Rooms 10 double, 9 with bath, one with shower; one single with bath and shower;

all rooms have central heating, phone, colour TV, coffee/tea kit, radio/alarm
Facilities sitting-room, bar, dining-room, conference room; croquet
Credit cards AE, DC, MC, V
Children welcome **Disabled** access easy to single bedroom on ground floor **Pets** welcome in bedrooms only
Closed 24 Dec to 1 Jan
Proprietors Andrew and Susan Tyrie

West Sussex

Manor house hotel, East Grinstead

Gravetye Manor

The country house hotel, now so much a part of the tourist scene in Britain, scarcely existed when Peter Herbert opened the doors of this serene Elizabethan house just over 32 years ago. It is scarcely surprising that in that time he and his team have got their act thoroughly polished; but it is remarkable that Gravetye is not in the least eclipsed by younger competitors. Standards in every department are unflaggingly high. Service consistently achieves the elusive aim of attentiveness without intrusion, while the ambitious food – eclectic, but predominantly French and English – is about the best in the county.

The pioneering gardener William Robertson lived in the house for half a century until his death in 1935. Great care is taken to maintain the various gardens he created and Robertson was also responsible for many features of the house as it is seen today – the mellow oak panelling and grand fireplaces in the calm sitting-rooms, for example. Bedrooms – all immaculately done out – vary in size from the adequate to the enormous, and prices range accordingly.

Nearby Bluebell Railway Line, 3 miles (5 km); Nyman's Gardens, 6 miles (10 km).

Vowels Lane, Near East Grinstead, West Sussex RH19 4LJ
Tel (0342) 810567
Location 4.5 miles (7 km) SW of East Grinstead by B2110 at Gravetye; in 30-acre grounds with ample car parking
Food & drink breakfast, lunch, dinner; restaurant and residential licence
Prices B&B £54-£86; dinner £22-£52
Rooms 12 double, 11 with bath, one with shower; 2 single, one with bath, one with shower; all rooms have central heating, TV, phone, radio, hairdrier
Facilities 2 sitting-rooms, bar, dining-room; Croquet, trout fishing **Credit cards** not accepted
Children welcome over 7, and babes in arms **Disabled** access difficult **Pets** not accepted **Closed** never
Proprietors Peter Herbert

West Sussex

Country house hotel, Storrington

Little Thakeham

We stray well outside our normal price limits here to embrace a house of irresistible character – an Edwin Lutyens Tudor-style manor house built in 1902-3 and considered one of his finest. The Ractliffs have been running it since 1980 as a refined and luxurious hotel of rare quality. The centrepiece is a double-height sitting-room with a vast fireplace and minstrel's gallery, and the furnishings – some designed by Lutyens himself – are of a high standard throughout. The Elizabethan theme continues into the part-paved, part-grassy gardens.

Nearby Parham House, 2.5 miles (4 km), Arundel Castle, 6 miles (10 km), Cissbury Ring, 5 miles (8 km); Sussex Downs.

Merrywood Lane, Storrington, West Sussex RH20 3HE
Tel (09066) 4416
Location 1.5 miles (2.5 km) N of Storrington, close to B2139; in garden and orchard with ample car parking
Food & drink full breakfast; lunch and dinner by arrangement; full licence
Prices B&B £52-£75; dinner £22.50

Rooms 9 double, all with bath; all rooms have central heating, colour TV with Teletext, phone
Facilities sitting-room, bar, restaurant; heated swimming-pool, tennis, croquet
Credit cards AE, DC, MC, V
Children welcome **Disabled** access fair **Pets** not accepted
Closed Christmas, New Year
Proprietors Tim and Pauline Ractliff

Country guest-house, Chichester

Crouchers Bottom

The Fodens have not explained the name of their converted farmhouse – a stalker's affliction, perhaps? – but they have told us that they aim to provide in it a relaxed and welcoming atmosphere for guests, and a reader writes to commend their success in this and other respects. Bedrooms (most of which are in a separate converted coach house, and in which there is no smoking) are 'very pretty, with lots of extra comforts', the Fodens 'charming and ever-helpful'.

Nearby Fishbourne Palace, Chichester Cathedral, 2 miles (3 km).

Birdham Road, Apuldram, Chichester, West Sussex PO20 7EH
Tel (0243) 784995
Location in countryside 2 miles (3 km) S of Chichester on the A286
Food & drink breakfast, dinner; residential and restaurant licence
Prices B&B £19-£30; dinner £12
Rooms 3 double, 2 with bath, all with shower; one family room with bath and shower;

all rooms have colour TV, tea/coffee kit, radio alarm, hairdrier
Facilities sitting-room with TV, dining-room
Credit cards MC, V
Children accepted
Disabled access easy – 2 ground-floor bedrooms
Pets not accepted **Closed** never **Proprietors** Ronald and Pamela Foden

East Sussex

The Twenty One

A reporter who had an "idyllic" stay in this tall Victorian town house in quiet Kemptown (on the quietly fashionable east side of the town) declares that "my mission in life is to find more places like this in Britain". Ours, too: since they opened up in 1979, Messrs Ward and Farquharson have shown that a small hotel can be beautifully furnished and caringly run without charging guests the earth.

The bedrooms are light and harmonious, and well equipped – one with a special emphasis on Victorian furnishings, including a splendid four-poster bed (but note that this room is one of those without en suite bathroom). Public rooms are smartly done out in a rich modern style, and the dining-room is particularly prettily decorated. Reports speak equally highly of Simone Ward's dinners – enterprising and rich four-course set meals with a French flavour – and the copious breakfasts (a professional taster even commends the coffee). The proprietors know just how to cosset guests without fussing over them unduly – "I asked whether they had a newspaper, and someone immediately rushed out and bought one for me" – but the place is run with a small staff so, delightful though it is, you cannot expect this kind of attention at all times.

Nearby Royal Pavilion, Aquarium and Dolphinarium, Volk's Electric Railway, all in Brighton.

21 Charlotte Street, Brighton, East Sussex BN2 1AG
Tel (0273) 686450
Location just off seafront road in Brighton; with free on-street parking
Food & drink breakfast, dinner (except Sun); residential licence
Prices B&B £15-£32; dinner £24
Rooms 7 double, 5 with shower; all rooms have central heating, colour TV, phone, tea/coffee kit, radio, hairdrier
Facilities sitting-room, dining-room
Credit cards AE, DC, MC, V
Children welcome over 12
Disabled not suitable
Pets accepted in bedrooms only, not left unattended
Closed mid-Dec to mid-Jan
Proprietors Stuart Farquharson and Simon Ward

East Sussex

Town hotel, Brighton

Topps

The Collins' complete renovation of these two terraced Regency houses may not have made the most of the character of the building, but it has certainly resulted in a hotel of exceptional comfort – the size of the bedrooms and the thorough equipment of the bathrooms come in for special commendation from visitors ("you could arrive without a suitcase and find everything you need"). There is a modest restaurant in the basement, painfully called Bottoms.

Nearby Royal Pavilion, seafront.

17 Regency Square,
Brighton, East Sussex BN1 2FG
Tel (0273) 729334
Location in heart of town
opposite West Pier; large
public car park opposite
Food & drink full breakfast,
dinner (except Wed and
Sun); residential and
restaurant licence
Prices B&B £32.50-£48;
dinner from £13.95;
reductions for 2 nights
Rooms 7 double, 5 single;
all with bath; all rooms have

central heating, colour TV,
phone, tea/coffee kit,
minibar, trouser-press,
hairdrier
Facilities bar, sitting-room,
dining-room
Credit cards AE, DC, MC, V
Children welcome
Disabled access difficult
Pets not accepted
Closed 24 Dec to 6 Jan
Proprietors Pauline and
Paul Collins

Country guest-house, Herstmonceux

Cleavers Lyng

Marylin Holden is one of the longest-serving proprietors in these pages: she has been running this picturesque tile-hung old house – dating from the 16thC, and sympathetically extended over the years – for close on 30 years. Son Neil is now part of the establishment, which is commended by a regular visitor for its warm atmosphere and plain but wholesome country cooking. Prices seem to be edging up more quickly than average, but remain sound value – particularly in view of the attractive setting on the edge of the South Downs.

Nearby Herstmonceux Castle (Observatory).

Church Road,
Herstmonceux, Hailsham,
East Sussex BN27 1QJ
Tel 0323 833131
Location 2 miles (3 km) S of
village, in countryside, next
to church; with parking for
15 cars
Food & drink breakfast,
lunch, tea, dinner
Prices B&B £13.35; DB&B
£19.95; reduced weekly rates
Rooms 6 double, 2 single;

all rooms have central
heating
Facilities dining-room with
bar, sitting-room with TV
Credit cards not accepted
Children welcome if well
behaved **Disabled** access
easy into most public rooms
Pets small well behaved
dogs accepted
Closed Christmas, New Year
Proprietors Marylin and
Neil Holden

East Sussex

Country guest-house, Telham

Little Hemingfold Farmhouse

Don't be misled by the word 'farmhouse': apart from the setting there is not much that is agricultural about this substantial, rambling building, part 17thC, part early Victorian. From small beginnings in the early 1980s, the previous owner Ann Benton built up her guest-house by converting the outbuildings around the neat, terraced courtyard into bedrooms to add to those in the main house. The Slaters took over in 1988.

The house has a peaceful setting in 40 acres of farm and woodland; it is surrounded by gardens, and overlooks a pretty 2-acre lake. Inside, the two comfortable sitting-rooms and the cosy dining-room all have log fires. So do four of the nine bedrooms accommodated in the outbuildings; all are individually furnished in pleasantly rustic style, and some have exposed beams.

The Slaters emphasize fresh ingredients in their cooking.
Nearby Bodiam Castle, 6 miles (10 km), Great Dixter, 6 miles (10 km); Rye within reach.

Telham, near Battle, East Sussex, TN33 0TT
Tel (04246) 4338
Location 1.5 miles (3 km) SE of Battle, off A2100; in 40-acre gardens, fields and woods, with ample car parking
Food & drink breakfast, light lunch, dinner; restaurant licence
Prices B&B £25; DB&B £38-£57; reductions for 2 nights or more
Rooms 10 double, 2 single; all with bath; all rooms have central heating, colour TV, phone, tea/coffee kit, radio clocks, electric blankets
Facilities 2 sitting-rooms, dining-room, bar; trout lake; boating, tennis, archery, croquet
Credit cards MC, V
Children welcome over 10
Disabled access very difficult
Pets small dogs accepted in garden rooms
Closed never
Proprietors Paul and Allison Slater

East Sussex

Town guest-house, Rye

The Old Vicarage

Ruth and Ernest Thompson built up a faithful following for their Tudor-Georgian house, taken over in 1988 by Paul and Julia Masters – a 'very friendly and helpful couple', to quote a reporter familiar with the old regime but very happy with the new. The house has an excellent position – central but peaceful, next to St Mary's church – but the new owners have set about giving it other attractions too. The bedrooms are now prettily decorated in Laura Ashley papers and fabrics, more of them have private bathrooms, and all have improved facilities. Breakfast includes home-made jams. Note that the cobbled streets hereabouts are awkward for anyone unsteady on their feet.

Nearby Great Dixter, 6 miles (10 km); Ellen Terry Museum.

66 Church Square, Rye, East Sussex, TN31 7HF
Tel (0797) 222119
Location on A259 near middle of town; with small walled garden, parking arrangements
Food & drink full breakfast, no licence
Prices B&B £16-£20
Rooms 4 double, 3 with shower; all rooms have central heating, TV, tea/coffee kit, hairdrier
Facilities sitting-room, dining-room
Credit cards not accepted
Children welcome over 12
Disabled not suitable
Pets not accepted
Closed never
Proprietors Paul and Julia Masters

Country house hotel, Netherfield

Netherfield Place

Netherfield Place gives the appearance of a Georgian mansion, but was built in 1924. It has been open as a hotel for seven years, the last four in the hands of the Colliers. The bedrooms are tastefully although fussily decorated, with fine views of the gardens. Public rooms are comfortable and stylish, although lacking the intimacy of less grand establishments.

Nearby Great Dixter, 6 miles (10 km), Bodiam Castle, 6 miles (10 km), Bateman's, 6 miles (10 km); Rye within reach.

Netherfield, Battle, East Sussex TN33 9PP
Tel (04246) 4455
Location 3 miles (5 km) NW of Battle, 2 miles (3 km) off A2100; in 30-acre grounds with parking for 30 cars
Food & drink full breakfast, lunch, dinner; full licence
Prices B&B £32.50-£55; dinner £16.95
Rooms 10 double, all with bath, 8 also with shower; 4 single, all with bath; all rooms have central heating, colour TV with Teletext, phone, radio
Facilities 2 sitting-rooms, bar, dining-room, tennis
Credit cards AE, DC, MC, V
Children welcome if well behaved **Disabled** access easy to dining-room, but no ground-floor bedrooms
Pets not generally accepted, but small breeds possibly by arrangement
Closed Christmas and New Year
Proprietors H and M Collier

East Sussex

Country hotel, Wallcrouch

Spindlewood

Robert Fitzsimmons and his parents have worked hard since 1979 to create an inviting country hotel in their rather austere Victorian building – it is now enlivened by a riot of colour in the herbaceous borders, overflowing hanging baskets adorn the glass-roofed loggia, and inside all is gradually becoming bright and colourful, as well. Bedrooms are all light and airy (some exceptionally spacious) with flowery wallpaper, thick new carpet, candlewick bedspreads, comfy armchairs and old-fashioned wooden furniture. The spanking new bathrooms are well decorated and generally spacious. Downstairs, the bar and the cosy wood-panelled sitting-room/library, with its large log fire, are more old-fashioned and homey than country-house; and the blue-and-brown dining-room is rather plainer than the chef's excellent cooking deserves. Harvey Lee Aram prepares dishes ('in the modern style') to order, and it is well worth the wait. The sound wine list merits unhurried consideration, too.

Nearby Bateman's, Scotney Castle, 4 miles (6 km).

Wallcrouch, Wadhurst, East Sussex TN5 7JG
Tel (0580) 200430
Location 9 miles (14.5 km) SE of Tunbridge Wells, on B2099, 2.5 miles (4 km) E of Wadhurst; in 5-acre gardens and woodland, with ample car parking
Food & drink full breakfast, lunch, dinner; residential and restaurant licence
Prices B&B £35-£45; dinner £12-£18; bargain breaks
Rooms 7 double with bath; 2 single, one with bath, one with shower; one family room with bath; all rooms have central heating, colour TV, radio/alarm, phone, tea/coffee kit, hairdrier
Facilities sitting-room, bar, dining-room
Credit cards AE, DC, MC, V
Children welcome if well behaved; cot, high-chair and high tea available
Disabled access easy only to dining-room
Pets guide dogs welcome
Closed 4 days at Christmas
Proprietors R V Fitzsimmons and Mr and Mrs R Fitzsimmons

East Sussex

New Inn

The New Inn is first and foremost a pub, and although its rooms do not match the standard of many of our other entries they are pleasant and inexpensive. Equally important, it is a thoroughly pleasant pub. The bars have some respectable wooden furniture, flagstone and carpeted floors, an array of dried flowers and horse brasses, and above all a friendly welcome for strangers. There is also a small garden and an area for families that is part of the pub rather than hidden away as is so often the case. It is described by landlords Richard and Eileen Joyce as "an eating pub rather than a drinking one".

Nearby Rye, 2 miles (3 km), Great Dixter, 7 miles (11 km).

German Street, Winchelsea, East Sussex TN36 4EN
Tel (0797) 226252
Location in middle of town, facing church; with garden, and parking for 16 cars
Food & drink full breakfast, lunch, dinner; full licence
Prices B&B £13.50-£16; dinner from £6; 10% reduction for 3 nights or more
Rooms 3 double; 3 family rooms, 2 with shower; all rooms have central heating, tea/coffee kit
Facilities 2 bars
Credit cards AE, DC, MC, V
Children welcome **Disabled** wheelchair access to saloon bar **Pets** not accepted
Closed Christmas Day and Boxing Day
Proprietors Mr and Mrs Richard Joyce

Powdermills

It is the extensive grounds, complete with lakes and woodland, which are perhaps the main attraction of this elegant Georgian house. The Cowplands are big in the antiques trade, and have assembled an interesting variety of period pieces – though without spoiling the comfortable, lived-in feel of the sitting-rooms. They are getting bigger in the hotel trade, too – as we prepared this edition, six new bedrooms had just been added. Julie Cowpland cooks dinners with a local flavour.

Nearby Bodiam, 6 miles (10 km), Bateman's, 8 miles (13 km).

Powdermill Lane, Battle, East Sussex TN33 0SP
Tel (04246) 2035
Location on S side of town; in 50-acre grounds with ample car parking
Food & drink full breakfast, tea, dinner; lunch by arrangement; full licence
Prices B&B £25-£37.50; dinner £11.50; low-season reductions; bargain breaks
Rooms 12 double, 2 suites; all with bath and shower; all rooms have central heating
Facilities sitting-rooms, sitting-room with TV, bar, library, dining-room, function room; outdoor swimming-pool, croquet, tennis, fishing; riding and golf nearby
Credit cards not accepted
Children welcome if well behaved **Disabled** access easy **Pets** dogs welcome if well behaved
Closed never
Proprietors Douglas and Julie Cowpland

West Kent

Country guest-house, Bethersden

Little Hodgeham

Most small hotels reflect the personality of their owner, but some are virtually extensions of that personality; Little Hodgeham falls squarely into the latter category. Erica Wallace dominates this picture-postcard Tudor house, and although evidence of her care, attention and hard work abounds, it is the vitality of her character that makes a lasting impression on guests. (Ms Wallace is not past putting a greeting card on the bed of a couple arriving for a wedding anniversary celebration and preparing heart-shaped mousses for that evening's first course.)

The lovingly restored house has just three bedrooms, all beautifully and carefully co-ordinated, right down to the choice of flowers. The split-level four-poster room is particularly striking. The sitting-room has a massive open fireplace, exposed beams and furnishings in complementary colours. The dining-room is small and intimate, the cooking displaying Erica Wallace's untutored 'natural feel for food'. The gardens, duck pond included, are immaculately kept.

Nearby Kent and East Sussex Railway, 6 miles (10 km); Sissinghurst Castle gardens, 8 miles (13 km).

Smarden Road, Bethersden, Kent TN26 3HE
Tel (023385) 323
Location 2 miles (3 km) NW of Bethersden, 8 miles (13 km) W of Ashford by A28; in garden, with car parking
Food & drink full breakfast, dinner; residential licence
Prices DB&B £35; reductions for 4 nights or more and children sharing parents' room
Rooms 3 double, 2 with bath, one with shower; all rooms have central heating, tea/coffee kit, hairdrier, radio
Facilities sitting-room, dining-room, TV room; carp fishing, small outdoor swimming-pool
Credit cards not accepted
Children accepted; usually fed earlier than adults
Disabled not suitable **Pets** accepted by arrangement
Closed Oct to mid-Mar
Proprietor Erica Wallace

West Kent

Manor house hotel, Cranbrook

Kennel Holt

You would be hard pressed to find a better-placed base for an exploration of south-east England than Cranbrook. And you certainly will not find a hotel which feels more at one with its Kentish setting than Kennel Holt – an Elizabethan manor of soft red brick and white wooden boards, set in secluded and flowery gardens.

It is a homely manor rather than a grand one, with capacious sofas before the open fires of its spacious, beamed sitting-rooms, and honest antiques dotted about bearing plants and flowers. The Misseldines took over in 1988 and, if their slogan is any guide ('You really couldn't feel more at home in a hotel'), are likely to maintain the welcoming atmosphere of the house. They have introduced one or two new facilities, but more importantly have a more relaxed attitude to mealtimes.

Chef Ian Bust cooks classic French and English dishes – and non-residents are catered for in a separate room. Prices include morning and afternoon tea, and a newspaper.

Nearby Sissinghurst Castle gardens, 3 miles (5 km), Hole Park, 5 miles (8 km); Weald of Kent; Rye within easy reach.

Goudhurst Road, Cranbrook, Kent TN17 2PT
Tel (0580) 712032
Location 1.5 miles (2.5 km) NW of Cranbrook, close to A262; in 5.5-acre gardens, with ample car parking
Food & drink full breakfast, dinner, snack lunch on request; residential and restaurant licence
Prices DB&B £56-£75; reduction for children sharing parents' room
Rooms 8 double, 5 with bath, 2 with shower; 2 single, both with separate bathroom; all rooms have central heating, colour TV, video, phone, radio/alarm, hairdrier
Facilities 2 sitting-rooms, dining-room; croquet
Credit cards AE, DC, MC, V
Children welcome, but those under 6 at proprietors' discretion
Disabled access difficult
Pets dogs accepted by arrangement
Closed 25-27 Dec
Proprietors Mr and Mrs D G Misseldine

West Kent

Star and Eagle

Reputed to be an old monastery building with connecting tunnels to the neighbouring church, the Star and Eagle has a magnificent location at the top of the pretty, bustling village of Goudhurst. The building is almost a visual cliché with its dark timbers, whitewashed walls, wooden balcony and latticed windows. Inside, dark wood and heavy beams are to the fore in both the restaurant and bar. Getting to any of the bedrooms is an adventure requiring much ducking of heads and bending of backs under very low beams, and up some awkward stairs. Look out, too, for some of the original 15thC plaster panels.

Nearby Sissinghurst Castle gardens, 5.5 miles (9 km).

High Street, Goudhurst, Kent TN17 1AL
Tel (0580) 211512
Location at top of High Street; ample car parking
Food & drink full breakfast, lunch, dinner; full licence
Prices B&B £25-£45; dinner from £8
Rooms 10 double, 8 with bath and shower; one single with bath; all rooms have central heating, colour TV, radio/ alarm, tea/coffee kit, phone, hairdrier
Facilities sitting-room, dining-room, bar
Credit cards AE, MC, V
Children welcome **Disabled** access difficult **Pets** not in bedrooms **Closed** never
Manager M Dimet

Moatenden Priory

Hidden down a quiet country lane off the main Headcorn-Sutton Valence road, Moatenden Priory is a small, slightly tumbledown building founded in 1224. Notable features are a Norman arched doorway, and an archetypal English rambling garden. The four bedrooms are all simply but adequately furnished in a restrained style that reflects the character of the house's charming owner, Mrs Deane. At weekends there are communal evening meals in the wooden-ceilinged dining-room, after which guests can relax in front of the massive open fire in the sitting-room. A friendly, relaxed and welcoming atmosphere at a bargain price. Smoking is not permitted.

Nearby Leeds Castle, 4 miles (6 km), Boughton Monchelsea Place, 4.5 miles (7 km), Sissinghurst Castle garden, 4.5 miles (7 km).

Headcorn, Kent TN27 9PT
Tel (0622) 890413
Location 6 miles (10 km) S of Maidstone on A274, 1.5 miles (2.5 km) N of village; in 2-acre garden with parking for 4 cars
Food & drink full breakfast, dinner Fri to Mon by arrangement; no licence
Prices B&B £12.50-£25; dinner £10
Rooms 3 double, one single; all rooms have central heating
Facilities sitting-room, dining-room/kitchen
Credit cards not accepted
Children welcome if kept under control **Disabled** not suitable **Pets** welcome
Closed Christmas
Proprietor Mrs J B Deane

West Kent

Tanyard

"Exactly the sort of place you are looking for – a most interesting building in a beautiful setting, not far from a busy town, run by a committed and sensitive proprietor and with top-class food."

This report from a regular visitor pays proper tribute to Tanyard's setting and the contribution Jan Davies makes to the well-being of her guests, but underplays the attractions of the house itself. It is a dream of a building – timber-framed, built around 1350 and entirely without symmetry, red tiles and muted yellow paint outside, sparkling white between the mellow exposed beams within – set in a lovely country garden with glorious views across the Weald of Kent.

It is furnished with a cheerful mix of modern and antique pieces – all very natural and home-like – and both the sitting-room and dining-room have large inglenook fireplaces. All the bedrooms are spacious, and at the top of the house is a large open-plan suite.

Jan Davies' dinners offer no choice, but preferences can be taken into account.

Nearby Boughton Monchelsea Place; Leeds Castle, 4 miles (6 km).

Wierton Hill, Boughton Monchelsea, near Maidstone, Kent ME17 4JT
Tel (0622) 744705
Location 4.5 miles (7 km) S of Maidstone, just off B2163; in 4-acre grounds with ample car parking
Food & drink full breakfast, dinner; residential licence
Prices B&B £25.88-£74.75; dinner £16.10
Rooms 4 double, 3 with bath, one with shower; one suite; all rooms have central heating, TV, phone, tea/coffee kit
Facilities dining-room, sitting-room
Credit cards AE, DC, MC, V
Children welcome over 6
Disabled not suitable
Pets not accepted
Closed mid–Dec to early Mar
Proprietor Jan Davies

West Kent

Inn, Smarden

The Bell

The Bell is a typical Kentish pub – weather-boarded and tile-hung outside, inglenook fireplaces, oak beams, stone floors and agricultural implements around the walls within. What makes it stand out from the crowd is the attractive small garden, with its wooden furniture and parasols, and the warm welcome from Mr and Mrs Turner, who have owned the pub for the last 14 years. The four rooms, simply but comfortably furnished, are equipped with a library's worth of paperbacks. Access is via a wrought-iron spiral staircase. Bed-and-breakfast rates are reasonable and the Bell's food has many admirers.

Nearby Sissinghurst Castle gardens, 4 miles (6 km), Leeds Castle, 7 miles (11 km); Kent Downs.

Bell Lane, Smarden, Kent
TN27 8PW
Tel (023377) 283
Location 8 miles (13 km) W
of Ashford, one mile (1.5
km) NW of village on
Headcorn road; with
ample car parking
Food & drink breakfast, bar
lunch, bar dinner; full licence

Prices B&B £12-£13
Rooms 4 double; all rooms
have TV, tea/coffee kit
Facilities bars, games room,
family room
Credit cards MC, V
Children welcome **Disabled**
access difficult **Pets** welcome
Closed Christmas Day
Proprietor Ian Turner

Town guest-house, Tenterden

West Cross House

Mr and Mrs May, who are both retired public servants, bought this Georgian town house (in an excellent position on Tenterden's wide, leafy main street) five years ago, and after much renovation opened it up primarily as a bed-and-breakfast establishment. The ground-floor sitting-room is light, spacious and well decorated, with an inglenook fireplace. The dining-room suffers slightly in comparison, being plainer and smaller; the bedrooms are comfortable, and reasonably priced; those at the front have double glazing to keep out traffic noise. Behind the house is a secluded walled garden.

Nearby Kent and East Sussex Railway; Hole Park, 2.5 miles (4 km).

2 West Cross, Tenterden,
Kent TN30 6JL
Tel (05806) 2224
Location at W end of town;
in walled garden with
adequate car parking at rear
Food & drink full breakfast,
dinner by arrangement;
residential licence
Prices B&B £12-£15; dinner £7
Rooms 4 double, one single,
2 family rooms; all rooms
have central heating, tea/

coffee kit
Facilities sitting-room,
dining-room
Credit cards not accepted
Children welcome if well
behaved; cot, high-chair
available **Disabled** not
suitable **Pets** well-behaved
dogs welcome, but not in
public rooms
Closed Nov to Feb
Proprietors Mr G and Mrs
M May

East Kent

Country guest-house, Chartham Hatch

Howfield Manor

"The usual, I'm afraid," said the previous owner of this charming house, in answer to our preliminary enquiries: "beams, inglenook fireplaces, candles and silver in the dining-room, lots of magazines and books." This list of ingredients may not be uncommon in small English hotels, and may not be a guarantee of charm; but it is not a bad start, and is the makings of a delectable dish. Martin Towns has been in charge since 1987, and has seen the change from home into hotel. There is now a 50-seat dining-room, and twice the original number of bedrooms. Time will tell whether the new formula works.

Nearby Canterbury Cathedral; Chilham Castle and gardens, 4 miles (6 km); the Kent Downs.

Howfield Lane, Chartham Hatch, Canterbury, Kent CT4 7HQ
Tel (0227) 738294
Location 2 miles (3 km) SW of Canterbury on A28; with ample car parking
Food & drink breakfast, lunch, dinner; residential licence
Prices B&B £27.50-£50; dinner from £18.95
Rooms 8 double, 2 single; all with bath and shower; all rooms have central heating, phone, alarm clock, hairdrier, trouser-press
Facilities sitting-room, library with TV, bar, dining-room, conference suite
Credit cards AE, DC, MC, V
Children welcome over 14
Disabled access difficult
Pets not accepted
Closed never
Proprietor Martin Towns

Town guest-house, Dover

Number One

One of the few properties of its vintage to survive the wartime bombing raids on Dover, this is a Georgian town house only minutes away from the Eastern Docks has become a well established favourite with cross-travellers who have need of break in their journey, or indeed who want to see something of Kent on the way. It is the Reidys' home, and has no pretensions to be anything more than a welcoming and comfortable home from home. Visitors remark on the Reidys' kindness, and readiness to adapt to the awkwardness of cross-Channel travel plans. We have a critical report of a damp basement room.

Nearby Canterbury within reach; France.

1 Castle Street, Dover, Kent CT16 1QH
Tel (0304) 202007
Location on E side of town, beneath Dover Castle; lock-up garage available or free car parking on street
Food & drink full breakfast; no licence
Prices B&B £12-£15
Rooms 3 double, 3 family rooms; all with shower; all rooms have colour TV, tea/coffee kit, hairdrier
Facilities sitting-room
Credit cards not accepted
Children welcome **Disabled** not suitable **Pets** small pets accepted by prior arrangement
Closed never
Proprietors John and Adeline Reidy

East Kent

Country guest-house, Hastingleigh

Woodmans Arms Auberge

The Campions' latest successful venture is a pink-painted 17thC inn – in practice open only to residents and their guests – in a delightfully secluded setting in a dead-end lane on the edge of the Downs. The low-ceilinged sitting-room and dining-room are furnished in charming cottagey style, the bedrooms prettily decorated. Susan's delectable dinners offer no choice until the dessert, but personal preferences can be taken into account; guests sit at separate tables, but this is nevertheless not a place for privacy. There is no smoking in the house.

Nearby Lympne Castle, 6 miles (10 km); Kent Downs.

Hassell Street, Hastingleigh, near Ashford, Kent TN25 5JE
Tel (023375) 250
Location 5 miles (8 km) W of Ashford, one mile (1.5 km) N of Hastingleigh; in large garden with parking for 6 cars
Food & drink full breakfast, tea, dinner; full licence
Prices B&B £25-£45; dinner £15
Rooms 3 double, all with bath, 2 also with shower; all rooms have central heating, colour TV, phone
Facilities bar, sitting-room, dining-room
Credit cards not accepted
Children welcome over 14
Disabled access difficult
Pets not accepted
Closed one week after Easter, 3 weeks Sep/Oct
Proprietors Susan and Gerald Campion

East Kent

Manor house hotel, St Margaret's-at-Cliffe

Wallett's Court

The Oakleys started doing bed and breakfast in their handsome old manor house in 1979, moved on to doing country suppers and now have a full-blown restaurant, open to non-residents. There are four compact, pine-furnished rooms in a converted barn, and a grander one in the main house, with abundant beams and brickwork in the best Kent tradition, and robust antique furniture. Both rooms and excellent value

Nearby Walmer Castle, 3 miles (5 km); Kent Downs.

West Cliffe, St Margaret's-at-Cliffe, Dover, Kent CT15 6EW
Tel (0304) 852424
Location 3 miles (5 km) NE of Dover on B2058, off A258; with garden and ample car parking
Food & drink full breakfast, dinner; residential and restaurant licence
Prices B & B £17.50-£40; dinner from £12.50 Mon-Fri, £18.50 Sat
Rooms 5 double, all with bath, 3 with shower; 2 family rooms, both with shower; all rooms have central heating, tea/coffee kit
Facilities sitting-room, dining-room, playroom, table-tennis
Credit cards MC
Children welcome
Disabled access difficult to dining-room; one annexe bedroom suitable **Pets** accepted in one bedroom, but not allowed in public rooms
Closed one week autumn and spring; Christmas
Proprietors C and L Oakley

Inn, St Margaret's-at-Cliffe

Cliffe Tavern

The father-and-son Westbys have built up the accommodation side of their business over the years, but the Cliffe Tavern nevertheless remains firmly a pub – with several real ales, and no sitting space except in the bars (and in the pretty walled garden). The white-painted clapboard pub itself dates from 1584. Most of the bedrooms are in the two annexes – one a cottage of similar vintage to the main house, the other recently built. All are simply furnished, but clean and of a fair size.

Nearby Deal, 5 miles (8 km).

High Street, St Margarets-at-Cliffe, Dover, Kent CT15 6AT
Tel (0304) 852749
Location 4 miles (6 km) NE of Dover, in middle of village; with walled garden, and ample car parking
Food & drink breakfast, lunch, dinner; full licence
Prices B & B £17.30-£26.30; dinner about £8
Rooms 10 double, 9 with bath, one with shower; 2 family rooms with bath; all rooms have central heating, colour TV, tea/coffee kit
Facilities 2 bars, dining-room
Credit cards AE, DC, MC, V
Children welcome if well behaved
Disabled access fairly easy – 5 ground-floor bedrooms with one or two small steps
Pets welcome if well behaved
Closed never **Proprietor** Christopher Westby

Berkshire

Inn, Yattendon

Royal Oak

'Hotel and restaurant,' says the sign on the front of this cottagey, mellow red-brick inn, lest you mistake it for a mere pub. Certainly, the Royal Oak is no longer a common-or-garden local: the Smiths, whose background is in smart London hotels and restaurants, have given it a style and elegance not usually associated with ale and darts. But the Oak does still have a small bar where residents and non-residents alike can enjoy a choice of real ales without having a meal.

Next in line along the terrace in which the Oak has been formed is the light, relaxed and comfortable sitting-room (with newspapers and books within easy reach of its sofas) and beyond that the dining-room with its elegant reproduction furniture and elaborate designer decoration. The bar/dining-room is less formal. Bedrooms are prettily decorated in fashionable style, the en suite bathrooms magnificently equipped with Victorian-style fittings including deep iron baths.

Richard Smith's cooking is inventive and expert, and the meals served in both the dining-room and the bar are ambitious – an amalgam of modern and more traditional dishes.

Nearby Basildon Park, 3 miles (5 km), Donnington Castle, 6 miles (10 km), Snelsmore Common, 6 miles (10 km).

The Square, Yattendon, near Newbury, Berkshire RG16 0UF
Tel (0635) 201325
Location 7 miles (11 km) NE of Newbury, in middle of village; walled garden and separate parking for 30 cars
Food & drink full breakfast, lunch, dinner; full licence
Prices B&B £27.50-£42; dinner from £17.50
Rooms 5 double, 4 with bath, one with shower; all rooms have colour TV, radio, phone, hairdrier

Facilities dining-room, sitting-room, 3-roomed bar/dining-room
Credit cards AE, MC, V
Children welcome if well behaved **Disabled** access easy to restaurant and bar but difficult to toilets and bedrooms **Pets** accepted by prior arrangement
Closed never
Proprietors Kate and Richard Smith

London

Town guest-house, Knightsbridge

L'Hotel

Opened in 1983 by David Levin, who is owner of the much-praised Capital Hotel next door, L'Hôtel adds a touch of glamour to the tarnished image of the big-city B&B. Some may baulk at paying high prices for a place with so few facilities (no room service or sitting-room), despite the pretty décor and professional staff. But others treasure the very fact that L'Hôtel is unaffected and simple, yet clearly in the luxury class. "We always stayed in top London hotels," said one glamorous guest, "but we find we miss none of their vast array of facilities here; nor do we miss the way they are monopolized by businessmen."

Far from being a businessman's enclave, this is a hotel which welcomes children – unusual for a small, up-market establishment – and sees husbands driven mad by their wives' habit of "just popping into Harrods" next door.

Bedrooms at L'Hôtel have been decorated by Margaret Levin in rustic yet feminine style. They vary hardly at all – none is large – but the three most pleasant are those which sport gas log fires. The reception area has a colonial American feel, with stencilled walls. Guests take breakfast in the smart cream-and-brown Metro wine bar in the basement, which is also open to non-residents and serves light French country dishes.

Nearby Hyde Park, Knightsbridge, Buckingham Palace.

28 Basil Street, London
SW3 1AT
Tel (01/071) 589 6286
Location between Sloane Street and Harrods; paying car park opposite
Food & drink breakfast; snacks, lunch, dinner available in wine bar
Prices B&B £45; suite £60
Rooms 11 double, one suite; all with bath and shower; all

rooms have central heating, radio, TV, phone, minibar, tea/coffee kit
Facilities wine bar
Credit cards AE, V
Children welcome **Disabled** not suitable **Pets** accepted by arrangement
Closed restaurant only, Sat dinner, Sun lunch and dinner
Proprietor David Levin

London

Town hotel, Marylebone

Dorset Square

Just a few years old, this striking hotel stands on the south side of the fine Regency garden square which was the original site of Lord's cricket ground. Outside is a discreet brass plaque bearing the hotel's name; inside, a delightful evocation of a traditional English country house – the work of co-owner Kit Kemp. The sensation that absolutely nothing has been left to chance may be slightly unnerving – even the receptionist is dressed in cricket flannels – but there is no denying that the whole effect is captivating. Colefax chintzes, striped wallpapers and clever paint effects are mixed with flair in the small public rooms, along with an abundance of flowers and pictures. Bedrooms – whose solid marble bathrooms include de luxe American showers which practically knock you over – are all fresh and supremely elegant, with not a jarring note to be found. In the basement is a countrified cream and blue-striped restaurant serving modern English dishes such as lobster sausage with saffron sauce.

Don't expect a sleepy, easy-going country-house atmosphere to go with the surroundings at Dorset Square. This is a slick city hotel with a carefully contrived image and a dynamic young management team.

Nearby Regent's Park, Madame Tussaud's, Oxford Street.

39 Dorset Square, London NW1 6QN
Tel (01/071) 723 7874
Location close to Marylebone station, in square with access to 3-acre private gardens, but no private car parking
Food & drink breakfast, lunch, dinner, full room service; full licence
Prices B&B £45-£133
Rooms 31 double, 6 single; all with bath and/or shower; all rooms have central heating, colour TV, clock/radio, minibar, phone
Facilities sitting-room, dining-room, bar
Credit cards AE, MC, V
Children welcome over 10
Disabled access easy to ground-floor bedrooms
Pets accepted by arrangement
Closed never
Manager Martin T Ball

London

Pembridge Court

This early Victorian town house offers friendly service and well-equipped, comfortable bedrooms with modern bathrooms. The standard rooms have recently been fully refurbished; the deluxe ones are notably spacious. A novel feature of the hotel is the large collection of framed Victorian fans, lace gloves and miscellaneous clothes on the walls. The basement restaurant and bar, Caps, is decorated with school and club caps.

Nearby Kensington Gardens, Kensington shops.

34 Pembridge Gardens,
London W2 4DX
Tel (01/071) 229 9977
Location a short walk N of
Notting Hill Gate, in
residential street with garage
for 2 cars; nearest tube
Notting Hill Gate
Food & drink breakfast,
snacks, dinner; restaurant
and residential licence
Prices B&B £40.25-£86.25;
dinner about £12
Rooms 14 double, all with
bath; 8 single, 2 with bath, 6
with shower; 2 family rooms,
both with bath; all rooms
have central heating, colour
TV, radio, phone.
Facilities restaurant, bar,
sitting-room
Credit cards AE, DC, MC, V
Children very welcome
Disabled access difficult,
though there is a lift **Pets**
accepted if well behaved
Closed never
Proprietors Paul Capra

Portobello Hotel

An established favourite with the music industry and other night owls, with a 24-hour bar and restaurant for the exclusive use of guests. Pastel decoration with cane armchairs in the bar, and garden chairs in the marble-tiled dining-room give a fresh, light air. The sitting-room is a mixture of styles, with modern sofas, a large leather-top desk, parlour palms in Victorian 'jardinières', and stripped French doors draped with brillant red livery. Bedrooms range from compact 'cabins' to spacious suites dominated by heavy, carved four-posters. Bathrooms are often small.

Nearby Kensington Gardens, Kensington High Street.

22 Stanley Gardens,
London W11 2NG
Tel (01/071) 727 2777
Location in residential area
north of Holland Park;
nearest tube: Holland Park
or Notting Hill Gate
Food & drink breakfast (in
room); other meals available
24 hours a day
Prices B&B £43.12-£71.30;
meals widely variable
Rooms 9 double, 9 single; all
with shower; 7 suites, 4 with
bath, 3 with bath and
shower; all rooms have
central air heating, colour
TV, phone, minibar
Facilities dining-room,
sitting-room, bar
Credit cards AE, DC, MC, V
Children welcome if well
behaved **Disabled** access
difficult **Pets** welcome if well
behaved
Closed one week at
Christmas
Manager John Ekperigin

London

Bed and breakfast guest-house, South Kensington

Number Sixteen

Although Michael Watson sold Number Sixteen in 1987, he keeps a watchful eye on it as a director of its parent company, and it remains one of London's most characterful luxury bed-and-breakfast establishments. The original building has spread along its early Victorian South Kensington terrace, to encompass three more adjoining houses, and major refurbishment has been undertaken by the new owners.

Public rooms and bedrooms alike are brimful of pictures, including a huge eye-catching abstract in the reception room. Downstairs there are always big bowls of fresh flowers – sweet peas or roses perhaps – and the large rear patio garden is well kept and full of colour. Inside, the decoration is traditional – past its first bloom perhaps, but harmonious. A series of small sitting-rooms, where drinks can be served, lead to a recently built garden room, from where, on summer days, you can sit and admire the profusion of flowers outside. Bedrooms are generously proportioned, comfortable though fairly simple, and largely furnished with period pieces; some have French windows opening on to the garden. Bathrooms are tiled and functional. Breakfast is served in your room.

Nearby South Kensington museums, Knightsbridge, Sloane Square, Kensington Gardens.

16 Sumner Place, London
SW7 3EG
Tel (01/071) 589 5232
Location just off Old
Brompton Road; small
garden, but no private car
parking; nearest tube South
Kensington
Food & drink breakfast;
residential licence
Prices B&B £50-£95
Rooms 28 double, 19 with
bath, 9 with shower; 4 single,
all with shower; all rooms
have central heating,
minibar, hairdrier, phone;
TV available
Facilities sitting-room, bar,
conservatory
Credit cards AE, DC, MC, V
Children accepted over 12
Disabled not suitable
Pets not accepted
Closed never
Manager Timothy McDonald

South-west Wales

Penally Abbey

The setting is the key attraction of this Gothic country house, converted to a hotel in 1985. It gives easy access to the lively little resort of Tenby, but stands secluded in its own extensive wooded gardens, giving views of the splendid Pembrokeshire coastline; when the weather permits, you can even enjoy the views while taking breakfast on the terrace. Food is freshly prepared, and satisfying. Most of the bedrooms have four-poster beds, and antique furniture dotted around.

Nearby Tenby; Pembrokeshire coast.

Penally, Nr Tenby,
Pembrokeshire, Dyfed
SA70 7PY
Tel (0834) 3033
Location in village 1.5 miles
(2.5 km) SW of Tenby;
with ample car parking
Food & drink breakfast,
dinner; residential and
restaurant licence
Prices B&B £32; DB&B £46
Rooms 8 double, one single,
2 family rooms; all with bath;
all rooms have central

heating, TV, phone
Facilities sitting-room,
dining-room, bar, billiards
room; indoor pool
Credit cards MC, V
Children accepted if well
behaved
Disabled access possible: 2
ground-floor bedrooms in
coach house
Pets not accepted
Closed never
Proprietors Mr and Mrs S T
and E Warren

Stone Hall

The Watsons bought this white-painted stone manor house in 1982, and opened their doors as a hotel and restaurant at the end of 1984. For Francophile gastronomes, it is becoming something of a Mecca, thanks to the guiding hand of Martine Watson, who not only is French but employs French chefs and waiters. The house retains its ancient character, with much stone and old oak in evidence. Bedrooms are notable mainly for their spaciousness.

Nearby St David's Cathedral; Pembrokeshire coast within reach.

Welsh Hook, Wolf's Castle,
Haverfordwest, Dyfed
SA62 5NS
Tel (0348) 840212
Location in countryside 1.5
miles (2.5 km) W of A40,
half-way between
Haverfordwest and
Fishguard; with ample car
parking
Food & drink full breakfast,
dinner; residential and
restaurant licence
Prices B&B £19.75-£28;
dinner £11-£11.50
Rooms 3 double, 2 with bath,

one with shower; 2 single,
one with bath, one with
shower; all rooms have
central heating, colour TV,
tea/coffee kit
Facilities sitting-room, bar,
2 dining-rooms
Credit cards AE, MC, V
Children welcome; meals
available at special times
Disabled access difficult
Pets not accepted
Closed never
Proprietors Alan and
Martine Watson

South-west Wales

Country hotel, Brechfa

Ty Mawr

This 16thC house in the deepest Dyfed outback is surrounded by nothing but sheep and wooded hillsides. Inside the long, low stone building, much thought has clearly gone into the cosy public rooms, in particular, which include an immaculate bar with rough stone walls and smart pine fittings, and a big stone-walled dining-room with more pine and lacy furnishings, sharing a huge open fireplace with the comfy sitting-room next door. But it was the delectable dessert table which impressed our inspector most. Bedrooms, recently redecorated, are well furnished in keeping with the country feel of the house.

Nearby Brecon Beacons, Cardigan Bay within reach.

Brechfa, Dyfed SA32 7RA
Tel (026789) 332
Location 10 miles (16 km) NE of Carmarthen, on B4310, in village; with garden, and ample car parking
Food & drink full breakfast, dinner, light lunch; full licence
Prices B&B £22.50-£40; dinner from £12.50; bargain breaks

Rooms 5 double, all with bath; all rooms have central heating
Facilities sitting-room, bar, dining-room
Credit cards MC, V
Children welcome – cot available; play area **Disabled** access reasonably easy **Pets** dogs welcome if well behaved
Closed never
Proprietors Flaherty family

Country hotel, Haverfordwest

Sutton Lodge

The decorative scheme of stripped pine and delicate country-style papers and fabrics suits this early 19thC house very well. The bedrooms are large and handsome, with splendid cast-iron baths and brass fittings, the public rooms calm and mellow. Breakfast is a wholesome feast, dinner chosen from a short, modest 'carte'; chef Stanford Moseley was previously at L'Escargot in London. A reporter commented that the atmosphere is "particularly pleasant for single travellers."

Nearby Pembrokeshire coast path; offshore islands.

Portfield Gate, Haverfordwest, Pembrokeshire SA62 3LN
Tel (0437) 68548
Location one mile (1.5 km) W of Haverfordwest; ample car parking
Food & drink full breakfast, dinner; residential and restaurant licence
Prices B&B £25-£27.50; dinner from £13.50; weekend breaks
Rooms 7 double, with bath; all rooms have central

heating, phone, colour TV, radio, tea/coffee kit
Facilities sitting-rooms, lounge, dining-room, conservatory
Credit cards not accepted
Children welcome over 12
Disabled access very good; ground-floor room takes wheel-chair
Pets at proprietors' discretion
Closed Jan
Proprietors Paul Rodwell and Stanford Moseley

South-west Wales

Fairyhill

From the time the hotel opened in April 1985, the Fraynes' great flair in looking after guests has helped to make Fairyhill well worth seeking out as a quiet and utterly civilized retreat, only about 15 minutes from the end of the M4.

Set in 24 acres of grounds – much of which is still semi-wild (the brochure unabashedly advertises a wildlife sanctuary) – the three-storey Georgian building has a series of spacious, simply furnished public rooms on the ground floor, leading to the conservatory-cum-dining-room, where assiduous and friendly local waitresses serve food from an interesting menu with distinctly 'nouvelle' touches – though there are interesting local dishes too, including cockles and laver bread. The sweet table is spectacular, reigned over (when our inspector stayed) by an old-fashioned Queen of Puddings. Bedrooms vary greatly in size and style, some being fairly modern, others more traditional – though they are all comfortable and well-equipped.

Nearby Loughor Castle, 7 miles (11 km); scenic coast of Gower Peninsula; Swansea within reach.

Reynoldston, Gower, near Swansea, West Glamorgan SA3 1BS
Tel (0792) 390139
Location 12 miles (19 km) W of Swansea, one mile (1.5 km) NW of village; in 24-acre park and woodland, with ample car parking
Food & drink breakfast, dinner, Sun lunch; restaurant and residential licence
Prices B&B £29.50-£59; dinner from £17
Rooms 9 double, all with shower, 3 also with bath; 3 single with shower; 2 family rooms with bath and shower; all rooms have central heating, colour TV, phone, tea/coffee kit
Facilities sitting-room, bar, 2 dining-rooms, conference room, sauna; trout fishing
Credit cards MC, V
Children accepted **Disabled** access easy to restaurant, but no ground-floor bedrooms **Pets** accepted
Closed 2 weeks Jan
Proprietors M and J Frayne

South-west Wales

Windsor Lodge

The care and attention the Rumbles have lavished on this blue-painted Georgian house is unusual in a provincial city hotel. The decoration is stylishly and confidently modern throughout, but there is a high order of comfort, too, in the relaxed sitting-room and adjoining conservatory, and in the spacious though rather dark dining-room. Some of the boldly decorated bedrooms and bathrooms are something of a squeeze, but they are comfortable and immaculately kept.

Nearby Vivian Art Museum (in Swansea); Gower peninsula.

Mount Pleasant, Swansea, West Glamorgan SA1 6EG
Tel (0792) 642158
Location close to middle of city, on NW side off A4118; in small garden, with adequate car parking
Food & drink full breakfast, lunch, dinner; restaurant and residential licence
Prices B&B £18.75-£32.20; dinner £10-£12.50
Rooms 10 double, 6 with bath; 8 single, 4 with bath, 4 with shower; all rooms have central heating, colour TV, phone, radio/alarm, tea/coffee kit
Facilities sitting-room, dining-room, bar, sauna
Credit cards AE, DC, MC, V
Children welcome **Disabled** access to public rooms fairly easy, but no ground-floor bedrooms
Pets welcome
Closed Christmas Day and Boxing Day
Proprietors Ron and Pam Rumble

Wolfscastle Country Hotel

Like the proprietor of Barlings Barn (page 93), Andrew Stirling is a qualified squash coach who has the luxury of (in this case) two courts he can call his own. The relaxed, unpretentious style of his well-run, much-extended Victorian house has won many friends – staff are picked for personality as much as skills – and its furnishings are gradually being improved. The wide-ranging menus use sound fresh ingredients.

Nearby Pembrokeshire coast.

Wolf's Castle, Haverfordwest, Dyfed SA62 5LZ
Tel (043787) 225
Location 8 miles (12 km) N of Haverfordwest on A40; with ample car parking
Food & drink full breakfast, bar lunch, dinner; restaurant and residential licence
Prices B&B £19-£27.50; dinner £12; 10% reduction for 4 nights or more
Rooms 12 double, 3 single; all with bath; all rooms have central heating, colour TV, radio/alarm, tea/coffee kit
Facilities sitting-room, bar, dining-room, banqueting-suite; squash, tennis
Credit cards AE, MC, V
Children welcome
Disabled not suitable
Pets small dogs accepted by arrangement
Closed never
Proprietor Andrew Stirling

Brecon Beacons & Wye

Inn, Llangynidr

The Red Lion

Ellie Lloyd came to this 15thC stone village pub in 1987, and lost no time in turning it into a thoroughly comfortable, relaxed place in which to stay – without frightening the locals out of the two large, informal bars, one boasting a fine array of dark-wood antiques. Leading off these are two rustic-style dining-rooms, with subdued lighting and bare stone walls. The most charming feature of all, though, is the bedrooms, which are simply decorated but have been furnished with a well-chosen variety of antiques and with just enough personal touches, including pot plants, to create a really welcoming atmosphere.

Nearby Brecon Cathedral, 6 miles (10 km); Brecon Beacons.

Llangynidr, near Crickhowell, Powys NP8 1NH	**Rooms** 5 double, 3 with shower
Tel (0874) 730223	**Facilities** 2 bars, 2 dining-rooms
Location 3 miles (5 km) W of Crickhowell, in upper village, off B4558; in garden, with car parks	**Credit cards** V
	Children welcome if well behaved
Food & drink breakfast, lunch, dinner; full licence	**Disabled** access difficult
	Pets not encouraged
Prices B&B £17.50-£25; dinner £15	**Closed** restaurant only Sun
	Proprietor Ellie Lloyd

Converted monastery, Llanthony

Abbey

Very much a place for fit outdoor types, this – not only because its remote setting is close to the excellent Offa's Dyke long-distance footpath, but also because going to bed may entail climbing 62 narrow spiral stairs up the one remaining tower of the old monastery of which the inn now forms a part. The rooms you reach thus are simple, with whitewashed walls and solid old wooden furniture – four-posters and half-testers. Three vaulted bays make up the dining-room, where freshly made, sound-value meals are served. Food is also available in the bar, down in a lower vaulted cellar, along with several real ales.

Nearby Llanfhangel Court, 5 miles (8 km); Brecon Beacons.

Llanthony, near Abergavenny, Gwent	rooms
Tel (0873) 890487	**Facilities** bar, dining-room
Location 10 miles (16 km) N of Abergavenny off B4423; with ample car parking	**Credit cards** not accepted
	Children welcome if well behaved – though unsuitable for toddlers
Food & drink full breakfast, lunch, dinner; full licence	**Disabled** access difficult – many steps
Prices B&B £17.50; dinner about £10; reduction mid-week	**Pets** dogs accepted if well behaved, with own bed
Rooms 3 double; 2 family	**Closed** Dec to Mar
	Proprietor Ivor Prentice

Brecon Beacons & Wye

Old Gwernyfed

Roger and Dawn Beetham ran this splendid Elizabethan manor house "very quietly" after taking over the lease from Roger's parents in 1979; but in 1986 the opportunity arose to buy Old Gwernyfed outright, and the two of them have since set about making it "the best personal small hotel around."

Happily, the improvements so far have not interfered with the historic character of the place. Decoration is kept to a minimum, and the slightly haphazard collection of grand old furniture goes on growing. Four new bedrooms, created where the kitchens used to be, have the same high ceilings and sense of space of the larger of the old rooms (which range in size from very small to positively enormous). The public rooms are especially impressive – the oak-panelled sitting-room is overlooked by a minstrel's gallery, the dining-room has a vast fireplace with a wood-burning stove. Period music is played as a background to Dawn's original and satisfying dinners ("designed for people who have just walked half of Offa's Dyke, says our inspector), with some choice at beginning and end.

Nearby Brecon Beacons, Hay-on-Wye, 5 miles (8 km).

Felindre, Three Cocks,
Brecon, Powys LD3 0SG
Tel (04974) 376
Location 11 miles (18 km) NE of Brecon, off A438, in open countryside; in 13-acre grounds and gardens, with ample car parking
Food & drink breakfast, dinner; packed lunch by arrangement; restaurant and residential licence
Prices B&B £17.50-£29.50; dinner £13; reductions for stays of 3 nights, and for children sharing parents' room

Rooms 9 double, 7 with bath, one with shower; 2 single, one with bath; 3 family rooms, all with bath
Facilities dining-room, sitting-room, games room, bar; table tennis, croquet
Credit cards not accepted
Children accepted if well behaved **Disabled** access difficult **Pets** accepted if well behaved, but not allowed in public rooms
Closed Jan and Feb
Proprietors Dawn and Roger Beetham

Brecon Beacons & Wye

Llanwenarth House

While the Weatherills have put tremendous efforts into rescuing this dignified house, they have taken great care to keep the personal touches. Their two young sons help look after the guests, while their mother, Cordon Bleu-trained, supervises the kitchen, where the emphasis is on home-grown and local ingredients. The well-furnished bedrooms and public rooms are notably spacious and comfortable, and many enjoy lovely views.

Nearby Brecon Beacons National Park; Offa's Dyke path.

Govilon, Abergavenny,
Gwent NP7 9SF
Tel (0873) 830289
Location 4 miles (6 km) SW
of Abergavenny, off A465;
in 9-acre grounds, with
ample car parking
Food & drink breakfast,
dinner; restaurant and
residential licence
Prices B&B £24.50-£39;
dinner £16; reductions for 2
nights or more
Rooms 5 double, 3 with bath,
2 with shower; all rooms
have central heating, TV,
phone, radio, tea/coffee kit
Facilities sitting-room,
dining-room; croquet
Credit cards not accepted
Children welcome over 5
Disabled access easy – one
ground-floor bedroom
Pets dogs accepted if well
behaved, but not in public
rooms
Closed Feb
Proprietors Bruce and
Amanda Weatherill

Crown at Whitebrook

There is a French flavour to this smartly-renovated and much-extended hotel (originally a 17thC inn), tucked away in a beautifully secluded wooded setting a mile from the Wye and recently taken over from the Jacksons by Roger and Sandra Bates. The cooking is French-inspired, and the ground-floor windows have gaily striped awnings. Inside, both sitting-rooms and dining-rooms are pleasantly rustic – though there are some flowers, candles and linen on the table – while the bedrooms are cheerfully modern in style. The previous owners gained a reputation for good food, which the Bates aim to maintain.

Nearby Wye Valley, Forest of Dean, Black Mountains.

Whitebrook, near
Monmouth, Gwent,
NP5 4TX
Tel (0600) 860254
Location 4 miles (6.5 km) S
of Monmouth on A466;
adequate car parking
Food & drink full breakfast,
lunch, dinner; full licence
Prices B&B £23-£35; dinner
£18.50
Rooms 12 double, all with
bath; all rooms have central
heating, colour TV, phone,
radio
Facilities sitting-room,
dining-rooms, small
conference room
Credit cards AE, DC, MC, V
Children accepted
Disabled access possible
Pets generally accepted
Closed Christmas Day and
Boxing Day
Proprietors Roger and
Sandra Bates

Mid Wales

Llwynderw

'Proprietor's background?,' we ask. 'Private,' answers Michael Yates. Fair enough, we say to ourselves – when you have been running one hotel for 20 years, what you did before is not particularly relevant.

What matters is that Michael Yates long ago got his hotel-keeping recipe clear. He offers a substantial secluded house high in the hills of mid-Wales (at night there is no sound, and no terrestial source of light is visible except the house) with no TV and no telephones, but charmingly individual bedrooms with modern bathrooms, cosy sitting-rooms with plenty of books and an amiable atmosphere throughout – though Llwynderw is clearly a hotel, with service to match the high prices. Food may be based in sound local ingredients but Mr Yates's chefs draw their inspiration widely for the obligatory five-course set dinners (no choice except at start and finish). Our inspector would have welcomed less of a hush in the dining-room.

Nearby Brecon Beacons, Powys Castle and Elan valley within reach.

Abergwesyn, Llanwrtyd Wells, Powys LD5 4TW
Tel (05913) 238
Location 4 miles (6 km) NW of Llanwrtyd Wells, surrounded by moorland; in garden, with ample car parking
Food & drink full breakfast, dinner; lunch by arrangement; residential and restaurant licence
Prices DB&B £50-£60

Rooms 9 double, 3 single, one suite; all with bath; all rooms have central heating
Facilities sitting-room, library, dining-room, card-room
Credit cards AE, MC
Children welcome, preferably over 10
Disabled access difficult
Pets accepted by arrangement
Closed Nov to Mar
Proprietor Michael Yates

Barlings Barn

Only two sounds disturb the peace of this secluded Welsh farmhouse – the baas of the sheep on the surrounding hillsides, and the thwacks, squeaks and anguished cries which accompany the game of squash. Terry Margolis is a qualified squash coach, and now has what he could never have had before quitting London in 1982: his own court, built to no-compromise standards. The same new building houses the sauna, solarium, and three of the bedrooms, while the modest pool is enclosed by an air bubble. The main cottage is charmingly rustic, with exposed oak beams and stone walls, and a wood-burning stove; it is run along house-party lines, with good home-cooked dinners (no choice, wine available) around a single grand table. Breakfast includes home-produced honey.

Nearby Riding, walking, fishing; Snowdonia.

Llanbrynmair, Powys
SY19 7DY
Tel (06503) 479
Location 2 miles (3 km) NE of Llanbrynmair in private lane off road to Pandy; with garden and ample car parking in lane
Food and drink breakfast, dinner; residential licence
Prices weekend breaks about £85 including sauna, squash and other facilities; reductions for children, and for groups of 10 or more

Rooms 6 double, 5 with shower; all rooms have central heating
Facilities 2 sitting-rooms, dining-room; squash, heated swimming-pool, sauna, solarium, massage
Credit cards not accepted
Children welcome; high tea available
Disabled not suitable
Pets not accepted
Closed never
Proprietors Terry and Felicity Margolis

Mid Wales

Lasswade House

A four-storey Edwardian house overlooking fields on the out-skirts of Llanwrtyd Wells. The Sharples took over here in 1988, inheriting decorations and furnishings that were not antique or sophisticated, but neat and well ordered. There is a spacious sitting-room with comfortable sofas; bedrooms are light and airy, with well-kept bathrooms. Diners can expect large helpings of mildly adventurous, mainly Welsh/English dishes and a choice of 30 or so wines which are well described and fairly priced.

Nearby RSPB bird reserves, mountain walks; Brecon Beacons.

Station Road, Llanwrtyd Wells, Powys LD5 4RW
Tel (05913) 515
Location SE of middle of village, close to railway station; in garden amid fields, with ample car parking
Food & drink breakfast, dinner; residential and restaurant licence
Prices DB&B £32.50
Rooms 8 double, 3 with bath, 5 with shower; all rooms have central heating, colour TV, phone, radio, alarm, tea/coffee kit
Facilities sitting-room, dining-room; outdoor swimming-pool
Credit cards MC, V
Children not accepted
Disabled access easy to dining-room and sitting-room only
Pets dogs welcome if well behaved
Closed never
Proprietors Sandy and Barry Sharples

The Ffaldau

We first came upon this solid house, sheltered by the Radnor-shire hills, shortly after the Knott's opened for business in the summer of 1985. We were welcomed into the kitchen, where preparations for dinner were aromatically under way, with encouraging warmth and openness, and it is no surprise that the Ffaldau is now firmly on its feet as both a restaurant and guest-house. Oak beams, log fires and pretty, country-style decorations give an inviting air to the house, which dates from around 1500. The bedrooms are rather small, but there is a cosy bar. Cooking is satisfying and mildly adventurous.

Nearby Llandrindod Wells, 4 miles (6 km).

Llandegley, Llandrindod Wells, Powys, LD1 5UD
Tel (059 787) 421
Location 4 miles (6.5 km) E of Llandrindod Wells on A44; ample car parking
Food & drink full breakfast, lunch, dinner; residential and restaurant licence
Prices B&B from £12; dinner from £10.50
Rooms 3 double, one with shower; all rooms have central heating, tea/coffee kit, hairdrier
Facilities sitting-room, bar, dining-room
Credit cards not accepted
Children welcome over 10
Disabled access easy but no ground-floor bedrooms
Pets by arrangement
Closed never
Proprietors L and S Knott

Lleyn Peninsula

Seaside hotel, Abersoch

Porth Tocyn

"An absolute winner," says a trusted correspondent, with rare lack of control, of this whitewashed, slate-roofed establishment looking out over the sea from the Lleyn peninsula. The Fletcher-Brewers, who have owned it for 40 years, call it a country house hotel; but it is not what most people would understand by the term. Porth Tocyn certainly contains as many antiques as the typical country house hotel, and is run with as much skill and enthusiasm as the best of them. But the building – an amalgam of several old lead miners' cottages, much extended over the years – makes for a cosy, home-like atmosphere. And the seaside position has naturally encouraged the Fletcher-Brewers to cater for families keen to enjoy the hotel's good food and great comfort – though Nick F-B is aware of the difficulties of catering well for children without interfering with the peace and privacy of other guests.

Nearby Plas Yn Rhiw, 6 miles (10 km); Criccieth Castle, 14 miles (23 km).

Bwlchtocyn, Abersoch, Pwllheli, Gwynedd LL53 7BU
Tel (075881) 2966
Location 2.5 miles (4 km) S of Abersoch; in 25 acres of farm land and gardens, with ample car parking
Food & drink breakfast, lunch, dinner, picnics; residential and restaurant licence
Prices B&B £23.75-£35.50; DB&B £36.10-£52.80
Rooms 13 double, 3 single, one family room; all with bath and shower; all rooms have central heating, TV, phone

Facilities cocktail bar, TV room, dining-room, 6 sitting-rooms; tennis, outdoor heated swimming-pool
Credit cards MC
Children welcome, but those under 7 take high tea instead of dinner
Disabled access easy – one step into hotel and 3 ground-floor bedrooms
Pets accepted by arrangement
Closed early Nov to week before Easter
Proprietors Fletcher-Brewer family

Snowdonia

George III

This 300-year-old inn, separated for a century from the nearby Mawddach estury by a railway line, now has direct access to the shore once again – and the bonus of space in the disused station building a few yards away for some spacious, well-furnished bedrooms to add to those in the main building. Gail Hall was brought up here, and obviously cherishes her home. The sitting-room has beams and an inglenook, while the main Welsh Dresser bar has wooden settles and oak tables; in summer the 'cellar' bar comes into play.

Nearby Fairbourne Railway, 6 miles (10 km); Snowdonia.

Penmaenpool, Dolgellau, Gwynedd LL40 1YD
Tel (0341) 422525
Location 2 miles (3 km) W of Dolgellau on A493; on edge of Mawddach estuary, with ample car parking
Food & drink breakfast, lunch (or snacks), dinner; full licence
Prices B&B £22-£66; dinner about £15; children sharing parents' room £5
Rooms 12 double, 10 with bath, one with shower; all rooms have central heating, colour TV, tea/coffee kit, trouser-press, hairdrier
Facilities sitting-room, 2 bars
Credit cards AE, CB, DC, MC, V **Children** welcome if well behaved
Disabled access good
Pets dogs and cats welcome if well behaved
Closed 2 weeks over Christmas and New Year
Proprietor Gail Hall

Gwernan Lake

This neat, whitewashed two-storey building overlooks its own 12-acre lake at the foot of Wales' second most famous mountain, Cader Idris. But the peace and quiet is second to none. Inside, the place feels almost Austrian, with pine-panelled walls and country-style furniture. The Coombers are recent arrivals here, but have kept up the hotel's tradition of providing good, interesting food using fresh local produce, while adding some (much-needed) en suite bathrooms.

Nearby Tal-y-Llyn Railway, 10 miles (16 km).

Cader Road, Dolgellau, Gwynedd LL40 1TL
Tel (0341) 422488
Location 2 miles (3 km) SW of Dolgellau, in open countryside; with 12-acre lake in wooded grounds, and ample car parking
Food & drink full breakfast, bar or packed lunch, evening meal; full licence
Prices B&B £15-£21; reductions for 3 or more nights; bargain breaks
Rooms 6 double, 3 single; all rooms have central heating
Facilities dining-room, sitting-room with TV, bar; trout fishing
Credit cards MC, V
Children accepted over 7
Disabled access possible to bar and dining-room
Pets not accepted
Closed never
Proprietors Ron and Gwen Coomber

Snowdonia

The Pen-y-Gwryd Hotel

High up in the desolate heart of Snowdonia, this small coaching inn is a place of pilgrimage for mountaineers – the team which made the first ascent of Everest in 1953 came here to train for the expedition (and still come back for reunions). Mr and Mrs Briggs, whose family have owned the hotel for the last 40 years, take pride in describing the hotel, its bedrooms, its food – even the Victorian bathrooms – as old-fashioned.

Nearby Snowdon Mountain Railway, 5 miles (8 km); Snowdonia.

Nant Gwynant, Gwynedd LL55 4NT
Tel (0286) 870211
Location 5 miles (8 km) SW of Llanberis, at junction of A498 and A4086, in isolated mountain setting, with garden and car parking
Food & drink full breakfast, bar lunch, tea, dinner; full licence
Prices B&B from £14; dinner from £9.50; reductions for 3 nights or more

Rooms 16 double; 3 single; one family room, with bath; all have central heating
Facilities sitting-room, bar, dining-room, games room
Credit cards not accepted
Children welcome
Disabled access easy **Pets** well-behaved dogs welcome
Closed early Nov to New Year; weekdays Jan and Feb
Proprietors Mr & Mrs C B Briggs and Mr & Mrs B C Pullee

Minffordd

"Minfford has the happiest atmosphere of all the places where I have stayed," says a reporter, "probably because the exceptional Pickles family itself is so happy."

The rambling, relaxed building is not remarkable, architecturally or decoratively. But the Pickles take a tremendous pride in making it as comfortable and welcoming to visitors as possible. Son Jonathan is the chef; he has established a reputation for his rich modern and traditional British dishes.

Nearby Ascent of Cader Idris; Talyllyn Railway, 5 miles (8 km).

Talyllyn, Tywyn, Gwynedd LL36 9AJ
Tel (065473) 665
Location 8 miles (13 km) S of Dolgellau at junction of A487 and B4405; parking for 12 cars
Food & drink full breakfast, dinner; residential and restaurant licence
Prices DB&B £33-£43; reductions for 2 nights or more and for children sharing parents' room;
Rooms 5 double, 4 with bath and shower, one with shower; one single, with shower; one family room, with bath and shower; all rooms have central heating, phone, radio, tea/coffee kit
Facilities bar, sitting-room, dining-room, sun room
Credit cards DC, MC, V
Children welcome over 3
Disabled access difficult
Pets not accepted
Closed Jan and Feb; also Nov, Dec and Mar except for weekends and Christmas
Proprietors Bernard, Jessica and Jonathan Pickles

Snowdonia

Country house hotel, Talsarnau

Maes-y-Neuadd

The name, pronounced "Mice-er-Nayath", means Hall in the Field, which is no longer a fair description of an amiable granite-built house set in grounds rich with rhododendrons and ringed by woods. But fields are not far away: all around is spell-binding hill scenery.

Maes-y-Neuadd is a civilized and welcoming country hotel, run with great care and flair by the four partners, all of them new to the business when they took over the hotel in 1981 and each of them now in charge of one aspect of it. Over the years they have refurbished the whole house, mixing antique and modern furniture with panache. Both public rooms and bedrooms vary in vintage and style, from cottagey to elegant Georgian; leather Chesterfields in the beamed 14th-century bar will not please purists.

The cooking is nowadays in the hands of Andrew Taylor, who will continue the hotel's tradition of satisfying and wide-ranging menus offering around nine alternatives at each course (vegetarian dishes included).

Nearby Ffestiniog Railway, 2.5 miles (4 km); Snowdonia.

Talsarnau, near Harlech, Gwynedd LL47 6YA
Tel (0766) 780200
Location 4 miles (6.5 km) N of Harlech, close to B4573; in 8-acre grounds with parking for 50 cars
Food & drink full breakfast, lunch, dinner; residential and restaurant licence
Prices B&B £34-£47.50; dinner £18.50; reduction for children sharing parents' room; winter breaks
Rooms 13 double, one with bath, 2 with shower, 10 with bath and shower; one single with shower; one suite; all rooms have central heating, colour TV, phone
Facilities sitting-room, bar, dining-room
Credit cards AE, DC, MC, V
Children welcome over 7, under 7 at proprietors' discretion **Disabled** access good – side entrance and one ground-floor bedroom
Pets accepted by arrangement
Closed Jan
Proprietors June and Michael Slatter, Olive and Malcolm Horsfall

North Wales coast

St Tudno

The Blands are meticulous in attending to every detail of this seafront house, which they have been improving for over 17 years. The pretty rooms, each decorated differently in designer wallpapers and matching fabrics, have found the balance between Victorian charm and modern facilities. A long list of thoughtful extras add to the comfort, including flowers and complimentary wine. The air-conditioned dining-room is light and inviting, with a profusion of plants and rattan chairs. The seasonally changing 'carte', based on the best local ingredients, deserves serious study in the comfortable bar, and the cooking is right on target. All of this would be difficult to resist even without the bonus of the hotel's young and helpful staff. There is a smoking ban in the period-style sitting-room and in the dining-room.

Nearby Conwy Castle, 3 miles (5 km), Bodnant Gardens, 7 miles (11 km); Snowdonia.

Promenade, Llandudno, Gwynedd LL30 2LP
Tel (0492) 74411
Location on seafront opposite pier and promenade gardens; with small garden and private parking for 6 cars; unrestricted street parking
Food & drink breakfast, lunch, dinner; residential and restaurant licence
Prices B&B £25-£40; dinner £16.50; reductions for children sharing parents' room; reduced DB&B rates for 2 nights or more
Rooms 17 double, all with bath; one single, with bath; 3 family rooms, all with bath; all rooms have central heating, colour TV, phone, radio/alarm, fridge, tea/coffee kit, hairdrier
Facilities bar, 3 sitting-rooms, dining-room; covered heated swimming-pool
Credit cards AE, MC, V
Children very welcome; baby-listening, cots, high chairs and high tea available (very young ones not welcome at dinner)
Disabled access fairly easy except for wheelchairs; lift/elevator to most bedrooms
Pets generally not accepted
Closed Christmas and New Year
Proprietors Martin and Janette Bland

Clwyd

The Hand Hotel

Surrounded by hills despite being 900 ft up in the highlands of Clwyd, the tiny village of Llanarmon DC (as it is often known) makes a blissfully peaceful retreat, and the Hand is entirely in character – a white-painted 16thC farmhouse with flowery terraces outside, beams and open fires within. The Alexanders moved here in 1982, and have evidently prospered – in the spring of 1987 they also took over the nearby West Arms. Reporters speak highly of them and their efficient, enthusiastic staff, and particularly of the food – a daily changing menu, more adventurous since the arrival of a new chef.

Nearby Chirk Castle 8 miles (13 km).

Llanarmon Dyffryn Ceiriog, near Llangollen, Clwyd, LL20 7LD **Tel** (069176) 666 **Location** 7 miles (11 km) S of Llangollen, in middle of village on B4500; ample car parking **Food & drink** full breakfast, bar meals for lunch/dinner, tea, dinner; full licence **Prices** B&B £29-£37; dinner £14.50; reductions for children under 10	**Rooms** 14 double, all with bath and shower; all rooms have central heating **Facilities** 2 sitting-rooms, dining-room, function room, tennis, fishing **Credit cards** AE, DC, MC, V **Children** welcome **Disabled** access easy **Pets** welcome but not in dining-room **Closed** 6 weeks from 1 Feb **Proprietors** Tim and Carolyn Alexander

Tyddyn Llan

The Kindreds converted this solid, unassuming house of mainly Georgian origin in the early 1980s, and it is now a calm and inviting house – with books and magazines on hand, and antiques and paintings dotted around. It is very much a home, despite the number of guests it can accommodate. Bridget's cooking is inventive and expert, the short menu embracing Mediterranean, Welsh and other influences.

Nearby Bala Lake and Railway, 8 miles (13 km); Snowdonia.

Llandrillo, near Corwen, Clwyd LL21 0ST **Tel** (049084) 264 **Location** 5 miles (8 km) SW of Corwen off B4401; with ample car parking **Food & drink** breakfast, lunch, tea, dinner; restaurant and residential licence **Prices** B&B £25.50-£34.50; DB&B £39.50-£48.50; reductions for 2 nights or more and for children	**Rooms** 9 double, 7 with bath, 2 with shower; all rooms have central heating, phone, radio, tea/coffee kit **Facilities** sitting-room, bar, restaurant, croquet, fishing **Credit cards** MC, V **Children** welcome **Disabled** not suitable **Pets** dogs accepted by arrangement, and not in public rooms **Closed** Feb **Proprietors** Bridget and Peter Kindred

Hereford & Worcester

Inn, Fownhope

The Green Man

This substantial old timber-framed inn successfully plays the dual roles of popular country pub and small hotel. Bedrooms vary widely: the four-poster room, with its exposed beams, is snugly traditional; others, which have been modernized, are light and airy. There is not much sitting space apart from the oak-beamed bars, but the large lawned garden has tables and benches. Modest but tasty food is served both in the bars and in the smartly converted barn which forms the dining-room.

Nearby Hellen's, 3 miles (5 km), Hereford, 6 miles (10 km).

Fownhope, near Hereford, Hereford and Worcester HR1 4PE
Tel (043277) 243
Location 8 miles SE of Hereford on B4224, in village; with garden and parking for 75 cars
Food & drink full breakfast, bar or packed lunch, tea, dinner, snacks; full licence
Prices B&B £18.25-£27.50; reductions for children sharing parents' room; winter breaks
Rooms 12 double, 4 with bath, all with shower; 3 family rooms, 2 with bath, all with shower; all rooms have central heating, tea/coffee kit, TV, trouser-press, hairdrier, phone
Facilities 2 bars, dining-room, sitting-room
Credit cards MC, V
Children welcome; cots, high-chairs available
Disabled access easy to public rooms and to ground-floor bedroom across courtyard
Pets welcome
Closed never
Proprietors Arthur and Margaret Williams

Country hotel, Great Malvern

Cottage in the Wood

Three buildings make up this glossy little hotel. There are bedrooms in all three, taking the hotel over our usual size limit; but the smartly furnished Georgian dower house at its heart is intimate, calm and comfortable. The setting is the key – superb views across the Severn Valley to the Cotswolds.

Nearby Malvern Hills; Eastnor Castle, 5 miles (8 km).

Holywell Road, Malvern Wells, Hereford and Worcester WR14 4LG
Tel (0684) 573487
Location 2 miles (3 km) S of Great Malvern on A449; ample car parking
Food & drink full breakfast, lunch, tea, dinner; residential and restaurant licence
Prices B&B £29.50-£47.50; dinner £17.50
Rooms 18 double, all with bath, 5 also with shower; 2 single, both with bath; all rooms have central heating, colour TV, phone, tea/coffee kit
Facilities sitting-room, bar, dining-room; conference suite
Credit cards MC, V
Children welcome; cots available **Disabled** not ideal – ground-floor bedrooms are in annexe **Pets** accepted but not in main building
Closed never
Proprietors John and Sue Pattin

Hereford & Worcester

Country guesthouse, Ledbury

Grove House

Although Grove House dates back to the 15thC it has the appearance of a Georgian farm manor-house, complete with courtyard, red-brick outhouses and stables. By keeping the number of rooms down to three, the Rosses have preserved entirely the atmosphere of a private home. (That the plumbing preserves one of the weaknesses of a private home – an occasional shortage of hot water – is less laudable but easily forgiven.)

The origins of the house are more evident inside, with timber framing in the walls of the heavily oak-beamed dining-room, and red oak panelling in the sitting room, where logs are burned in winter. The bedrooms are large, comfortable and carefully furnished with antiques – two with four-posters – and our anonymous inspector records with delight that hot water bottles are slipped between the crisp cotton sheets in the late evening. There are fresh cut flowers, and towels are not stinted.

Ellen Ross is an excellent cook who aims higher than is usual in such small establishments, aided by the produce of her own large vegetable garden. After help-yourself drinks in the sitting-room, dinner is served at a single long table.

Nearby Eastnor Castle, 1.5 miles (2.5 km); Malvern Hills.

Bromsberrow Heath,
Ledbury, Herefordshire
HR8 1PE
Tel (053181) 584
Location 3 miles (5 km) S of
Ledbury off A417, close to
M50; ample car parking
Food & drink full breakfast,
dinner; no licence
Prices B&B £21-£26;
dinner £15
Rooms 3 double, all with
bath, one also with shower;
all rooms have central
heating, TV, tea kit, clock/
radio, hairdrier
Facilities sitting-room,
dining-room; tennis, riding,
outdoor swimming-pool,
boating-pond
Credit cards not accepted
Children accepted
Disabled not suitable
Pets can stay in car
Closed 17 Dec to 4 Jan
Proprietors M and E Ross

Hereford & Worcester

Country house hotel, Ledbury

Hope End

Of the many couples who have given up other careers to run small hotels listed in this guide, no others have done so with quite such clear-eyed vision, individual flair and tireless dedication as the Hegartys. It was 1975 when Patricia inherited the shell of Hope End – a handsome red-brick 18th-century house with exotic embellishments which had been the childhood home of Elizabeth Barrett – and 1979 before she and husband John were ready to open their doors. They quickly established Hope End as one of the most distinctive and satisfying hotels in the country.

Whereas many country house hotels are made in a single mould, Hope End is the Hegartys' own creation; their watchwords are simplicity and quality – whether in Patricia's excellent cooking (employing a striking range of home-grown vegetables and herbs, and often milk or yoghurt from their own goats) or in the stylishly understated furnishings and furniture (some of itantique, some stripped pine, some locally crafted). All the bedrooms are inviting, but the biggest are splendidly spacious.

Dinner offers no choice, so culinary conservatives should check Patricia's plans.

Nearby Eastnor Castle, 5 miles (8 km); Malvern Hills; Worcester, Hereford, and Gloucester all within easy reach.

Hope End, Ledbury,
Hereford and Worcester
HR8 1JQ
Tel (0531) 3613
Location 2.5 miles (4 km)
N of Ledbury; in 40 acres of
wooded parkland with
ample car parking
Food & drink full breakfast,
dinner; residential and
restaurant licence
Prices DB&B £55-£120;
reduction for more than
2 nights

Rooms 9 double, all with
bath; all rooms have central
heating, tea/coffee kit, phone
Facilities 3 sitting-rooms,
dining-room
Credit cards MC, V
Children welcome over 12
Disabled access difficult
Pets not accepted
Closed Mon and Tue night,
and last week Nov to last
week Feb
Proprietors John and
Patricia Hegarty

Hereford & Worcester

Country guest-house, Ullingswick

The Steppes

There are candles on the tables for dinner in the charmingly old-world dining-room here, and men are expected to wear ties to enhance the sense of occasion. Tricia Howland serves fixed four-course 'gourmet' meals, with the option of choosing from a 'carte' instead (provided you give plenty of notice). Bedrooms are tastefully furnished and immaculately kept.

Nearby Hereford, 7 miles (11 km); Wye valley.

Ullingswick, near Hereford,
Hereford and Worcester
HR1 3JG
Tel (0432) 820424
Location 9 miles (14.5 km)
NE of Hereford off A417, in
countryside; car parking
Food & drink full breakfast,
bar lunch, dinner;
residential licence
Prices DB&B £29-£41
Rooms 5 double, 2 with bath
and shower, 3 with shower;
all rooms have central
heating, colour TV, tea/
coffee kit, radio, phone
Facilities 2 sitting-rooms,
dining-room with bar, cellar
bar
Credit cards not accepted
Children welcome over 12
Disabled access easy – no
steps **Pets** dogs accepted, but
not in public rooms
Closed mid-Dec to mid-Jan,
except Christmas to New
Year **Proprietors** Henry and
Tricia Howland

Country home hotel, Bromsgrove

Grafton Manor

This ancient red-brick manor house is very much a family affair – father John and twins Nicola and Simon in the kitchen, mother June and elder son Stephen running the front of house. They opened as a restaurant in 1980, and the imaginative four-course dinners are still the best for miles around; a newly created formal herb garden behind the house makes its contribution. Bedrooms are richly furnished and thoroughly equipped, and the heart of the house is the lofty old Great Parlour, now the bar/sitting room complete with Steinway grand piano.

Nearby Hagley Hall, 6 miles (10 km).

Grafton Lane, Bromsgrove,
Hereford and Worcester
B61 7HA
Tel (0527) 579007
Location 2 miles (3 km) SW
of Bromsgrove off B4090;
in 11-acre gardens, with
ample car parking
Food & drink breakfast,
lunch, dinner; residential
licence
Prices B&B £40.50-£73;
dinner £23
Rooms 6 double, one single,
one suite; all with bath; all
rooms have central heating,
colour TV with teletext,
radio/alarm, hairdrier,
phone **Facilities** sitting-room/bar,
dining-room; fishing,
croquet, clay pigeon
shooting
Credit cards AE, DC, MC, V
Children welcome if well
behaved **Disabled** access
difficult **Pets** not accepted;
kennels can be provided
Closed never
Proprietors Morris family

Hereford & Worcester

Country guest-house, Welland

Holdfast Cottage

"Cottage" seems to be stretching things a bit – and yet, despite its size, this Victorian farmhouse does have the cosy intimacy of a cottage. This gives the new managers here a head start towards the friendly informality they seek to maintain. Inside, low oak beams and a polished flagstone floor in the hall conform to the cottage requirement; beyond there, headroom improves – though flowery decoration emphasizes the cottage status. Bedrooms are light and airy, with carefully co-ordinated fabrics and papers, though bathrooms are definitely small. Outside, the veranda with its wisteria keeps the scale of the house down. The garden beyond – again, scarcely cottage-style – adds enormously to the overall appeal of the place, with its lawns, shrubberies, fruit trees and delightful 'wilderness'.

The daily-changing 'carte' is based on traditional English dishes with a strong French influence, employing the best local produce.

Nearby Eastnor Castle, 4 miles (6 km); Worcester, Hereford and Gloucester all within easy reach.

Welland, near Malvern,
Hereford and Worcester
WR13 6NA
Tel (0684) 310288
Location 4 miles (6.5 km) S
of Great Malvern on A4104;
with ample car parking
Food & drink full breakfast,
dinner; residential and
restaurant licence
Prices B&B from £32;
dinner about £18; bargain
breaks
Rooms 6 double, all with
bath; 2 single, one with bath,
one with shower; all rooms
have central heating, colour
TV, radio/alarm, phone,
hairdrier, trouser-press
Facilities sitting-room, bar,
dining-room, conservatory;
croquet
Credit cards MC
Children welcome over 10
Disabled access difficult
Pets not allowed indoors;
kennel in garden
Closed Jan
Managers Philip Harris and
Diane Brown

Hereford & Worcester

Butchers Arms

Good beer and good food, along with a classical country-pub atmosphere, are what keep people rolling up at this black-and-white half-timbered inn out in the rolling Hereford countryside. There is a choice of properly kept real ales in the low-ceilinged bars, and a range of excellent home-made snack meals – but Bill Griffiths reserves his more ambitious dinner-party dishes for the separate dining-room, where the carte changes monthly. The bedrooms are small but much above the pub average in comfort and trimmings. There is a pleasant patio garden, with views across the countryside.

Nearby Hereford Cathedral 7 miles (11 km); Wye Valley.

Woolhope, Herefordshire.
HR1 4RF
Tel (043277) 281
Location 7 miles (11 km) SE of Hereford off B4224, just outside village; in gardens with ample car parking
Food & drink full breakfast, bar meals, dinner Wed to Sat and every evening during winter; full licence
Prices B&B £16.50-£20.50; dinner from £9.50

Rooms 3 double, all rooms have central heating, TV
Facilities 2 bars, dining-room
Credit cards not accepted
Children accepted over 14
Disabled access to public rooms only
Pets not accepted in house
Closed never
Proprietor Bill Griffiths

Rhydspence Inn

The Wallingtons, who left this black-and-white half-timbered inn in 1986, had gained a high reputation for their food and hospitality. The Glovers' chef doesn't yet enjoy the same recognition, but in other ways the inn has improved – in particular, the bedrooms have been 'demodernized', the modern fitments being replaced by traditional furniture. The building remains much as it always was – in the Glovers' words, full of "genuine creaks, groans, draughts and atmosphere". The intimate, rambling, beamed bars remain free of Space Invaders, and real ales and ciders can still be enjoyed in front of a roaring fire.

Nearby Brecon Beacons, Black Mountains, Wye valley.

Whitney-on-Wye, Hereford and Worcester HR3 6EU
Tel (04973) 262
Location 4 miles (6 km) NE of Hay-on-Wye, on A438; in one-acre grounds with ample car parking
Food & drink breakfast, lunch, dinner; full licence
Prices B&B £20; dinner £9
Rooms 4 double, all with bath; one single, with

shower; all rooms have central heating, colour TV, tea/coffee kit
Facilities 2 bars, 2 dining-rooms, breakfast room
Credit cards AE, MC, V
Children welcome **Disabled** reasonably easy access
Pets not accepted
Closed never
Proprietors Peter and Pamela Glover

West Gloucestershire

Country guest-house, Awre

The Old Vicarage

Some visitors to this handsome Georgian vicarage marvel at the Bulls' juggling act – keeping the guests, hens, herbs and vines happy all at once. Others have prescribed concentration on fewer goals. But there is agreement that the Old Vicarage is a warm, welcoming house, full of character as well as flowers and antiques. There is a pretty sitting-room, and bedrooms are simply furnished but charmingly decorated, with plenty of flowers. The Bulls are enthusiastic cooks, and offer quite a wide choice of traditional and innovative dishes at dinner – served in dinner-party style at a single table. Although they do not possess a licence, they will happily uncork wine at no charge.

Nearby walks to river Severn; Forest of Dean, Wye valley.

Awre, Newnham,
Gloucestershire GL14 1EL
Tel (0594) 510282
Location 3 miles (5 km) SE of
Newnham, off A48, on edge
of village; in 4-acre grounds,
with adequate car parking
Food & drink full breakfast,
dinner; no licence
Prices B&B £15.50-£17.50;
dinner £11.50
Rooms 3 double, one with
shower; 2 single; all rooms
have tea/coffee kit
Facilities sitting-room,
dining-room
Credit cards not accepted
Children accepted over 11
Disabled access difficult
Pets accepted
Closed Christmas
Proprietors May and Nick
Bull

Country guest-house, Clearwell

Tudor Farmhouse

The chatty Reids are both eager to please guests now that they have completed several years' continuous work on their lovely 14thC stone farmhouse. It is prettily decorated and neatly furnished as a result, and all the bedrooms now have bathrooms en suite. Some have four-posters. The sitting- and dining-rooms have exposed stone and beams, and the former an open fireplace. When we visited, Sheila served an excellent fixed meal, but there is now a thriving 'à la carte' restaurant and professional kitchen staff. Breakfast is a minor feast.

Nearby Monmouth Castle, 5 miles (8 km); Wye valley.

Clearwell, near Coleford,
Gloucestershire GL16 8JS
Tel (0594) 33046
Location 5 miles (8 km) SE of
Monmouth on B4231;
parking for 15 cars
Food & drink full breakfast,
dinner; residential and
restaurant licence
Prices B&B £17.50-
£39.50; dinner £7.50
Rooms 8 double, one suite,
all with bath; all rooms have
central heating, colour TV,
tea/coffee kit, radio/alarm,
phone
Facilities sitting-room/bar,
dining-room, conservatory
Credit cards MC, V
Children welcome if well
behaved **Disabled** access
easy **Pets** not accepted,
except in cottage
Closed never
Proprietors Sheila and
James Reid

West Gloucestershire

Country hotel, Corse Lawn

Corse Lawn House

This tall, red-brick Queen Anne house, set back across common land from what is now a minor road, must have been one of the most refined coaching inns of its day. Should you arrive in traditional style, you could still drive your coach-and-four down the slipway into the large pond in front of the house, to cool the horses and wash the carriage .

The Hines have been here since the late 1970s, first running the house purely as a restaurant, later opening up four rooms and in 1987 adding a new rear extension (carefully designed to blend with the original building) to provide half a dozen more, as well as extra dining-room space. The Falstaffian Denis Hine – a member of the famous French Cognac family – extends a warm welcome to guests while his English wife Baba cooks. Her repertoire is an eclectic mix of English and French, modern and provincial dishes, all carefully prepared and served in substantial portions; there are fixed-price menus (with a vegetarian alternative) at both lunch and dinner as well as a 'carte', and they are notably good value – as are the interesting bar meals.

Bedrooms (in the old house, at least) are large, with a mixture of antique and modern furnishings, and the atmosphere of the house calm and relaxing. Breakfasts are a home-made feast.
Nearby Tewkesbury Abbey, 5 miles (8 km); Malvern Hills.

Corse Lawn,
Gloucestershire GL19 4LZ
Tel (045278) 479
Location 5 miles (8 km) W of Tewkesbury on B421; in 12-acre grounds with ample car parking
Food & drink full breakfast, lunch, tea, dinner; full licence
Prices B&B £32.50-£50; dinner £19.75
Rooms 10 double, all with bath and shower; all rooms have central heating, colour TV, phone, tea/coffee kit, hairdrier, trouser-press
Facilities sitting-room, bar, dining-room, conference room; croquet, putting
Credit cards AE, DC, MC, V
Children welcome if well behaved **Disabled** access easy to public rooms and 2 ground-floor bedrooms **Pets** dogs allowed in bedrooms
Closed never
Proprietors Denis and Baba Hine

West Gloucestershire

Drakestone House

Drakestone House takes you back to turn-of-the-century rural England – an Edwardian country house complete with dovecote; landscaped gardens bordered by neatly trimmed yew hedges; and views of green fields and the Welsh mountains in the distance. There's a warm welcome from Hugh and Crystal St John-Mildmay, whose family home this is. They serve breakfast before a log fire on chilly days, and trays of tea in the friendly sitting-room.

Nearby Slimbridge Wildfowl Trust, 4 miles (6 km), Owlpen Manor, 4 miles (6 km); Cotswold villages.

Stinchcombe, near Dursley, Gloucestershire, GL11 6AS
Tel (0453) 2140
Location 3 miles (5 km) NW of Dursley, off B4060; ample car parking in courtyard
Food & drink full breakfast; dinner by prior arrangement; no licence, take your own wine
Prices B&B £16; dinner £10; reduction for children

Rooms 3 double, one with shower; all rooms have central heating
Facilities sitting-room, dining-room
Credit cards not accepted
Children welcome
Disabled access difficult
Pets not allowed in house
Closed Nov to Mar
Proprietors Hugh and Crystal St John-Mildmay

Halewell

Elizabeth Carey-Wilson opened her lovely Cotswold-stone house to guests in the early 1980s, and has managed to keep the atmosphere of a gracious family home entirely intact. The house, part of it an early 15th-century monastery, forms a picture-postcard group around a courtyard. Mrs Carey-Wilson treats her guests as friends. Breakfast is whenever you will, but she serves her set dinner – usually a roast or a grill – at a single table at a set time (couples are split).

Nearby Chedworth Roman Villa, 1.5 miles (2.5 km).

Withington, near Cheltenham, Gloucestershire GL54 4BN
Tel (024289) 238
Location 6 miles (10 km) SE of Cheltenham between A40 and A435, on edge of village; ample car parking
Food & drink full breakfast, dinner; residential licence
Prices B&B £29-£41; dinner £12; reductions for 2 nights or more, and for children
Rooms 6 double, all with bath, some also with shower;

all rooms have central heating, colour TV, radio, tea/coffee kit
Facilities 2 sitting-rooms, bar, dining-room; heated outdoor swimming-pool (summer), trout lake
Credit cards not accepted
Children welcome
Disabled access good – specially constructed ground-floor suite **Pets** accepted by arrangement
Closed never
Proprietor Elizabeth Carey-Wilson

Cotswolds

Country guest-house, Broad Campden

Malt House

It is easy to miss this 17thC Cotswold house (in fact a conversion of three cottages) in a tiny hamlet comprising little more than a church and a pub. Once found, the Malt House is delightful – beamed with low ceilings, antique furniture and leaded windows overlooking a dream garden where two mad, tame chickens scamper about.

Pat Robinson has time to chat, running the house with unnoticeable efficiency with the help of two local girls. The bedrooms are comfortable and prettily decorated, with pleasant old furniture and in some cases brass beds. All around the house there are piles of books about the countryside, wine and cooking, and novels of all styles.

Meals are normally conceived as a big happy family occasion, taking place at a communal table, but separate tables are available for those who want them. Breakfast is thoroughly British and jolly good too. Dinner is a fixed multi-course meal of ambitious new English cooking, and there is a similarly high-flown wine list. Simple food is served in the pub around the corner.

Nearby Batsford Park Arboretum, 3 miles (5 km), Sezincote Garden, 4.5 miles (7 km); Snowshill Manor, 5 miles (8 km), Stratford-upon-Avon, 12 miles (19.5 km); Cotswold villages; Cheltenham.

Broad Campden, Chipping Campden, Gloucestershire GL55 6UU
Tel (0386) 840295
Location one mile (1.5 km) SE of Chipping Campden, just outside village; in 4.5-acre paddocks, orchard and garden, with ample car parking
Food & drink full breakfast, dinner; restaurant licence
Prices B&B £23.50-£32.50; dinner from £17.50

Rooms 5 double, 4 with bath; one single; all rooms have central heating, colour TV, tea/coffee kit
Facilities 2 sitting-rooms, dining-room; croquet
Credit cards MC, V
Children welcome if well behaved; high tea provided
Disabled access difficult
Pets not accepted
Closed 24 to 26 Dec
Proprietor Mrs Pat Robinson

Cotswolds

Country hotel, Broadway

Collin House

John and Judith Mills (she a trained cook, he an engineer-businessman) bought this hotel in 1981; they thought it was just the kind of place they loved staying in – small and personal – and that is how they have aimed to keep it.

It is not the most beautifully furnished house you will come across; the dining-room and the sitting-room lack style, and some of the bedroom furniture is rather routine. But there are compensations. A key attraction is the cosy lounge-bar (very much a cross between those two animals), with low linen-covered armchairs around the huge inglenook where a log fire blazes at the merest excuse. The bedrooms are spacious and comfortable, and neatly decorated. The food represents sound value and has a distinctly English character. And in summer the spacious, open garden comes into its own, with its small pool.

If the folder in your room does not have enough ideas about how you might spend the day, just ask the Millses.

Nearby Snowshill Manor, 2.5 miles (4 km); Batsford Park Arboretum, 6 miles (10 km); other Cotswold villages.

Collin Lane, Broadway,
Worcester WR12 7PB
Tel (0386) 858354
Location one mile (1.5 km) NW of Broadway, off A44; in spacious grounds with ample private car parking
Food & drink full breakfast, bar lunch, dinner Mon to Sat; full lunch and supper on Sun; residential and restaurant licence
Prices B & B £30.50-£34.50; dinner £13-£15; reductions for 7 nights or more; bargain breaks
Rooms 6 double, 5 with bath, one with shower; one single, with shower; all rooms have central heating, tea/coffee kit
Facilities sitting-room, bar, dining-room; outdoor swimming-pool, croquet
Credit cards MC, V
Children welcome; by prior arrangement under 6
Disabled access not easy, except to public rooms
Pets not allowed in bedrooms or dining-room
Closed 24 to 27 Dec
Proprietors John and Judith Mills

Cotswolds

Bed and breakfast guest-house, Broadway

Mill Hay

On the edge of Broadway, but out of the way of the tourist hordes, Mill Hay offers a truly luxurious country-house atmosphere at comparatively modest prices. Surrounded by neatly trimmed gardens, the house has considerable charm; behind the lattice windows are comfy sofas and a sizeable stone fireplace. Bedrooms range from a cosy single, with a four-poster bed and Victorian lithographs on the walls, to a spacious double with a king-size bed. English breakfast is served in Continental fashion at a breakfast bar in the kitchen. Friendly service complements the comfort.

Nearby Snowshill Manor, 2.5 miles (4 km), Sezincote Garden, 6 miles (10 km).

Snowshill Road, Broadway, Hereford and Worcester WR12 7JS
Tel (0386) 852498
Location on SW fringes of village, 5 miles (8 km) SE of Evesham; in gardens, with ample car parking
Food & drink breakfast; no licence
Prices B & B £20-£25
Rooms 3 double; one single; one suite with bath; all rooms have central heating, tea/coffee kit
Facilities 2 sitting-rooms (one with TV)
Credit cards MC, V
Children welcome if well behaved
Disabled no special facilities
Pets not accepted
Closed never
Proprietors H and R Will

Country hotel, Burford

Bay Tree

Sir Lawrence Tanfield, Elizabeth I's unpopular Lord Chief Baron of the Exchequer, may have lacked charm, but he did not lack judgement. He built his house in a delightfully peaceful corner of Burford, away from the busy, sloping high street. The new owners, Select Hotels, have so far taken care to respect the antiquity of this rambling, relaxed building, which has numerous cosy sitting corners well furnished with antiques – and tea still arrives at the fireside on a silver tea service.

Nearby Minster Lovell Hall, 5 miles (8 km); Cotswold villages.

Sheep Street, Burford, Oxfordshire OX8 4LW
Tel (099382) 3137
Location in side street of town, at junction of A40 and A424; parking for 20 cars
Food & drink full breakfast, lunch, dinner; full licence
Prices B & B £32-£47.50; dinner £15.75; reductions for children sharing parents' room
Rooms 18 double, 2 single, 2 family rooms; all with bath and shower; all rooms have central heating, colour TV, phone, hairdrier
Facilities 3 sitting-rooms, 2 bars
Credit cards AE, DC, MC, V
Children welcome
Disabled access easy to dining-room only
Pets not accepted
Closed never
Manager Rupert Duffin

Cotswolds

Manor house hotel, Cheltenham

Greenway

The mellow, intimate feel of this polished Cotswold manor house wins it a place here, despite high prices, and the number of rooms (some of which are in a converted coach house). Even where the furnishings lack the patina of age, they are harmonious and comfortable, and both the public rooms and the bedrooms are more than usually spacious. There are no better local alternatives to the cooking here.

Nearby Witcombe Roman Villa, 3 miles (5 km), Gloucester, 5 miles (8 km); Cotswolds.

Shurdington, Cheltenham, Gloucestershire GL51 5UG
Tel (0242) 862352
Location 3 miles (5 km) SW of Cheltenham, off A46; in 37-acre grounds with ample car parking
Food & drink full breakfast, lunch (except Sat), afternoon tea, dinner; residential licence
Prices B&B £47.50-£75
Rooms 16 double, all with bath, 15 with shower; 2 singles with bath; all rooms have colour TV, phone
Facilities sitting-room, bar, 3 dining-rooms; croquet; helipad
Credit cards AE, DC, MC, V
Children welcome over 7
Disabled access easy to restaurant and public areas; ground-floor bedrooms in coach house annexe
Pets not accepted
Closed 28 Dec to 6 Jan
Proprietor Tony Elliott

Town hotel, Chipping Campden

Kings Arms

The Kings Arms Hotel presents a varied face to the world; part Georgian, part 17thC, but all in warm Cotswold stone. Although the hotel is no secret, it represents unusual value for this area. All the bedrooms are charmingly decorated, and the best are no less than thoroughly comfortable. In sitting-room and dining-room log fires and tastefully muted colours complement the original style of the building; in the lively, low-ceilinged bar, solid country furniture rounds off the traditional atmosphere. The walled garden bursts with colour in summer.

Nearby Hidcote Manor Garden, 2.5 miles (4 km), Batsford Park Arboretum, 4 miles (6.5 km).

The Square, Chipping Campden, Gloucestershire GL55 6AW
Tel (0386) 840256
Location in main square; in one-acre gardens, with ample public car parking in square
Food & drink full breakfast, snack lunch, dinner, Sun lunch; restaurant and residential licence
Prices B&B £20-£25; dinner from £10; bargain breaks
Rooms 11 double, 2 with bath; 3 single
Facilities sitting-room, bar, dining-room
Credit cards MC, V
Children welcome
Disabled access easy to dining-room, but no ground-floor bedrooms
Pets accepted, but not allowed in public rooms
Closed never
Managers S and L Earnshaw

Cotswolds

Fleece

The Tudor-fronted Fleece is a former coaching inn which has undergone major refurbishments in recent years. The result is plush bedrooms decorated in pastels with every facility, including telephone extensions in the bathrooms. The dining-room has also been elegantly redecorated and offers an impressive menu. The sitting-room and bar retain their old world charm and draw a crowd of faithful locals. Across the entrance passage a wine bar caters for a predominantly younger clientele.

Nearby Corineum Museum (in Cirencester); Barnsley Park, 4 miles (6 km); Cotswold villages.

Market Place, Cirencester, Gloucestershire GL7 2NZ
Tel (0285) 658507
Location in market square; limited car parking at rear
Food & drink full breakfast, lunch, dinner; full licence
Prices B&B £36.45-£60.95; dinner £13.95
Rooms 21 double, 2 single; all with bath; all rooms have central heating, trouser-press, colour TV, radio, hairdrier, phone, tea/coffee kit
Facilities sitting-rooms (one with bar), dining-room, wine bar
Credit cards AE, DC, MC, V
Children welcome **Disabled** access good **Pets** allowed in bedrooms only
Closed Christmas day
Manager Stephen Davenport

Lamb Inn

Richard and Kate Cleverly's inn is not a luxurious place, but it epitomizes what this guide is all about – it is run with energy, verve and good humour; the features of the 300-year-old inn are retained and extensions have been made using original stone and beams; respectable beers such as Wadworths 6X, Tanglefoot and Flowers IPA are on tap; the furniture is comfortable; the bedrooms are well equipped; there is a delightful garden; the food is home-cooked, and it is very reasonably priced.

Nearby Stow-on-the-Wold, 5 miles (8 km), Burford, 6 miles (10 km), Shipton-under-Wychwood, 9 miles (14 km).

Great Rissington, Bourton-on-the-Water, Gloucestershire GL54 2LJ
Tel (0451) 20388
Location 4 miles (6 km) SE of Bourton-on-the-Water, 3 miles (5 km) N of A40; in gardens with ample car parking
Food & drink full breakfast, light (or packed) lunch, dinner; full licence
Prices B&B £16-£25; dinner from £8
Rooms 9 double, 4 with bath, 2 with shower; all rooms have central heating
Facilities sitting-room with TV, bar; indoor heated swimming-pool
Credit cards MC, V
Children welcome, but not in bar **Disabled** not suitable
Pets dogs welcome in bedrooms if well behaved
Closed Christmas day
Proprietors Richard and Kate Cleverly

Cotswolds

Mill House

With furnishings that are repro or modern rather than antique, Mill House is not the last word in intimacy or character. But the Cotswold stone building is welcoming and comfortable – with a notably spacious and stylish sitting-room, friendly bar and bright bedrooms – and immaculately kept. There is ambitious Anglo-French cooking, and a formidable wine-list. The Barnetts are unable to resist the villainous addition of a 10 per cent service charge.

Nearby Chastleton House, 3 miles (5 km); Cotswold villages.

Kingham, Stow-on-the-Wold, Oxfordshire OX7 6UH
Tel (06087) 8188
Location 4.5 miles (7 km) E of Stow-on-the-Wold, in Kingham village, close to B4450; in own grounds with ample car parking
Food & drink full breakfast, lunch, dinner, bar snacks; full licence
Prices B&B £32.50-£42.50; dinner £15.75; reductions for children under 10 sharing parents' room; bargain breaks

Rooms 20 double, all with bath and shower; one family room with bath; all rooms have colour TV, phone, radio, tea/coffee kit
Facilities lounge-bar sitting-room, dining-room; trout stream
Credit cards AE, DC, MC, V
Children welcome over 5
Disabled access easy to dining-room but difficult to bedrooms **Pets** not accepted
Closed never
Proprietors John and Valerie Barnett

Old Farmhouse

A highly individual family-run small hotel decorated in keeping with its origins as a 16thC farmhouse. All the rooms differ in style but are uniformly comfortable; those in the Old Stables are larger and more luxurious than those in the main building, but have less character. Food is a highlight here.

Nearby The Slaughters, 1.5 miles (2.5 km).

Lower Swell, Stow-on-the-Wold, Gloucestershire GL54 1LF
Tel (0451) 30232
Location one mile (1.5 km) W of Stow-on-the-World on B4068, in middle of village; with walled garden and ample car parking
Food & drink full breakfast, light lunch, dinner, full lunch on Sun; residential and restaurant licence
Prices B&B £18.25-£27.50; DB&B £28.50-£36.50; reductions for 2 or more

nights
Rooms 12 double, 10 with bath, 9 also with shower; one family room with bath and shower; all rooms have central heating, colour TV, radio/alarm, tea/coffee kit
Facilities sitting-room, bar, dining-room
Credit cards MC, V
Children welcome; high tea provided under 6 **Disabled** access easy only to family room **Pets** by arrangement
Closed Christmas to late Jan
Proprietors R and R Belsham

Cotswolds

Manor house and farm, Shipston-on-Stour

Longdon Manor

Jane Brabyn usually gives precise directions to her guests before they arrive, as this spectacular Elizabethan manor house is hidden deep in the countryside, amidst barns, stables and acres of corn.

The first glimpse of the interior is its magnificent entrance hall, complete with huge flagstones, which dates back to the 14thC. Now, it is used primarily as a sitting-room, where guests can relax surrounded by old oak furniture and a marvellous collection of musical instruments – and is used for monthly concerts which are a real treat for visitors. The hall overlooks delightful gardens, housing a 17thC dovecote and leading to various walks.

The four bedrooms are large, comfortable and all very different in character and furnishings – one boasting a large, circular bath – and all reflecting the splendour and slight eccentricity of the house. The emphasis is very much on informality – guests can expect to share the dinner table not only with one another but also with the Brabyn family and friends. If you want wine, remember to take it – the nearest off-licence is quite a trek.

Nearby Hidcote Manor garden, 5 miles (8 km); Stratford-upon-Avon, 8 miles (13 km); Cotswold villages.

Shipston-on-Stour,
Warwickshire CV36 4PW
Tel (060882) 235
Location 3 miles (5 km) W of Shipston, one mile (1.5 km) N of B4035; on working farm with ample car parking and garages
Food & drink full breakfast, tea, dinner by arrangement; no licence
Prices B & B £20-£28; dinner £12-£15
Rooms 3 double, all with bath, one also with shower; all rooms have central heating; tea/coffee kit on request
Facilities sitting-room, dining-room
Credit cards not accepted
Children welcome if well behaved **Disabled** access easy; no ground-floor bedrooms but shallow stairs
Pets not accepted
Closed Dec to Feb
Proprietor Jane Brabyn

Cotswolds

Inn, Shipton-under-Wychwood

Lamb Inn

The original Cotswold stone cottages that comprise the Lamb have been cleverly converted and modernized without losing their character. Everything is immaculate, pristine and tasteful, with lawns that look like astroturf. The Lamb is much favoured, for its food, which is outstanding both for quality and value – the three-course dinner is served in the oak-floored bar as well as in the charming dining-room. The wine list features sound-value bin ends and keeps prices low. Lynne and Hugh Wainwright are friendly hosts and their training within the Savoy group stands them in good stead here. Rooms are individually named, beamed and well appointed.

Nearby Cotswold villages; Oxford within reach.

High Street, Shipton-under-Wychwood, Oxfordshire OX7 6DQ
Tel (0993) 830465
Location in village, off A361; in garden with ample car parking
Food & drink full breakfast, lunch, dinner; full licence
Prices B & B £24; dinner from £14
Rooms 5 double, all with bath, 3 also with shower; all rooms have central heating, TV, tea/coffee kit, radio/alarm
Facilities bar, dining-room
Credit cards AE, MC, V
Children welcome over 14
Disabled access difficult
Pets not accepted
Closed Christmas week
Proprietors Hugh and Lynne Wainwright

Inn, Shipton-under-Wychwood

The Shaven Crown

An imposing limestone building built around a courtyard garden, the Shaven Crown dates back to 1384, and many of the original features are intact – most impressively the medieval hall, with its stunning beamed ceiling, which is the residents' sitting-room. Since we inspected the hotel, much has apparently changed for the better – in particular, the bedrooms have all been refurbished, and the bar has log fires. The menu is a sophisticated French-style one, and there is an impressive wine list. Breakfast is an excellent feast.

Nearby North Leigh Roman Villa, 6 miles (10 km).

Shipton-under-Wychwood, Oxfordshire OX7 6BA
Tel (0993) 830330
Location in middle of village; ample car parking
Food & drink full breakfast, lunch, dinner; full licence
Prices B & B £24-£42; dinner from about £8.50; reduced weekly rates, bargain breaks
Rooms 7 double, with bath; one single, with bath; one family room, with bath; all rooms have central heating, TV, tea/ coffee kit
Facilities restaurant, bar, medieval hall; bowling green
Credit cards MC, V
Children welcome
Disabled good access – one ground-floor bedroom
Pets allowed in bar but not in bedrooms
Closed never
Proprietors T D W Brookes and M Brookes

Cotswolds

Country guest-house, Lower Brailes

Feldon House

The Withericks both escaped the world of commercial catering to renovate their charming house on the fringes of the Cotswolds. For most travellers, Feldon House is a bed-and-breakfast establishment – and a thoroughly welcoming and comfortable one it is, too. But it is even more attractive to those who opt to take lunch or dinner. Allan Witherick does not run a restaurant in the conventional sense, but caters for single parties of up to 12 in the small dining-room and up to three couples in the conservatory. His fixed menus (which can of course take account of individual preferences) tend towards English food, based on fresh ingredients, all delightfully presented.

The house is a modest one with a red-brick Victorian façade. Inside, it has been carefully decorated, with stripped woodwork, muted colours and antique furniture. Bedrooms are pretty and comfortably furnished, and each provides creature comforts such as electric blankets, bottles of mineral water, sweets, books, magazines and tissues. Two rooms with bath have recently been created in the old coach house. The gardens, front and rear, are leafy and colourful, and beautifully kept without being formal. A delightful place, and a good alternative to the pricier hotels in and around Stratford-upon-Avon.

Nearby Upton House and gardens, 5.5 miles (9 km), Broughton Castle, 8 miles (13 km); Cotswold villages, Stratford-upon-Avon.

Lower Brailes, near Banbury, Oxfordshire OX15 5HW
Tel (060885) 580
Location 10 miles (16 km) W of Banbury on B4035, in middle of village; in garden with parking for 9 cars
Food & drink full breakfast, lunch, dinner; restaurant and residential licence
Prices B&B £17.50-£35; dinner £16.50; reductions for 2 nights or more
Rooms 2 double with bath; all rooms have central heating, clock; hairdrier and trouser-press available
Facilities 2 sitting-rooms, dining-room, conservatory, dining-room
Credit cards MC, V
Children welcome over 11
Disabled access difficult
Pets accepted, but not in public rooms
Closed never
Proprietors Allan and Maggie Witherick

Cotswolds

Swalcliffe Manor

Judith and Francis Hitching opened the doors to their beautiful and historic house to guests in 1985 – and have not looked back. No wonder. Swalcliffe Manor boasts a host of unrivalled features – a Tudor great hall with huge log fireplace, a fine medieval undercroft, an enormous Georgian sitting-room, a dining-room with a long Elizabethan refectory table, and bedrooms which are widely different but all captivating, with views over the secluded gardens. Judith runs the house almost single-handed – though "Francis is a good butler" – and has won awards for her gourmet cooking. Dinner might include scallops with ginger and onions, boned and stuffed chicken *en croute*, elderflower sorbet and raspberry coulis. Breakfast is large, and comes complete with home-made jams.

Nearby Upton House, 5 miles (8 km); Stratford-upon-Avon and Cotswold villages within reach.

Swalcliffe, Banbury, Oxfordshire, OX15 5EH
Tel (029578) 348
Location 5 miles (8 km) W of Banbury, next to church; in 4.5-acre grounds, with ample car parking
Food & drink full breakfast, tea, dinner; no licence
Prices B&B £15-£25; dinner from £14
Rooms 3 double, 2 with bath, one with separate bathroom (one four-poster bedroom); all rooms have central heating, tea/coffee kit
Facilities sitting-rooms, dining-room, great hall with piano and TV; croquet, swimming-pool
Credit cards not accepted
Children welcome over 7 if well behaved
Disabled not suitable: steep stairs, polished floors
Pets dogs tolerated, but not allowed in dining-room
Closed mid-Dec to Mar
Proprietors Judith and Francis Hitching

Manor Farm Barn

Bed and breakfast only, and for no more than six people – but nonetheless difficult to resist. This lovely old Cotswold-stone barn has been comfortably converted and beautifully furnished. It is run with exemplary care and good humour by Mrs Florey and it enjoys a peaceful rural setting in a hamlet.

Nearby Minster Lovell Hall, 6 miles (10 km); Cotswolds.

Taynton, Burford, Oxfordshire OX8 4UH
Tel (099382) 2069
Location 1.5 miles (2.5 km) NW of Burford, close to A424; parking for six cars
Food & drink full breakfast; no licence
Prices B&B £20-£25
Rooms 3 double, all with bath and shower; all rooms have central heating, TV, tea/coffee kit, hairdrier
Facilities sitting-room
Credit cards not accepted
Children welcome over 10 if well behaved
Disabled access difficult
Pets not accepted
Closed Christmas to New Year
Proprietors Mrs J Florey

Cotswolds

Country house hotel, Tetbury

Calcot Manor

This 15thC Cotswold farmhouse has been functioning as a hotel only since 1984, but the Ball family – father Brian and son Richard professionally trained, mother Barbara a dedicated amateur – settled immediately into a confident stride, providing the highest standards of comfort and service while preserving a calm and relaxed atmosphere. The lovely old house itself was a sound choice – its rooms are spacious and elegant without being grand – and the setting amid lawns and old barns, surrounded by rolling countryside, is all you could ask for. The furnishings and decorations are carefully harmonious, with rich fabrics and pastel colours, but are a little lacking in character (you know you are in a hotel and not a home).

Food is a highlight. When Brian Ball hired the young Ramon Farthing as chef in 1986, he called him "a star of the future"; within a year his original and satisfying cooking had earned the hotel a prized Michelin star.

Nearby Chavenage, 1.5 miles (2.5 km), Owlpen Manor, 3 miles (5 km), Westonbirt Arboretum, 4 miles (6 km); Cotswold villages.

Near Tetbury,
Gloucestershire GL8 8YJ
Tel (066689) 391
Location 3 miles (5 km) W
of Tetbury on A4135; in
4-acre grounds with ample
car parking (4 under cover)
Food & drink full breakfast,
lunch, dinner; residential
and restaurant licence
Prices B&B £42.50-£55;
dinner £28
Rooms 13 double, all with
bath and shower (4 with spa
bath); all rooms have central
heating, colour TV, phone,
radio, hairdrier
Facilities 2 sitting-rooms,
dining-room; heated
outdoor swimming-pool,
croquet
Credit Cards AE, DC, MC, V
Children welcome over 12
Disabled access good to all
ground-floor public rooms;
4 ground-floor bedrooms,
one specially equipped
Pets not accepted
Closed one week after New
Year
Proprietors Brian and
Barbara Ball

Cotswolds

The Close

The Close has a fine 16thC façade, an elegant sitting-room (once an open courtyard, but now covered in with a Georgian domed roof), and Adam ceilings in the dining-room, which looks out on to the pleasant walled garden at the back. The hospitality, however, is thoroughly up to date, with modern English cooking and plenty of extras in the bedrooms; over the last couple of years several new rooms have been added at the quieter rear of the hotel, and all have been smartly refurbished.

Nearby Badminton House, 6 miles (10 km).

Long Street, Tetbury, Gloucestershire GL8 8AQ
Tel (0666) 52272
Location in middle of town on A433; large car park at rear
Food & drink full breakfast, lunch, dinner; residential and restaurant licence
Prices B & B £47.50-£110; dinner £25.50; reduction for children

Rooms 15 double, all with bath; all rooms have central heating, phone, radio, colour TV
Facilities 3 sitting-rooms, 2 dining-rooms; croquet
Credit cards AE, DC, MC, V
Children very welcome over 10 **Disabled** access difficult
Pets not accepted
Closed never
Manager David Broadhead

Lords of the Manor

A delightful house, dating from the 17th century but with major additions in the 18th and 19th, resulting in a range of bedrooms from cosy to elegant, with prices stepping up in line. The glory of the place is its setting, in one of the most unspoilt and peaceful parts of the Cotswolds, with the little river Eye meandering through the grounds on its way to join the Thames. Chef Richard Mundy, a fairly recent recruit, is a disciple of the famous Raymond Blanc.

Nearby Sezincote gardens, 5 miles (8 km); Cotswold villages; Stratford-upon-Avon within reach.

Upper Slaughter, Bourton-on-the-Water, Cheltenham, Gloucestershire GL54 2JD
Tel (0451) 20243
Location 2 miles (3 km) SW of Stow-on-the-Wold; in 7.5-acre grounds with parking for 20 cars
Food & drink breakfast, lunch, dinner; full licence
Prices B & B £40-£57.50; dinner from £22; bargain breaks
Rooms 14 double with bath; one single with shower; all rooms have central heating,

phone
Facilities bar, sitting-room, dining-room; croquet, trout fishing
Credit cards AE, DC, MC, V
Children welcome aged 2 or over **Disabled** access fairly good – 2 ground-floor bedrooms (but one is down 3 steps); 3 steps to bar and sitting-room **Pets** dogs accepted, but not allowed in public rooms
Closed never
Manager Richard Young

Oxfordshire

Town guest-house, Henley-on-Thames

Regency House

The key feature of this elegant house is its setting, right beside one of the most charming urban stretches of the upper Thames (just above Henley Bridge): most of the large, comfortable and stylishly decorated rooms have superb views of the river and the beautiful countryside beyond. The dining-room has become more important of late; it is open to non-residents and has recently been enlarged, taking over what was the sitting-room. There is now a 'lovely' garden-room bar and terrace.

Nearby Thames valley; Windsor Castle, 10 miles (16 km).

4 River Terrace, Henley-on-Thames, Oxfordshire RG9 1BG
Tel (0491) 571133
Location 100 yds above Henley bridge, on town side of the Thames; car parking on street outside, or in nearby public car park
Food & drink full breakfast; lunch by arrangement, dinner; residential licence
Prices B&B £22.50-£38; dinner £15; weekend reductions off-season
Rooms 4 double, 3 with bath, one with separate shower; one single with shower; all rooms have central heating, TV, radio, phone, tea/coffee kit, minibar
Facilities bar, dining-room
Credit cards AE, V
Children accepted, but more suitable for those over 12
Disabled access difficult
Pets not accepted
Closed Christmas Day and Boxing Day
Proprietors Wyn Peters and Ann Ducker

Town hotel, Woodstock

Feathers

An amalgam of four tall 17th-century town houses of mellow red brick, rescued from decay by Gordon Campbell-Gray. The public rooms are full of character, the individually decorated bedrooms elegant and comfortable – though some are on the small side. Antiques, pictures, books, flowers and plants abound. Even the 'controlled imaginative English' food is highly regarded. A few years ago Mr C-G took a back seat and standards slipped; but he is now firmly in control again.

Nearby Blenheim Palace; Oxford, 7 miles (11 km).

Market Street, Woodstock, Oxfordshire OX7 1SX
Tel (0993) 812291
Location in middle of town; with courtyard garden and limited private car parking
Food & drink breakfast, lunch, dinner; full licence
Prices B&B £46-£50; dinner from £18.50
Rooms 14 double, 13 with bath, one with shower; 2 single, both with shower; all rooms have central heating, colour TV, phone, radio
Facilities bar, 2 sitting-rooms, dining-room
Credit cards AE, DC, V
Children welcome
Disabled access difficult
Pets accepted by arrangement
Closed never
Proprietor Gordon Campbell-Gray

Northamptonshire

Country hotel, Paulerspury

Vine House

This old, family-owned farmhouse in a tiny Northamptonshire village, only quite recently converted into a hotel and restaurant, was and is a very welcome development in an area where good hotels are thin on the ground. It was taken over in 1988 by Christine and Karen Snowdon.

The kitchen, now under the supervision of Karen and her colleague Jon Stanbury, remains at the heart of the hotel and its success. Everything possible is home-made, from the bread and preserves at breakfast to the petit-fours and chocolates served with coffee after dinner. There are fixed-price menus of three, four or six courses – all available at lunch and dinner and all changed twice a month – as well as an extensive 'carte'. The dining-room is attractively cottagey, with white linen against warm Burgundy-papered walls, and there is a pleasant little bar for pre-dinner drinks.

The hotel's six spotless bedrooms, all individually decorated in country style, are named after grape varieties. Back rooms have views over the pleasant walled garden. The only flaw is that the shower rooms (in sharp contrast to the bedrooms themselves) are decidedly small.

Nearby Silverstone, 5 miles (8 km), Buckingham, 9 miles (14 km).

100 High Street, Paulerspury, Towcester, Northamptonshire NN12 7NA
Tel (032733) 267
Location 3 miles (5 km) SE of Towcester, in village off A5; with ample car parking
Food & drink full breakfast, lunch, dinner; restaurant and residential licence
Prices B&B £29.50-£49; dinner from £13.95
Rooms 5 double, 4 with shower, one with bath; one single, with shower; all rooms have central heating, colour TV, radio/alarm, phone, tea/coffee kit
Facilities sitting-room, bar, dining-room
Credit cards MC, V
Children welcome **Disabled** access easy to public rooms only **Pets** not in public rooms
Closed Sat, Sun, Mon, lunch
Proprietors Christine and Karen Snowdon

Bedfordshire

Manor house hotel, Flitwick

Flitwick Manor

Built 1638, altered 1730, 1780, 1840, 1872 (wing), modernized 1936, converted to hotel 1984. So reads Somerset Moore's summary of the history of his red-brick house, which presents a mainly Georgian face to modern-day visitors. The Moores, drawing on long experience in the hotel and restaurant business, have quickly established their new enterprise as something of an oasis in the desert of Bedfordshire.

An authentically crunchy tree-lined drive leads to the house, which overlooks parkland extending beyond its own substantial gardens. The several public rooms are highly individual – the mellow panelled bar sitting-room, the library with ornamental plaster, the dining-room in elegant Regency style, the music room newly done out in Gothic style. Bedrooms are spacious and beautifully furnished in varying traditional styles, with many antique pieces.

The cooking is refreshing, with a pronounced emphasis on seafood (and game in season); as well as the 'carte', there are fixed-price menus of shellfish and vegetarian dishes.

Nearby Woburn Abbey, 4.5 miles (7 km); Chilterns.

Church Road, Flitwick,
Bedfordshire MK45 1AE
Tel (0525) 712242
Location 2 miles (3 km) S of
Ampthill, on S side of village,
close to A5120; in 6.5-acre
grounds with ample car
parking
Food & drink breakfast,
lunch, dinner; full licence
Prices B & B £50-£125;
dinner £15-£25
Rooms 11 double, all with
bath; 4 single, all with bath;
all rooms have central
heating, colour TV, phone,
radio, hairdrier
Facilities dining-room, bar,
library, sitting-room, music
room; croquet, putting,
tennis, fishing
Credit cards AE, MC, V
Children welcome if well
behaved **Disabled** access
good – separate entrance for
wheelchairs; 3 ground-floor
rooms
Pets welcome (but charged
for)
Closed Christmas
Proprietors Somerset and
Hélène Moore

Warwickshire

Chapel House

The Robertses have now finished extending this predominantly Georgian building – the peaceful but rather small sitting-room has been enlarged, along with the adjacent conservatory. The house is a successful blend of period elegance and modern comforts. The light and airy Garden Room has a single large table used mainly for breakfast; the main dining-room has elegantly laid separate tables, and is open to non-residents in the latter part of the week. David Roberts himself is in charge of the kitchen, and does a sound job with fresh ingredients. The second-floor bedrooms, in cottage style, are welcoming.
Nearby Coventry and Lichfield within reach.

Friars Gate, Atherstone, Warwickshire CV9 1EY
Tel (0827) 718949
Location 5 miles (8 km) NE of Nuneaton; off A5, in town square; car parking in street
Food & drink full breakfast, dinner; restaurant licence
Prices B&B £21.50-£31.50, dinner from £9.50
Rooms 6 double, all with bath and shower; 6 single, 4 with bath, 2 with shower; all rooms have central heating, colour TV, phone, radio
Facilities sitting-room, 2 dining-rooms
Credit cards DC, MC, V
Children welcome, but not in restaurant under 8
Disabled access easy
Pets not accepted **Closed** Christmas **Proprietors** David and Pat Roberts

Mallory Court

Allan Holland and Jeremy Mort have put the emphasis in this converted country manor – built at the turn of the century in Lutyens style – unashamedly on luxury, from the oak-panelled dining-room, where the tables are laid with silver and crystal, to the spacious, individually decorated bedrooms. The menu is small and imaginative, and is uncompromisingly expensive.
Nearby Warwick Castle, 2 miles (3 km), Kenilworth Castle, 5 miles (8 km), Stratford-upon-Avon, 9 miles (14.5 km).

Harbury Lane, Bishops Tachbrook, Royal Leamington Spa, Warwickshire CV33 9QB
Tel (0926) 330214
Location 2 miles (3 km) S of Leamington, just off A452; in 10-acre grounds, with ample parking and garages for 3 cars
Food & drink breakfast, lunch, tea, dinner; full licence
Prices B&B £40-£125 (double occupancy – single occupancy on application); dinner from £33
Rooms 8 double, all with bath, 4 also with shower; one suite, with bath; all rooms have central heating, colour TV, hairdrier, radio
Facilities sitting-rooms, dining-room, garden room; outdoor swimming-pool, tennis, squash, croquet
Credit cards MC, V
Children welcome over 12
Disabled access difficult
Pets not accepted
Closed never
Proprietors Allan Holland and Jeremy Mort

Warwickshire

Town hotel, Stratford-upon-Avon

Stratford House

For a central position in Stratford, this lovely old Georgian house is hard to beat – a mere stone's throw from the Royal Shakespeare Theatre, with the rest of historical Stratford right on the doorstep. Its previous owners ran Stratford House as a B&B place for many years before adding a restaurant in 1986. Sylvia Adcock 'retired' from a larger hotel in 1987 to take it over; she has had the rooms redecorated, but some are on the small side. The sitting-room at the front of the house is intimate and home-like, while the Shepherd's Garden Restaurant at the back has a delightful conservatory, which opens on to a flowery walled garden where diners can eat alfresco, if the weather permits. John George's cooking is geared to a short, mildly adventurous and regularly changing menu.

Nearby Shakespeare's birthplace and tomb, Royal Shakespeare Theatre (all in Stratford); Warwick, Cotswolds within reach.

Sheep Street, Stratford-upon-Avon, Warwickshire CV37 6EF
Tel (0789) 68288
Location in middle of town, with walled courtyard; free car parking can be arranged nearby
Food & drink full breakfast, lunch, dinner; residential and restaurant licence
Prices B&B £20-£50; dinner from £15; bargain breaks
Rooms 8 double, 6 with bath, 2 with shower; one single, with shower; one family room, with bath; all rooms have central heating, colour TV, tea/coffee kit, phone, radio/alarm
Facilities dining-room, sitting-room, bar
Credit cards AE, DC, MC, V
Children welcome, preferably over 5
Disabled access easy – 3 ground-floor bedrooms (though no wide doorways)
Pets not accepted
Closed Christmas
Proprietor Sylvia Adcock

Derbyshire

Riverside

This Georgian-style L-shaped stone house, originally part of the Chatsworth estate, has been a hotel since the early 1980s, when the Taylors took over. It is smartly furnished, mostly with good reproduction antiques, and the menu served in the spacious, somewhat formal dining-room is notably ambitious, reflecting the wide experience of chef Jeremy Buckingham.

Nearby Chatsworth and Haddon Hall, 4 miles (6 km).

Fennel Street, Ashford-in-the-Water, Bakewell, Derbyshire DE4 1QF
Tel (062981) 4257
Location 2 miles (3 km) NW of Bakewell off A6, at top of village main street; in one-acre gardens, with parking for 25 cars
Food & drink full breakfast, dinner Mon-Sat; Sun lunch, cold table in evening; residential and restaurant licence
Prices B & B £35; dinner from £17.50; bargain breaks

Rooms 7 double, 4 with bath, 3 with shower; all rooms have central heating, colour TV, radio/alarm, tea/coffee kit, phone
Facilities sitting-room, cocktail bar, 2 dining-rooms
Credit cards AE, MC, V
Children welcome, but not young babies **Disabled** access easy to public rooms only
Pets small dogs only, by prior arrangement
Closed never
Proprietors Roger and Sue Taylor

Wind in the Willows

The whimsical name honours not Kenneth Graham's classic but a tree in the garden. Peter and Anne Marsh – who are brother and mother of Eric Marsh of the Cavendish at Baslow (opposite entry) – spent six years upgrading their Victorian guest-house before relaunching it under the new name in 1987, and an excellent job they made of it. All the bedrooms are thoroughly comfortable, but the Erika Louise room has a truly magnificent Victorian half tester and a splendid period-style bathroom.

Nearby Peak District.

Derbyshire Level, Glossop, Derbyshire SK13 9PT
Tel (04574) 68001
Location 1 mile (1.5 km) E of Glossop off A57; in 5-acre grounds, with parking for 12 cars
Food & drink full breakfast, dinner; restaurant licence
Prices B & B £25-£55; dinner £15
Rooms 6 double, one with bath, 5 with shower; one family room, with shower; one suite with bath and

shower; all rooms have central heating, phone, clock, radio/alarm, tea/coffee kit, hairdrier, trouser-press; TV on request
Facilities sitting-room, bar/study, dining-room
Credit cards AE, MC, V
Children not discouraged
Disabled access difficult to bedrooms
Pets not accepted
Closed never
Proprietors Peter Marsh and Anne Marsh

Derbyshire

Country house hotel, Baslow

Cavendish

A posh, West End name and mini-bars in each of 24 bedrooms? The Cavendish doesn't sound like a personal small hotel. But the smart name is not mere snobbery – it is the family name of the Duke of Devonshire, on whose glorious Chatsworth estate the hotel sits (and over which the bedrooms look). And neither the hotel's size nor its equipment interferes with its essential appeal as a polished but informal country house – thanks to the care and enthusiasm of Eric Marsh and his staff.

The solid stone building is plain and unassuming. Inside, all is grace and good taste – the welcoming entrance hall sets the tone, with its paintings, linen-covered sofas before an open fire, and elegant antique tables standing on a brick-tile floor. Bedrooms are consistently attractive and comfortable, but vary in size and character – older ones are more spacious.

The Paxton Room, as the elegant restaurant is called, claims to have a 'controversial' menu; it is certainly ambitious and highly priced, and yet has not met with the approval of the food-guide establishment. Perhaps chef Nick Buckingham (who has been here since the start in 1975) is too original for his own good.

Nearby Chatsworth, 1.5 miles (2.5 km); Haddon Hall, 4 miles (6 km); Peak District.

Baslow, Derbyshire DE4 1SP
Tel (024688) 2311
Location 10 miles (16 km) W of Chesterfield on A619; in extensive gardens with ample car parking
Food & drink breakfast, lunch, dinner; full licence
Prices B&B £36-£68.50; dinner from £18; extra bed or cot £5
Rooms 24 double, all with bath and shower; all rooms have central heating, colour TV, phone, tea/coffee kit, clock radio, minibar, hairdrier
Facilities dining-room, bar, sitting-room; putting-green
Credit cards AE, DC, MC, V
Children welcome
Disabled access difficult
Pets not accepted
Closed never
Proprietor Eric Marsh

Derbyshire

Riber Hall

Twenty years ago, Alex Biggin rescued this sturdy Elizabethan manor from the verge of dereliction, furnished it sympathetically, and opened it as a restaurant – to the applause of local gourmets, who are not spoilt for choice of ambitious and competent French cooking. The bedrooms came later – created in outbuildings across an open courtyard and ranging from the merely charming and comfortable to the huge and delightful, with deep armchairs. Exposed timbers and stone walling, and antique four-posters are the norm, and all the thoughtful trimmings you could wish for are on the hand (even down to miniature sherries).

The dining-room is elegantly traditional, and much the better for its light new decoration; the small sitting-room through which it is reached is a fine place to sit before an open fire on a wild night (umbrellas are provided to get you across the courtyard), isolated from the world as well as insulated from the storm. Friendly and accommodating local lasses serve meals in one and drinks in the other.

And you still have the hope that by morning the storm will have cleared, so that you can enjoy the delicious seclusion of the luxuriant walled garden.

Nearby Chatsworth House, Haddon Hall, Hardwick Hall, all 7 miles (11 km).

Matlock, Derbyshire, DE4 5JU
Tel (0629) 582795
Location 3 miles (5 km) SE of Matlock by A615; take minor road S at Tansley: in extensive grounds with adequate car parking in courtyard
Food & drink breakfast, lunch, dinner; restaurant and residential licence
Prices B & B £35-£65; dinner about £23; 2–day breaks from £96 Oct-Apr
Rooms 11 double, all with bath and shower (5 with whirlpools) no twin beds, most four-posters; all rooms have central heating, minibar, colour TV, hairdrier, tea/coffee kit, trouser-press
Facilities sitting-room with bar service, conservatory, dining-room; tennis
Credit cards AE, DC, MC, V
Children not under 10
Disabled not suitable
Pets not accepted
Closed never
Proprietor Alex Biggin

Lincolnshire

Town guest-house, Lincoln

D'Isney Place

Anyone who aspires to run a small town hotel would do well to start by taking a close look at this delightful red-brick Georgian house in a quiet street a few yards from Lincoln cathedral. From the moment they arrived, back in 1978, David and Judy Payne were determined that everything about their venture should be of the best – the well-co-ordinated decorations and fabrics, the antiques, the breakfasts served on bone china in the tremendously comfortable and stylish bedrooms, and above all the private-house-style welcome extended to the guests. What cannot be of the best simply is not provided – which applies particularly to dinner, for which guests are pointed towards one of the excellent restaurants within walking distance, though some sandwiches and snacks are laid on. A recent visitor quibbled over the "garish" decoration of her bathroom, but was delighted by everything else – including the opportunity to have breakfast gazing out of her bedroom window over the peaceful walled garden (open to guests) which boasts a 700-year-old tower from the old Cathedral Close wall.

Nearby Cathedral, Bishop's Palace, Usher Gallery.

Eastgate, Lincoln,
Lincolnshire LN2 4AA
Tel (0522) 538881
Location in middle of city,
just E of cathedral; with large
walled garden and adequate
car parking
Food & drink full breakfast,
snacks at night; no licence
Prices B & B £30-£37;
Rooms 14 double, 12 with
bath (2 with spa bath, one
with Turkish steam shower),
2 with shower; 2 single, one
with bath, one with shower; 2
family rooms, both with

bath; all rooms have central
heating, colour TV, radio,
phone, tea/coffee kit; some
rooms have hairdrier
Facilities short tennis in
summer
Credit cards AE, DC, MC, V
Children welcome; cots
available
Disabled access good –
wheelchair ramp and wide
doors; ground-floor
bedrooms **Pets** welcome
Closed never
Proprietors David and Judy
Payne

Essex

Country guest-house, Dedham

Dedham Hall

A night or two in Dedham can cost a small fortune, but it will not if you stay with the Slingos in their pretty pink-washed farmhouse, set in a garden-cum-smallholding. The house dates from the 15th century, and is sympathetically furnished and decorated; beams and antiques abound, and one of the comfortable sitting-rooms looks out on to a secluded walled garden. A barn has been converted for painting courses throughout the year.

Nearby Castle House (in Dedham).

Dedham, Colchester, Essex
CO7 6AD
Tel (0206) 323027
Location 5 miles (8 km) NE of Colchester, one mile (1.5 km) from A12; in 6-acre grounds with parking for 15 cars
Food & drink full breakfast, dinner; residential licence
Prices B&B £15.50-£32; dinner £12
Rooms 9 double, 3 with bath, 4 with shower; 2 single, one with shower; one family room, with bath; all rooms have central heating, tea/coffee kit
Facilities bar, 2 dining-rooms, 2 sitting-rooms
Credit cards not accepted
Children accepted, but not specially catered for
Disabled access difficult for wheelchairs although there are 3 ground-floor bedrooms **Pets** not accepted
Closed Christmas to Feb
Proprietors Elizabeth and Bill Slingo

Bed and breakfast guest-house, Dedham

Maison Talbooth

For lavish comfort this rather plain-looking Victorian house is hard to beat. The bedrooms have flamboyant fabrics, luxury drapes, king-size beds, fruit and flowers; and the bathrooms thick fluffy towels, gold taps and circular sunken baths. The French doors of an elegantly furnished sitting-room open out on to two beautiful acres of landscaped garden and beyond that the lush pastures of Constable country. Down the road Le Talbooth, a half-timbered weaver's cottage also under the Milsom management, provides the gastronomic highlight of the area. But a light snack will be willingly served in your room.

Nearby Castle House (in Dedham); Dedham Vale.

Stratford Road, Dedham, Colchester, Essex CO7 6HN
Tel (0206) 322367
Location 5 miles (8 km) NE of Colchester, W of village; in 2-acre grounds with parking for 12 cars
Food & drink breakfast and light snacks in rooms
Prices B&B £45-£70; dinner from £30
Rooms 10 double, all with bath (2 with spa bath); all rooms have central heating, colour TV, minibar
Facilities sitting-room; croquet, lawn chess
Credit cards AE, MC, V
Children welcome if well behaved **Disabled** easy access – 5 ground-floor rooms **Pets** not accepted
Closed never
Proprietor Gerald Milsom

Essex

Country house hotel, Dedham

Dedham Vale

Dedham Vale is the youngest offspring of Gerald Milsom's family of East Anglian hotels and restaurants. The rooms are not as sumptuous as those of the Maison Talbooth, but they are certainly a cut above average and some guests prefer the absence of the ritzy Talbooth touches. Although no two bedrooms are exactly alike, flowing floral curtains, thick carpets and elegant painted furniture are features of them all. Bathrooms are white and plain – no sunken baths or jacuzzis here.

The Edwardian house is creeper-clad and stands amid three acres of immaculately tended lawns and flower beds in a quiet spot in the Vale of Dedham. The theme is the outdoors – from the murals of Suffolk landscapes in the bar to the conservatory-like dining-room where the profusion of cascading plants, the glass dome, the crisp yellow tablecloths and the white laquered chairs create the illusion of eating alfresco. It is an exceptionally lovely setting at any time of day – and you eat well too. Specialities are succulent grills and spit roasts cooked on 'the largest rotisserie in Britain' and – the latest addition – authentic Indian dishes.

Nearby Castle House (in Dedham); Dedham Vale.

Stratford Road, Dedham, Colchester, Essex CO7 6HW
Tel (0206) 322273
Location 5 miles (8 km) NE of Colchester, off A12, one mile (1.5 km) W of village; in 3-acre grounds with ample car parking
Food & drink breakfast, lunch (except Sat), dinner (except Sun); restaurant licence
Prices B&B £30-£50; dinner from £25
Rooms 6 double, all with bath; all rooms have central heating, radio, phone, colour TV
Facilities sitting-room, bar, dining-room; golf and tennis nearby
Credit cards AE, DC, MC, V
Children welcome
Disabled access difficult – 4 steps to restaurant and no ground-floor bedrooms
Pets not accepted
Closed never
Proprietor Gerald Milsom

West Essex

Manor house hotel, Broxted

Whitehall

The Keanes opened the doors of Whitehall – their first such venture – only five years ago; but already they have established a high reputation for food and hospitality.

It is a splendid house. The public rooms are uniform only in being thoroughly comfortable. The bar has a modern feel, decorated in grey and with abundant motor racing memorabilia. The sitting-room, now extended and decorated in pastel shades has (like the entrance hall) comfortable, prettily covered chester-field sofas, and pictures on the walls. But the 'pièce de résistance' is the dining-room, with its exposed oak beams and window frames, a fine view over the garden and a truly remarkable brick chimney snaking up to the vaulted ceiling. The Keanes have wisely not attempted to decorate this room in its own style, but to complement it with simple bentwood and cane chairs and peach linen. It is an appropriate setting for the studied and stylish cooking of daughter Paula – limited-choice menus in modern French post-'nouvelle' fashion.

'The Team', as the Keanes like to call themselves and their senior staff, are a successful blend of amateur caring and professional skills.

Nearby Mole Hall wildlife park, 3 miles (5 km), Audley End House, 6 miles (10 km).

Church End, Broxted, Essex CM6 2BZ
Tel (0279) 850603
Location 4 miles (6.5 km) SW of Thaxted on B1051; in walled garden with ample car parking
Food & drink full breakfast, lunch, dinner; restaurant licence
Prices B & B £40-£75; dinner £23.50
Rooms 11 double, all with bath; all rooms have central heating, colour TV, phone, radio, hairdrier, trouser-press
Facilities sitting-room, bar, conference room, dining-room; outdoor heated swimming-pool, tennis
Credit cards AE, MC, V
Children welcome over 5
Disabled access good to ground-floor rooms, with ramps **Pets** not accepted
Closed 26-31 Dec
Proprietors Keane family

Cambridgeshire

Town hotel, Cambridge

Cambridge Lodge

The location of Cambridge Lodge is not ideal – neither peaceful nor convenient for the shops or sights. But it has the advantage over other, more central hotels of a car park and a pretty garden – and its rooms are effectively double-glazed. It is also an immaculately cared-for hotel, both inside and out. The lawn is neatly trimmed, flowers flow from hanging baskets, and the mock-Tudor façade is well kept. Inside, dark beams and pink furnishings create a cosy effect. Bedrooms, in floral fabrics, are on the small side, but plush and comfortable.

Nearby Fitzwilliam Museum, County Museum, Colleges.

Huntingdon Road, Cambridge, Cambs CB3 0DQ
Tel (0223) 352833
Location on A1307 leading out of city; in one-acre garden with parking for 20 cars
Food & drink full breakfast, lunch, dinner; restaurant and residential licence
Prices B&B £27.50-£40; dinner £17.95; reductions for weekends in winter
Rooms 10 double, 2 with bath, 8 with shower; one single, with shower; all rooms have central heating, colour TV, radio/alarm, phone, tea/coffee kit, hairdrier
Facilities sitting-room with bar, dining-room, conference room
Credit cards AE, DC, MC, V
Children welcome, but preferably not at dinner
Disabled access easy
Pets in bedrooms only
Closed never
Manager Sheila Hipwell

Town guest-house, Cambridge

Parkside Guest House

The welcome from John Sutcliffe and Shirley Heaton could not be more friendly, and their helpfulness is boundless. If you ask for breakfast at 1.30 pm following a May Ball they will be happy to oblige – and what is more the choice will include nearly 40 different cereals. Bedrooms are light, bright and comfortable and always contain plants and flowers.

Nearby University Colleges, Fitzwilliam Museum.

25 Parkside, Cambridge, Cambridgeshire CB1 1JE
Tel 0223 311212
Location close to middle of city; overlooking Parker's Piece; parking for 5 cars
Food & drink full breakfast, lunch, high tea, dinner; residential licence
Prices B&B £20-£23.50; dinner £9
Rooms 4 double, one with shower; 5 single, 3 with shower; 2 family rooms, one with shower; all rooms have central heating, colour TV, radio, phone
Facilities sitting-room with bar, dining-room, laundry room
Credit cards not accepted
Children welcome if well behaved; cots and high-chairs available **Disabled** access reasonable – ground-floor single bedroom
Pets by arrangement
Closed never
Proprietors John Sutcliffe and Shirley Heaton

Cambridgeshire

Duxford Lodge

This Georgian house, completely gutted in the course of its recent conversion to a hotel, scrapes into these pages as a 'useful in the area' entry. The painted-cane chairs and strategically placed potted plants, reproduction antiques and thick fitted carpets spell 'hotel' in large letters. But it is thoroughly comfortable and relaxed, and some of the bedrooms are particularly pretty. Food is in the light, modern style.

Nearby Air Museum; sights of Cambridge.

Ickleton Road, Duxford, Cambridgeshire CB2 4RU
Tel (0223) 836444
Location 9 miles (14 km) S of Cambridge, in village; with ample car parking
Food & drink full breakfast, lunch, dinner; restaurant and residential licence
Prices B&B £30-£50; dinner from £16; weekend breaks
Rooms 12 double, all with bath and shower; 4 single, 3 with bath, one with shower; all rooms have central heating, phone, colour TV, radio/alarm, tea/coffee kit; 11 rooms have minibar, trouser-press, hairdrier
Facilities bar, sitting-room, dining-room, conference room
Credit cards AE, DC, MC, V
Children welcome, but not allowed in dining-room after 8.30pm **Disabled** access reasonable **Pets** welcome in bedrooms only
Closed several days at end Dec, but open for Christmas and New Year's Eve
Manager Patricia Evans

Swynford Paddocks

This smart, white-painted country house has a scandalous past – it was allegedly the scene of the affair between the poet Byron and his half-sister Augusta. But the owners' pursuit of complete comfort rather than the preservation of character leaves you in no doubt that you are in a hotel – albeit a hotel of considerable appeal, with immaculately decorated and spacious bedrooms, a relaxed air about its harmoniously furnished lounge/bar and intimate panelled restaurant, beautiful gardens and friendly staff.

Nearby Cambridge, 6 miles (10 km), Newmarket, 6 miles (10 km).

Six Mile Bottom, Newmarket, Suffolk CB8 0UE
Tel (063870) 234
Location 6 miles (10 km) SW of Newmarket on A1304; with ample car parking
Food & drink full breakfast, lunch, tea, dinner; full licence
Prices B&B £40-£60; dinner from £17; weekend breaks
Rooms 12 double, 3 single; all with bath; all rooms have central heating, colour TV, radio/alarm, phone, minibar, trouser-press, hairdrier
Facilities sitting-room, bar, dining-room, conference room; croquet, tennis, putting, giant chess
Credit cards AE, DC, MC, V
Children welcome **Disabled** access easy to ground floor
Pets welcome, but not in public rooms
Closed never
Manager Tony Derrett

Cambridgeshire

Country guest-house, Melbourn

Melbourn Bury

This gracious manor house, dating mainly from Victorian times, although of much earlier origin, offers an intimate retreat only 20 minutes' drive from Cambridge. The white-washed and crenellated house, with roses round the door, has a delightful setting in mature parkland with its own lake and gardens.

All the public rooms are furnished with antiques, but have just the right degree of informality to make the house feel like a lived-in home and not a museum – not surprising, when you learn that Sylvia Hopkinson's family have been here for 150 years. As well as an elegant drawing-room, there is a splendid Victorian billiards room (full-size table) incorporating a book-lined library, and a sun-trap conservatory.

The three bedrooms are spacious and comfortably furnished in harmony with the house; particularly delightful is the 'pink room' which looks out over the lake and the garden; it is a profusion of Sanderson prints and antiques, and has a large bathroom.

The Hopkinsons' dinner-party food – home-made, down to the ice creams and sorbets – is served dinner-party style around a large mahogany table in the dining-room.

Nearby University colleges and Fitzwilliam Museum, in Cambridge; Wimpole Hall, Audley End within reach.

Melbourn, near Royston, Hertfordshire SG8 6DE
Tel (0763) 61151
Location 10 miles (16 km) SW of Cambridge, on S side of village off A10; in 5-acre gardens with ample car parking
Food & drink full breakfast, dinner; residential licence
Prices B&B £30-£40; dinner £12.50
Rooms 3 double, 2 with bath, one with shower; all rooms have central heating, TV, clock/radio
Facilities 2 sitting-rooms, dining-room, billiard room
Credit cards AE, V
Children welcome over 8
Disabled not suitable
Pets not accepted
Closed Christmas, New Year and Easter
Proprietors Anthony and Sylvia Hopkinson

Suffolk

Black Lion

Long Melford is a famously attractive Suffolk village, and the Black Lion is at the heart of it, overlooking the green. It was lifted out of the ordinary by the previous owners, Luke and Amelia Brady, who ran it from 1986 to 1989, when the Erringtons took over. It is an elegant early 19thC building, decorated and furnished with great sympathy, taste and lightness of touch. The Erringtons have brought with them their existing restaurant operation, the Countrymen, which offers 'modern cuisine with a strong classical influence' and wide-ranging wine list.

Nearby Melford Hall and Kentwell Hall.

The Green, Long Melford, Suffolk CO10 9DN
Tel (0787) 312356
Location in village 3 miles (5 km) N of Sudbury, overlooking village green; with car parking
Food & drink breakfast, lunch, dinner
Prices B&B £22.50-£40; dinner from £15
Rooms 8 double, one single and one family room; all with bath; all rooms have central heating, phone, TV, tea/coffee kit
Facilities sitting-room, 2 dining-rooms, bar
Credit cards MC, V
Children welcome if well behaved; baby-listening and cot provided **Disabled** no special facilities **Pets** not accepted in public rooms
Closed never **Proprietors** Janet and Stephen Errington

Pipps Ford

A reader recommends enthusiastically this glorious half-timbered Tudor house in flowery gardens, which Raewyn Hackett-Jones has been running as a guest-house since the early 1980s. She lays great stress on the quality of her meals, producing her own ham, bread, honey, vegetables and countless other ingredients.

The bedrooms are delightful and full of character, with log fires burning downstairs when necessary.

Nearby Blackenham Woodland Garden, 5 miles (7 km).

Needham Market, Nr Ipswich, Suffolk IP6 8LJ
Tel (044979) 208
Location in countryside one mile (1.5 km) E of Needham Market, down private road off roundabout where A140 meets A45; with car parking
Food & drink full breakfast, dinner; residential licence
Prices B&B DB&B £28-£37; B&B by arrangement
Rooms 6 double, all with bath and shower; 2 single, sharing shower room; all rooms have central heating, tea/coffee kit, radio/alarm
Facilities sitting-room, dining-room, 2 TV rooms; tennis, outdoor pool, fishing
Credit cards not accepted
Children accepted
Disabled rooms and lounge in stable on one floor
Pets not accepted in house, but can stay in car
Closed Christmas to New Year; no dinner on Sun
Proprietor Raewyn Hackett-Jones

Suffolk

Hintlesham Hall

"The most beautiful building in East Anglia," says Ruth Watson, thus making one of the few extravagant claims for Hintlesham Hall which does not (quite) stand up to scrutiny. The house is beautifully decorated and sumptuously furnished, sensibly mixing the antique, the reproduction and the modern; the cooking is elaborate, indulgent and expert. With recent development the hotel is no longer small; but it is still charming.

Nearby Dedham, 6 miles (10 km).

Hintlesham, near Ipswich, Suffolk IP8 3NS
Tel (047387) 268
Location 3 miles (5 km) W of Ipswich on A1071; in 23-acre grounds with ample car parking
Food & drink full breakfast, lunch, tea, dinner; restaurant licence
Prices B & B £40-£125; dinner from £28.50
Rooms 33 double, all with bath and shower; all rooms have central heating, colour TV, phone, radio
Facilities sitting-room, bar, billiard room; tennis, croquet, riding
Credit cards AE, DC, MC, V
Children accepted under one year and over 10 – others only by arrangement
Disabled access difficult **Pets** not accepted in hotel
Closed never **Proprietors** David and Ruth Watson

Edgehill

The Rolfes have achieved a happy combination of old and new in their handsome Georgian town house: a flagstoned hall, open fireplaces and chandeliers downstairs; bedrooms (some of which are surprisingly spacious) decorated with modern floral wallpaper, matching fabrics and thick pile carpets. A fair-sized sitting-room opens on to a walled flower-garden. Dinner is a cosy affair in a small but elegant room. Vegetables come straight from the kitchen garden and everything is home-made – including traditional English puddings.

Nearby Hadleigh Castle; Castle House, 6 miles (10 km); Dedham.

2 High Street, Hadleigh, Ipswich, Suffolk IP7 5AP
Tel (0473) 822458
Location 9 miles (14.5 km) W of Ipswich, in middle of town; with walled garden and car park at rear
Food & drink breakfast, dinner if pre-booked; residents licence
Prices B & B £16-£27.50; dinner £10; bargain breaks
Rooms 7 double, 3 with bath, 3 with shower; 2 single; 2 family rooms, one with bath, one with shower; all rooms have central heating, TV
Facilities sitting-room, dining-room
Credit cards not accepted
Children welcome; cot and high-chair provided
Disabled access difficult
Pets welcome
Closed one week Christmas to New Year
Proprietors Angela and Rodney Rolfe and Betty Taylor

Suffolk

Restaurant with rooms, Lavenham

The Great House

The ancient timber-framed houses, the fine Perpendicular 'Wool Church' and the high street full of antiques and galleries makes Lavenham a high-spot on any tourist itinerary of East Anglia.

The Great House in the market place was built in the heyday of the wool trade but was extensively renovated in the 18thC and looks more Georgian than Tudor – at least from the outside. It was a private house (lived in by Stephen Spender in the 1930s) until John Spice, a Texan brought up in Suffolk, had the bright idea of turning it into a restaurant with rooms. Its food (predominantly French) is the best for miles, and if you can secure one of its three bedrooms it is also a delightful place to stay. All are different, but they are all light, spacious and full of old-world charm, with beams and antiques. Each has its own fireplace and sitting area, with sofa or upholstered chairs. The dining-room is dominated by an inglenook fireplace which formed part of the original house. In winter log fires blaze, in summer French doors open out to a pretty courtyard, paved with stone, for drinks, lunch or dinner. Fixed-price lunches are sound value.

Nearby Little Hall (in Lavenham), Melford Hall, 4 miles (6 km), Gainsborough's House, Sudbury, 5.5 miles (9 km).

Market Place, Lavenham, Suffolk CO10 9QZ
Tel (0787) 247431
Location 16 miles (26 km) NW of Colchester, in middle of village; garden at rear, with public car parking
Food & drink full breakfast, lunch, tea, dinner; full licence
Prices B&B £23-£50; dinner from £11.75; reduction for 2 nights or more, and for children sharing parents' room
Rooms 3 family-size suites, all with bath; all rooms have central heating, phone, colour TV, tea/coffee kit
Facilities sitting-room/bar, dining-room, patio
Credit cards MC, V
Children very welcome; cot and high chair provided, free baby-listening **Disabled** access difficult **Pets** welcome
Closed last 3 weeks of Jan
Chef-manager Régis Crépy

Suffolk

Country guest-house, Otley

Otley House

Otley House has become one of the better-known examples of the 'country house party' establishments. Guests have the run of the relaxed but elegant house – 16thC but outwardly Georgian – including the grand piano in the candle-lit dining-room and the full-size snooker table. Lise Hilton's Danish origins shine through in her cooking – as in her intolerance of the slightest speck of dirt. Although there is a licence, there is no bar – 'guests are just given what they wish for.'

Nearby Woodbridge, 6 miles (10 km); Suffolk coast.

Otley, near Ipswich, Suffolk
IP6 9NR
Tel (047339) 253
Location 7 miles (11 km) N of Ipswich on B1079; ample car parking
Food & drink full breakfast, dinner (except Sun); residential licence
Prices B&B £15-£42; dinner £12.50
Rooms 4 double, all with bath; one single; with separate bathroom; all rooms have central heating, radio, hairdrier
Facilities 2 sitting-rooms (one with TV), dining-room, billiard room, hall; croquet
Credit cards not accepted
Children welcome over 12
Disabled access not easy, though wide staircase
Pets can be left in cars
Closed mid-Dec to mid-Feb
Proprietors L and M Hilton

Inn, Southwold

The Crown

We have conflicting reports of this refurbished inn, the flagship of Adnams – brewers to this part of the world, and wine merchants to a much wider clientele – but there is no doubt that overall the 'ayes' have it. The hotel is a comfortably unpretentious place, with an oak-panelled bar at the back still popular with locals as well as the main bar/sitting-room, where the food served bears no resemblance to normal 'bar snacks'. In the dining-room, too, Jason Wright's cooking is original and (usually) highly successful, with particular emphasis on fish. Bedrooms are unremarkable – small (some very small) but neat; Sunday brunch, sadly, is no more.

Nearby Suffolk Wild Life Country Park, 6 miles (10 km).

High Street, Southwold, Suffolk IP18 6DP
Tel (0502) 722275
Location in middle of town; with ample car parking, some covered
Food & drink breakfast, lunch, dinner; full licence
Prices B&B £20.50-£26; dinner £13-£15
Rooms 9 double, 6 with bath, 2 with separate bath, one with shower; 2 single, both with bath; one family room, with separate bath; all rooms have central heating, TV, phone
Facilities dining-room, 2 bars, function room
Credit cards AE, MC, V
Children welcome **Disabled** access possible to ground floor **Pets** welcome, but not allowed in dining-room
Closed never
Manager Simon Hawkins

North Norfolk

Converted windmill, Cley-next-the-Sea

Cley Mill

Imagine staying in a 'real' windmill. That is the sense of adventure that Cley Mill can induce even in the most world-weary. Memories of 'Swallows and Amazons' or the 'Famous Five' crowd in as you climb higher and higher in the mill, finally mounting the ladder to the look-out room, accompanied by the resident cat.

The sitting-room on the ground floor of the Mill is exceptionally welcoming – it feels well used and lived in, with plenty of books and magazines, comfy sofas, TV and an open fire. Bedrooms in the Mill feel rather like log cabins – much wood in the furniture and fittings – and there are wide views from the little windows out across the Blakeney Marshes to the sea. They are pretty rooms, with white lace bedspreads, and bathrooms ingeniously fitted in to the most challenging nooks and crannies.

Carolyn Hederman is a friendly woman who sees the Mill primarily as a 'classy guest-house' rather than a hotel, and does not mind a bit if you simply take B&B – though she happily cooks for guests who would like dinner, too. 'Good country cooking' is how she describes it, and just right, too, after a day in the fresh air. Take your own drink – no corkage charged.

Nearby Sheringham Hall, 6 miles (10 km), Cromer Lighthouse, 10 miles (16 km); Norwich within reach.

Cley-next-the-Sea, Holt, Norfolk NR25 7NN
Tel (0263) 740209
Location 7 miles (11 km) W of Sheringham on A149, on N edge of village; in garden, with ample car parking
Food & drink full breakfast; dinner on request; no licence
Prices B&B £17-£18; dinner £10; reductions for 3 or 7 nights
Rooms 2 double, one with bath, one with shower; one single; one family room, with bath
Facilities sitting-room, dining-room
Credit cards not accepted
Children welcome if well behaved **Disabled** access difficult **Pets** welcome if house-trained
Closed mid-Jan to end Feb
Proprietor Carolyn Hederman

North Norfolk

Country guest-house, Great Snoring

Old Rectory

Though presumably the words have a quainter etymology, Great Snoring lives up to its name. There is no shop, the last pub has closed, and it is easy to drive through the village without noticing the Old Rectory, hidden behind high stone walls beside the church. This seclusion is the pride of Rosamund Scoles, her husband and parents, who have been running the red-brick parsonage as a hotel since 1978.

'Hotel' is scarcely the right word for this relaxed retreat. There is no reception desk, no row of keys, no signs. Although Mrs Scoles herself makes the early morning tea round of the richly and individually furnished bedrooms, you are left to your own devices in the large sitting-room with its hotch-potch of comfortable old chairs (plus a few less comfortable-looking newer ones).

In the dining-room, heavy velvet drapes hang at the stone mullioned windows, and fresh flowers are arranged on each of the tables. The dinner menu is English (Mrs Scoles' mother does most of the cooking) and some may find it restricted – though guests are consulted before the one main course dish is chosen.

Nearby Walsingham Abbey, 1.5 miles (2.5 km), Holkham Hall, 8 miles (13 km); Norfolk Heritage Coast; Norwich within reach.

Barsham Road, Great Snoring, Fakenham, Norfolk NR21 0HP
Tel (0328) 820597
Location 3 miles (5 km) NE of Fakenham, in hamlet; in 1.5-acre garden with ample car parking
Food & drink full breakfast, dinner; restaurant and residential licence
Prices B & B £33-£45; dinner £14.60
Rooms 6 double, one single; all with bath; all rooms have central heating, colour TV, phone
Facilities sitting-room, dining-room
Credit cards AE, DC
Children accepted over 12
Disabled access difficult
Pets not accepted
Closed Christmas Day and Boxing Day
Proprietors Rosamund and William Scoles, Norah and Ronald Tooke

North Norfolk

Inn, Blickling

Buckinghamshire Arms

This 350-year-old inn has blossomed under Nigel Elliot, who ran hotels with hundreds of bedrooms before taking over this one with only three. Part of the appeal of the place is its next-door neighbour, Blickling Hall – a superb National Trust pile (the grounds open year-round, house only in summer). But the Arms itself is an exceptionally amiable place to stay, particularly if you are keen on real ales – there is a choice of four or five, served in a quaint 'snug' bar and in the larger but still rustic lounge bar. Food in the bars and restaurant is satisfying. There are tables on the neat lawns in summer.

Nearby Blickling Hall; Holt Woodlands Park, 8 miles (13 km).

Blickling, near Aylsham, Norwich, Norfolk NR11 6NF
Tel (0263) 732133
Location 1.5 miles (2.5 km) NW of Aylsham on B1354; with large private car park
Food & drink breakfast, bar lunch, dinner; full licence
Prices B&B £24-£38; dinner from £14.50; reductions for children
Rooms 3 double; all rooms have four-poster bed, colour TV, tea/coffee kit
Facilities dining-room, lounge bar, smaller bar
Credit cards AE, DC, MC, V
Children welcome, but not allowed in bars **Disabled** easy access to bars and restaurant, but not to bedrooms **Pets** accepted by arrangement
Closed Christmas Day
Proprietor Nigel Elliott

Country house hotel, Grimston

Congham Hall

There is much about this white 18thC Georgian house that impresses. The spacious bedrooms and public areas are luxuriously furnished, the service is solicitous and efficient. Our inspector found his dinner (in the modern British style) to be "commendable in every respect." But he also found the atmosphere genteel (a jacket for men is requested at dinner); the once flawed central heating system has now been put right.

Nearby Sandringham, 4 miles (6 km); Norwich within reach.

Grimston, King's Lynn, Norfolk PE32 1AH
Tel (0485) 600250
Location 6 miles (10 km) NE of King's Lynn near A148; in 40-acre grounds with parking for 50 cars
Food & drink full breakfast, lunch (except Sat), dinner; residential and restaurant licence
Prices B&B £38.50-£80; full breakfast £2 extra; dinner £25; weekend breaks
Rooms 9 double, all with bath; one single, with shower; one suite; all rooms have central heating, TV, phone, radio
Facilities 2 sitting-rooms, bar, dining-room; jacuzzi, swimming-pool, tennis, croquet
Credit cards AE, DC, MC, V
Children welcome over 12
Disabled access easy to restaurant
Pets not allowed
Closed never
Proprietors Christine and Trevor Forecast

North Norfolk

Country guest-house, Heacham

Holly Lodge

Mrs Piper planted 2,000 wallflowers in her garden in 1986, and the result at the time of our first inspection in 1987 was wonderful. That give you an idea of the sort of effort she makes to look after her guests at Holly Lodge.

This 16thC Elizabethan building, standing back from the road in its pretty gardens in the unprepossessing village of Heacham, has served as a sleeping place more than once in its history. It was built as a dormitory for visiting monks, and was probably once called Holy – not Holly – Lodge. The monastic theme is echoed in some of the pictures and other treasures that decorate this lovely house, but that is where it stops. Today's overnight guests sleep in pretty, comfortable rooms, some with four-poster beds; they dine in elegant surroundings from a menu which makes the most of local Norfolk products (asparagus, crab, duck . . .); they relax in small, comfortable sitting-rooms with open fires to induce post-prandial well-being.

Holly Lodge has the feel of being the home of someone who has their share of decorative taste and some beautiful possessions – but at the same time of being expertly and professionally run. Mrs Piper is full of information about the area, and now offers the additional attraction of outings in a carriage drawn by two white ponies.

Nearby Sandringham, 5 miles (8 km); King's Lynn within reach.

Heacham, near King's Lynn, Norfolk PE31 7HY
Tel (0485) 70790
Location 3 miles (5 km) S of Hunstanton, off A149, on edge of village; in 1.5 acre gardens with ample car parking
Food & drink full breakfast, dinner; residential and restaurant licence
Prices B&B £25-£35; dinner from £10; 2- and 3-day bargain breaks
Rooms 6 double, 5 with bath. one with shower; all rooms have central heating
Facilities 2 sitting-rooms, dining-room
Credit cards MC, V
Children accepted over 12
Disabled not suitable **Pets** accepted by arrangement if well behaved
Closed Jan and Feb
Proprietor Lesley Piper

Country house hotel, Felmingham

Felmingham Hall

Like the Joyces before them, the new owners run this gracious Elizabethan house in a very low-key way, but nothing is missing either – and the staff are careful to find time to talk to their guests. Wood-burning stoves were lit and welcoming on the chilly summer evening of our visit: curling up on a sofa after dinner in the elegant sitting-room was a positive treat.

Bedrooms are mostly huge, with room for comfortable armchairs and sofas. First-floor rooms are high-ceilinged and traditional, second-floor ones more modern and plush in a very tasteful way (some sharing a sitting area between two rooms – pleasant if you are with friends).

The new regime has inherited an interesting and reasonably priced wine list. You make your choice from this and the menu in the wine cellar bar – a rather dark, unexceptional place where you are also encouraged to take post-dinner drinks. Dinner is four generous courses from a daily menu with choices; cooking is simple but competent – and the choice of desserts would satisfy the greediest. Remember that next day you face a real 'country' breakfast.

Nearby woodland walks in grounds; Blickling Hall, 6 miles (10 km), the Broads, 6 miles (10 km); Norwich within reach.

Felmingham, North
Walsham, Norfolk
NR28 0LP
Tel (069269) 228
Location 3 miles (5 km) W of
North Walsham on B1145,
signposted from village; in
16-acre grounds, with ample
car parking
Food & drink full breakfast,
lunch, dinner; residential
and restaurant licence
Prices DB&B £35.50-£40;
reductions for 3 or 7 nights

Rooms 12 double, 2 single;
all with bath; all rooms have
central heating, colour TV,
tea/coffee kit, phone
Facilities 2 sitting-rooms,
bar, dining-room;
swimming-pool
Credit cards AE, MC
Children welcome over 12
Disabled access difficult
Pets not accepted, but local
kennels can be arranged
Closed never
Proprietors Consilium Ltd

North Norfolk

Country hotel, Shipdham

Shipdham Place

Justin de Blank, with his wife Melanie, opened this charming 17thC rectory in 1979 as a 'restaurant with rooms' – a label which they continued to use despite increasing numbers of bedrooms and the evident comfort of the place, and which persists under the new owners.

The modest vicarage atmosphere has been retained, together with many of the original features, though there are concessions to contemporary taste in the stripped pine doors and panelling. Laura Ashley prints and cane furniture prevail in the (mostly) airy bedrooms. Paintings and books abound, notably in the sitting-room, with its cosy log fire and deeply upholstered chairs and sofas. Here, as elsewhere, the impression is very much of a home furnished over the years rather than a set of furniture requisitioned in one go. You help yourself to pre-dinner drinks, recording your consumption.

French windows lead out to the garden with its brick patio, croquet lawn and dried-up moat. Beyond these are herb, fruit and vegetable gardens. Tina Poulton supervises the kitchen, and produces a daily changing menu of inventive dishes.

Nearby East Dereham, 5 miles (8 km); Norwich within reach.

Church Close, Shipdham, near Thetford, Norfolk IP25 7LX
Tel (0362) 820303
Location 5 miles (8 km) SW of East Dereham on A1075 in middle of village; adequate car parking
Food & drink full breakfast, lunch, dinner; residential and restaurant licence
Prices B&B £20-£66; dinner £16.50-£18.50
Rooms 8 double, all with bath and central heating
Facilities sitting-room, dining-room, conference room; croquet, pétanque
Credit cards MC, V
Children welcome if well behaved
Disabled access not easy; 2 steps at entrance
Pets well-behaved dogs accepted by arrangement
Closed never
Proprietors Tina and Alan Poulton

Lancashire

Northcote Manor

In a part of the world where there are few satisfactory alternatives, this late-Victorian mill-owner's house stands out for a combination of good food and comfortable surroundings. The young Craig Bancroft built up the reputation of the hotel as its manager during the early 1980s, and bought the business in 1986; the (also young) chef, Nigel Haworth, is now his partner, underlining the importance of the restaurant. He produces a frequently changing menu of modern, ambitious and innovative dishes, beautifully presented. The few bedrooms take second place, but have been refurbished and re-bathroomed.

Nearby Browsholme Hall, 8 miles (13 km); Gawthorpe Hall, 8 miles (13 km).

Northcote Road, Langho, Nr Blackburn, Lancashire BB6 8BE
Tel (0254) 40555
Location north of village, off A59; with ample car parking
Food & drink full breakfast, lunch, dinner; afternoon tea on request; residential and restaurant licence
Prices B&B £30-£50; dinner from £25
Rooms 5 double, 3 with bath, 2 with shower; one single with bath; all rooms have central heating, phone, TV, radio, tea/coffee kit
Facilities sitting-room, bar, dining-room, restaurant
Credit cards AE, DC, MC, V
Children welcome **Disabled** no special facilities **Pets** dogs welcome, not in public rooms
Closed 25 and 26 Dec, 1 Jan
Proprietors Craig Bancroft and Nigel Haworth

The River House

"A rare example of old-fashioned, small-scale high quality in the otherwise brash Fylde," says a reporter of this comfortable Victorian house in a peaceful setting on the banks of a tidal creek. Bedrooms are cosy and well equipped, and the house as a whole is friendly and welcoming, with plenty of period pieces, paintings and bric-a-brac. But the emphasis is on food, which is richly international and based on excellent ingredients.

Nearby Blackpool; many golf courses.

Skippool Creek, Thornton-le-Fylde, near Blackpool, Lancashire FY5 5LF
Tel (0253) 883497
Location one mile (1.5 km) SE of Thornton, off A585; parking for 20 cars
Food & drink full breakfast, lunch, dinner; restaurant and residential licence
Prices B&B £25-£50; dinner about £30
Rooms 4 double, one with bath and shower; all rooms have central heating, TV, phone, radio, tea/coffee kit, trouser-press, hairdrier
Facilities sitting-room, bar, dining-room, conservatory
Credit cards AE, MC
Children welcome if well behaved **Disabled** access difficult **Pets** welcome if well behaved
Closed never, but booking essential; restaurant closed Sun
Proprietors B and C Scott

West Yorkshire

Restaurant with rooms, Otley

Pool Court

Leeds and Bradford are not over-endowed with good hotels, large or small, so a well-run restaurant with rooms a short drive from either is welcome news in any event. But this is no ordinary RWR: the food at Pool Court has for decades been regarded as the best for miles around; the recently added bedrooms, like the dining-room, are immaculately furnished with great elegance (and equipped with every imaginable extra – including a copy of the long wine-list); and the whole operation is run with admirable flair, friendliness and minute attention to detail. Though there is no separate lounge, there is a welcoming small bar – and most of the rooms are spacious. Breakfast is a magnificent meal in itself.

Nearby Harewood House and gardens 4.5 miles (7 km); Leeds.

Pool-in-Wharfedale, West Yorkshire, LS21 1EH
Tel (0532) 842288
Location 3 miles (5 km) W of Otley by A659, just S of Pool on A658; in extensive gardens, with ample private parking
Food & drink breakfast, dinner Tue-Sat; full licence
Prices B&B £37.50-£79; cheaper Mon
Rooms 5 double, with bath; one single with shower; all rooms have central heating, colour TV, clock/radio, wall safe, minibar, phone, hairdrier
Facilities dining-room, bar, sitting-room
Credit cards AE, DC, MC, V
Children welcome ('often better behaved than the adults')
Disabled difficult
Pets not allowed; can be accommodated locally
Closed 2 weeks from Christmas Day, 2 weeks Summer
Proprietor Michael Gill

Humberside

Manor house hotel, Winteringham

Winteringham Fields

The name is as romantically bleak as anything conceived by the Brontë sisters, but the house is quite different: an amiable stone manor house dating from the 16thC, decoratively Victorian inside. Germain Schwab is a Swiss master chef; he and his wife, who runs the front of house, moved here in 1988 after running a restaurant near York for eight years. They have already created an exceptionally alluring formula.

Nearby Normanby Hall, 6 miles (10 km); Thornton Abbey, 13 miles (21 km).

Winteringham, South Humberside DN15 9PF
Tel (0724) 733096
Location in middle of village on south bank of Humber, 4 miles (6 km) W from Humber bridge on A1077; with ample car parking
Food & drink breakfast, lunch, dinner; residential and restaurant licence
Prices B&B £30-£48; lunch £12, dinner around £20
Rooms 4 double, all with bath and shower; all rooms have central heating, colour TV, phone
Facilities sitting-room, dining-room, restaurant
Credit cards MC, V
Children welcome in dining-room over age 10
Disabled access difficult
Pets not accepted; arrangements can be made with local kennels **Closed** first fortnight in Mar, first week in Aug, 4 days at Christmas
Proprietors G and A Schwab

Country house hotel, Walkington

The Manor House

This late-Victorian house may not be what most people expect a manor house to be, but that can be forgiven. Under the practised eye of chef-patron Derek Baugh and his wife, it has made an exceptionally civilized hotel. The furnishings are opulent, with a sprinkling of antiques and plenty of rich fabrics in carefully harmonized colours. The original conservatory, which serves as a dining-room, is a particular highlight. Bedrooms are notably spacious, with smart bathrooms. Food is elaborately modern.

Nearby Beverley Minster, 4 miles (6 km); Skidby Windmill Museum, 4 miles (6 km).

Northlands, Walkington, North Humberside HU17 8RT
Tel (0482) 881645
Location on the Newbald road NW of Walkington, 4 miles (6 km) SW of Beverley
Food & drink breakfast, dinner; lunch by arrangement; residential licence
Prices B&B £37.50-£65; full English breakfast £5.50 extra, dinner £21.50
Rooms 6 double, all with bath; all rooms have central heating, phone, colour TV, tea-coffee kit, minibar
Facilities sitting-room, dining-room, conservatory
Credit cards MC, V
Children accepted over 12
Disabled no special facilities
Pets accepted by arrangement
Closed Christmas day
Proprietors D and L Baugh

Western Dales

Country hotel, Arncliffe

Amerdale House

Definitely a place to watch, this – taken over recently by an enthusiastic, friendly young couple who are gradually improving on the swirling patterned carpets, plush pink sofas and gilt mirrors they inherited. The setting is one of the most seductive in all the Dales: on the fringe of a pretty village nestling in a lonely valley, wide meadows in front, high hills behind. Food (the owners are ex-restauranteurs) is in the modern English style.

Nearby Wharfedale, Wensleydale, Ribblesdale, Pennine Way.

Arncliffe, Littondale, Skipton, North Yorkshire BD23 5QE
Tel (075677) 250
Location 6 miles (10 km) NW of Grassington, 3 miles (5 km) off B6160; with parking for 20 cars
Food & drink full breakfast, dinner; residential and restaurant licence
Prices B&B £26-£36; DB&B £34-£44; reductions for 7 nights or more, and for children sharing parents' room; bargain breaks
Rooms 12 double, 5 with bath, 4 with shower; all rooms have colour TV, tea/coffee kit
Facilities sitting-room, bar, dining-room
Credit cards MC, V
Children welcome **Disabled** access easy to ground floor only **Pets** dogs not allowed in hotel but free kennelling
Closed Dec to Feb
Proprietors Nigel and Paula Crapper

Country hotel, Bainbridge

Riverdale House

Anne Harrison's converted row of cottages is in the best tradition of the unpretentious country hotel – bedrooms freshly decorated, in simple tasteful style (those in the main building more spacious than the rather cramped ones which have been added at the back), and first-class country cooking (with a bit more adventure in the starters and desserts than the main courses) served in a tea-shop-style dining-room with polished tables. Service is friendly, but unceremonious to the point of offending those who like things to be done formally.

Nearby Aysgarth Falls, 4 miles (6 km); Upper Dales Folk Museum, Hawes, 6 miles (9 km); Yorkshire Dales.

Bainbridge, Leyburn, North Yorkshire DL8 3EW
Tel (0969) 50311
Location off A684 on village green; with small garden and parking on road
Food & drink full breakfast, packed lunch, dinner
Prices DB&B £24.50-£30; reductions for children
Rooms 14 double, 10 with bath or shower; all rooms have central heating, colour TV, tea/coffee kit
Facilities 2 sitting-rooms (one with TV), bar/dining-room
Credit cards not accepted
Children welcome
Disabled access very difficult
Pets not welcome
Closed Dec to Feb; weekdays Nov and Mar
Proprietor Mrs A Harrison

Country guest-house, Hawes

Rookhurst

The setting of Rookhurst, on the straggly edge of the hamlet of Gayle, is uninspiring (though it affords fine views). But once inside, it is immediately clear that this guest-house is something out of the ordinary.

Rookhurst was renovated almost single-handedly by its previous owners, the Jutsums. It is an idiosyncratic delight – part high Victorian, part Georgian, part country farmhouse – and they furnished it in equally individual style. The new owner, Iris VanDerSteen, has inherited some of the furnishings, and has set about replacing in appropriate style the pieces that have gone.

The dining-room and sitting-room are comfortably spacious, with Gothic stone-mullioned bay windows. All the bedrooms are fun, several with impressive four-posters or half-testers; prettiest is the delightful 'bridal suite' in the farmhouse wing of the house. Its bathroom is a gem, fitted with a complete 1903 Royal Doulton suite – bath, basin and lavatory, all gleaming brass and polished mahogany. The other rooms vary from the imposing Victorian to the cosy Georgian.

Nearby Pennine Way, Wharfedale, Ribblesdale.

Gayle, Hawes, Wensleydale, North Yorkshire DL8 3RT
Tel (09696) 67454
Location 0.5 miles (one km) S of Hawes, just off A684; in 0.75-acre garden, with large car park
Food & drink full breakfast, tea, dinner; residential and restaurant licence
Prices B&B £29-£34; DB&B £38-£43; reductions for 3 nights or more
Rooms 5 double, all with bath; 2 bridal suites; all rooms have central heating, colour TV, radio/clock, hairdrier, tea/coffee kit
Facilities sitting-room, dining-room
Credit cards not accepted
Children not accepted
Disabled access difficult
Pets not allowed in hotel, but may be kept in car
Closed Jan
Proprietor Mrs Iris S VanDerSteen

Western Dales

Country house hotel, Hawes

Simonstone Hall

Although converted only quite recently from a private house by Mr and Mrs Jeffryes, Simonstone Hall has something of the gentle, slightly faded feel of a much longer-established hotel: uncommonly large bedrooms with comfy furniture and beds, old-fashioned decoration, rather muddled layout and a courteous staff dressed neatly in black and white.

Dogs are particularly welcome here: there is a small charge for taking them, but in return they are treated as guests. Canines and humans alike cannot fail to be uplifted by the hotel's splendid views.

Nearby Pennine Way, Wharfedale, Ribblesdale.

Hawes, North Yorkshire DL8 3LY
Tel (0969) 667255
Location 1.5 miles (2.5 km) N of village on Muker road; ample car parking
Food & drink breakfast, bar lunch, tea, dinner; full licence
Prices B&B £28-£34.75; dinner from £14.50
Rooms 9 double, one family room; all with bath and shower; all rooms have central heating, colour TV, tea/coffee kit
Facilities bar, 2 sitting-rooms, garden room
Credit cards AE, DC, MC, V
Children welcome
Disabled easy access to ground floor but no lift
Pets not in dining-room
Closed never
Proprietors John and Mrs S K Jeffryes

Country guest-house, Grassington

Ashfield House

In the pleasant Dales touring area of Grassington, this is a modest guest-house tucked at the end of a cobbled 'fold' off the main square. It consists of three 17thC cottages knocked together. The rooms are all different – a white lacey duvet cover here, an amusing tartan carpet there – all simple and clean. Downstairs, in the two sitting-rooms, are comfortable chairs. In the evenings guests wax comradely as they anticipate Linda Harrison's abundant portions of country food, served at 7 pm.

Nearby Skipton Castle, 7 miles (11 km); Yorkshire Dales.

Grassington, near Skipton, North Yorkshire BD23 5AE
Tel (0756) 752584
Location close to main square; parking for 7 cars
Food & drink full breakfast, dinner; residential licence
Prices DB&B £22.75-£25.75; half-price for children aged 4-10 sharing parents' room
Rooms 6 double, 2 with shower; one family room; all rooms have central heating, tea/coffee kit
Facilities 2 sitting-rooms, one with bar, dining-room
Credit cards not accepted
Children welcome if well behaved **Disabled** access difficult **Pets** not accepted
Closed Jan
Proprietors Keith and Linda Harrison

Western/Eastern Dales

Sheppard's Hotel

As the name perhaps suggests, this is very much a Sheppard family affair – run by father, mother, three sons and one daughter (at the last count). They started in the bed-and-breakfast business in 1978, and in 1982 opened this more elaborate enterprise after spending a year in the red-brick buildings of Church Farm. The style is simple and wholesome – stone floors and brick walls in the dining room, stripped pine, plain walls and country prints in the bedrooms.

The food is the highlight – wide-ranging and satisfying, and not over-expensive.

Nearby Yorkshire Dales, North York Moors.

Church Farm, Front Street, Sowerby, Thirsk, North Yorkshire YO7 1JF
Tel (0845) 23655
Location next to Sowerby village green
Food & drink full English breakfast, Sunday lunch, dinner; lunch by arrangement
Prices B&B £17.50-£38; dinner £15-£18
Rooms 4 double, 2 with bath, one with shower; 3 family rooms, one with bath, one with shower; all rooms have central heating, TV
Facilities sitting-room, bar
Credit cards MC, V
Children accepted over age 10
Disabled access difficult
Pets not accepted
Closed first week in Jan
Proprietors Olga and Roy Sheppard and family

Woodlands

This double-fronted early Edwardian house makes a friendly, comfortable and sound-value country retreat. The interior is spacious and spotlessly kept, and many rooms have antiques, though the overall effect is home-like rather than elegant. You will be greeted as one of the family, and the well prepared set menus are mildly adventurous.

Nearby Malham, 7 miles (11 km), Ingleton, 10 miles (16 km); Yorkshire Dales.

The Mains, Giggleswick, Settle, North Yorkshire BD24 0AX
Tel (07292) 2576
Location on outskirts of village, N of A65; in gardens with parking for 10 cars
Food & drink full breakfast, dinner; residential and restaurant licence
Prices B&B £19-£22; DB&B £28.75-£31.75; weekend breaks
Rooms 7 double, 2 with bath, one with shower; 2 single; all rooms have central heating; 3 rooms have TV, radio, trouser-press
Facilities 2 sitting-rooms (one with TV), dining-room
Credit cards not accepted
Children accepted over 12
Disabled access fair – 3 ground-floor bedrooms
Pets not allowed in house
Closed Christmas, New Year
Proprietors Roger and Margaret Callan

Eastern Dales

Country house hotel, Jervaulx Abbey

Jervaulx Hall

This low stone house sits in the grounds of the lovely flower-covered ruins of Jervaulx Abbey – an exceptionally pleasing setting for a stroll before breakfast or dinner.

The house is early Victorian, with spacious bedrooms and bathrooms and a comfortable lived-in feel. There is a large hall-cum-sitting-room, with a help-yourself drinks table in one corner, and an attractive drawing-room where after-dinner coffee is served.

In the afternoon, tea can be taken on the front terrace overlooking the abbey.

John Sharp welcomes his guests with a hand-shake – many of them old faces returning for the umpteenth time – introduces them to one another over drinks, and presides over dinner. It is served punctually at eight and consists of a somewhat limited straightforward menu – a cold mousse to start, perhaps, followed by a well-cooked roast or creamy chicken dish.

Nearby Jervaulx Abbey; Middleham Castle, 3 miles (5 km); Yorkshire Dales.

Jervaulx, Ripon, North Yorkshire HG4 4PH
Tel (0677) 60235
Location 5 miles (8 km) SE of Leyburn on A6108; in 8-acre grounds with parking for 15 cars
Food & drink full breakfast, afternoon tea, dinner; residential and restaurant licence
Prices DB&B £45-£47; reduced weekly rates; reductions Nov to Easter; reductions for children

Rooms 8 double, all with bath; all rooms have central heating, tea/coffee kit, hairdrier
Facilities 2 sitting-rooms, dining-room, croquet
Credit cards not accepted
Children welcome
Disabled access easy – no steps and one ground-floor bedroom
Pets dogs welcome, but must not be left unattended in bedrooms
Closed Dec to Feb
Proprietor John A Sharp

Eastern Dales

Old Hall

Once the servant's wing of Jervaulx Hall (page 153) the Old Hall enjoys the same proximity to the ruins of Jervaulx Abbey. It is a sturdy stone house which faces a slightly ramshackle courtyard. Ian Close, an estate clerk of works, and his wife Angela, retired florist and housewife, bought it in a derelict state, and together they have created a country home which could grace the pages of a glossy magazine. Everywhere, bedrooms and bathrooms included, there are pictures and antique collections to catch the eye, as well as attractive wall-papers and materials cleverly mixed to create a warm, mellow air, enhanced by Mrs Close's magnificent flower arrangements.

The Closes emphasize that the Old Hall is no more than a private home which accommodates a few paying guests. They make a point of joining their guests in the drawing room (notice the fireplace built of tiles made for the Abbey's high altar) for sherry at 7.15 each evening, and eat dinner with them around the large oak table in the dining-room. "Mostly though," says Mrs Close, "everyone ends up in the kitchen" – which is Victorian with a great black range, and full of the delicious smells of her perfect home cooking.

Nearby Jervaulx Abbey; Middleham Castle, 3 miles (5 km); Swaledale, Wensleydale.

Jervaulx Abbey, Ripon, North Yorkshire HG4 4PM
Tel (0677) 60313
Location 5 miles (8 km) SE of Leyburn on A6108; in 5-acre grounds with ample parking
Food & drink full breakfast, packed lunch, dinner; no licence
Prices B & B £26; dinner £14
Rooms 2 double, one single; all with bath and shower; all rooms have central heating, tea/coffee kit
Facilities sitting-room, dining-room
Credit cards not accepted
Children welcome
Disabled access difficult
Pets welcome
Closed never
Proprietors Ian and Angela Close

Eastern Dales

Country hotel, Markington

Hob Green

Hob Green is the former family home of its owners, and though the front aspect of the house is uninspiring, the rear stone elevation is more impressive. All the public rooms, including a peaceful sun room, are on this side, with long French windows giving on to the terrace and enjoying uninterrupted views of rolling fields and woods.

Inside, there is an attractive, prettily curtained dining-room, and a main hall which uses Hill and Knowles American folk wallpaper to great effect; what a pity that the sofas and chairs are so dully uniform throughout – leaving no doubt that you are in a hotel. Bedrooms and bathrooms are not large but thoughtfully equipped (though don't be tempted to sing too loud in the bath: some of the partitions are thin).

As well as holidaymakers, Hob Green attracts some business visitors to nearby Harrogate (which has an enormous conference centre); perhaps that is why the prices are a little higher than they might be – the bar tariff particularly so. On our visit we found the cooking over-ambitious. Perhaps this is not always the case.

Nearby Fountains Abbey, 2 miles (3 km), Ripley Castle, 3 miles (5 km), Ripon, 4.5 miles (7 km), Knaresborough Castle, 6 miles (10 km).

Markington, Harrogate, North Yorkshire HG3 3PJ
Tel (0423) 770031
Location 6 miles (10 km) NW of Harrogate, off A61, one mile (1.5 km) outside village; in gardens, with ample car parking
Food & drink breakfast, lunch, dinner; residential and restaurant licence
Prices B&B £31.25-£53; suite £95; dinner from £14.50
Rooms 8 double, 3 single, one suite; all with bath and shower; all rooms have central heating, colour TV, phone, tea/coffee kit, hairdrier, minibar
Facilities sitting-room, sun room, dining-room; croquet
Credit cards AE, DC, MC, V
Children welcome **Disabled** access to public rooms by special ramp, but no ground-floor bedrooms
Pets dogs accepted, but not allowed in public rooms
Closed never
Manager Gary Locker

Eastern Dales

Bank Villa

In the best tradition of British guest-houses, Bank Villa is unpretentious, well-run, comfortable and home-like. Bedrooms are pleasant (a few have showers) and the bathroom is a vivid yellow and blue with a huge mirror. Downstairs the fabric-covered walls are a warm terracotta colour and the dining-room spacious. Although Bank Villa is situated in a rather dull corner of Masham, its terraced garden, with summerhouse and conservatory, overlooks the river Ure. Messrs Gill and Van der Horst serve a generous English breakfast, and a well-cooked evening meal at 7.30 pm.

Nearby Jervaulx Abbey, 4 miles (6 km), Thorpe Perrow Arboretum, 4 miles (6 km); Fountains Abbey within reach.

Masham, Ripon, North Yorkshire HG4 4DB
Tel (0765) 89605
Location 9 miles (14.5 km) NW of Ripon on A6108, at entrance to village; limited car parking
Food & drink full breakfast, dinner; residential and restaurant licence
Prices B&B £12.50-£15; dinner £10; reduced weekly rates

Rooms 7 double, 4 with shower; all rooms have central heating
Facilities 2 sitting-rooms, dining-room
Credit cards not accepted
Children accepted over 5
Disabled access difficult
Pets dogs accepted by arrangement
Closed Nov to Feb
Proprietors Phillip Gill and Anton van der Horst

The Miller's House

Something of a transformation has been apparently wrought by the new owners of this elegant Georgian house set back from Middleham's cobbled market square. The public rooms have been smartened up, with new furniture and sumptuous drapes. The bedrooms and bathrooms too have been improved – and one has been equipped with a richly festooned four-poster and a splendid Victorian bath. A professional chef has been installed in the kitchen, and produces a daily changing menu offering several choices at each course.

Nearby Middleham Castle; Jervaulx Abbey, 3 miles (5 km).

Market Place, Middleham, North Yorkshire DL8 4NR
Tel (0969) 22630
Location just off market square, 2 miles (3 km) S of Leyburn; parking for 8 cars
Food & drink breakfast, picnic lunch, dinner; residential licence
Prices B&B £24.50-£27; dinner £12
Rooms 5 double, all with

bath; one single, with shower; all rooms have central heating, colour TV, tea/coffee kit, phone, radio/alarm
Facilities sitting-room, dining-room; croquet
Credit cards MC, V
Children welcome over 11
Disabled no special facilities
Pets not accepted **Closed** Jan
Proprietors Judith and Crossley Sutherland

Eastern Dales

Country house hotel, Northallerton

Kirkby Fleetham Hall

An entire village had to be bulldozed to make way for the sweeping landscaped gardens of Kirkby Fleetham, and the helpless residents rehoused a mile away. Fortunately, local resentment at this insensitive approach to home improvement has faded in the intervening two and a half centuries.

The house and garden were rescued from decay in 1980 by the previous owners, the Grants. Roderick and Janine Richman came here only a couple of years ago. The house – to all appearances Georgian, but with much older origins – is now a relaxed and welcoming home, gracious but not intimidating. It is beautifully and confidently decorated, and furnished with a sensible mix of antiques and appropriate reproductions. Bedrooms are pretty and spacious (most have sitting areas), and equipped with abundant pampering extras. The dining-room is splendid, with candles on polished tables and rich drapes framing long windows overlooking the lake.

A professional kitchen prepares dishes to order 'in the nouvelle style', using vegetables and herbs from Kirkby Fleetham's own walled garden, and the new owners claim to maintain the reputation David Grant established for the breadth and depth of his wine list.

Nearby Bedale Hall, 4 miles (6 km), Thorpe Perrow Arboretum, 5.5 miles (9 km); Yorkshire Dales, North York Moors.

Kirkby Fleetham,
Northallerton, North
Yorkshire DL7 0SU
Tel (0609) 748711
Location 5 miles (8 km) W of
Northallerton, 2.5 miles (4 km)
E of A1, just N of village;
in 30-acre grounds with
ample car parking
Food & drink breakfast,
dinner; Sun lunch;
residential and restaurant
licence
Prices B & B £41-£65;
dinner £23

Rooms 22 double, all with
bath; all rooms have central
heating, colour TV, radio,
phone
Facilities 3 sitting-rooms,
dining-room
Credit cards AE, DC, MC, V
Children welcome **Disabled**
access difficult **Pets** dogs
accepted by arrangement,
but not allowed in public
rooms or to be left unattended
Closed never
Proprietors Roderick and
Janine Richman

Eastern Dales

Town guest-house, Richmond

Howe Villa

This handsome Georgian house is reached by driving through an unappealing old paper mill which used to house Tom Berry's dry-cleaning works. Anita is a mother of three who has turned her natural flair as a hostess to good advantage since the children grew up. She started in 1979 offering bed-and-breakfast, soon found a demand for her honest dinners and has since steadily acquired the skills to support more ambitious menus. The house is elegantly decorated and immaculately kept – bedrooms on the ground floor and fine public rooms on the first floor where they enjoy a fine view across the Swale.

Nearby Richmond Castle, 1.5 miles (2.5 km), Easby Abbey, 2.5 miles (4 km); Yorkshire Dales.

Whitcliffe Mill, Richmond, North Yorkshire DL10 4TJ
Tel (0748) 850055
Location 0.75 miles (one km) W of Richmond, close to A6108; in large garden by river, with ample car parking
Food & drink full breakfast, dinner; no licence
Prices DB&B £31.50
Rooms 4 double, 2 with shower, 2 with bath and shower; all rooms have central heating, colour TV, radio, tea/coffee kit, hairdrier
Facilities sitting-room, dining-room
Credit cards not accepted
Children welcome over 12
Disabled access difficult
Pets not accepted
Closed Nov to mid-Mar
Proprietor Anita Berry

Restaurant with rooms, Ripon

The Old Deanery

In the lee of Ripon cathedral, the Old Deanery is a popular restaurant which happens to have a couple of bedrooms to let – large, floral and unpretentious, with one equally roomy bathroom across the corridor. The house itself is delightfully creaky and – in the best sense of the word – unmodernized. Muted colours, wood panelling, ancient curtains and splendid old sofas and chairs all add to the charm. There is a comfortable bar for pre-dinner drinks and a large, impressive drawing room where your coffee is served. In the restaurant you can expect good bistro food, swiftly and willingly served.

Nearby Cathedral; Fountains Abbey, 3 miles (5 km).

Minster Road, Ripon, North Yorkshire HG4 1QS
Tel (0765) 3518
Location close to cathedral in middle of town; in garden, with adequate car parking
Food & drink breakfast, lunch, dinner; restaurant licence
Prices B&B £35-£50; dinner £15
Rooms 2 double, both with bath
Facilities sitting-room, bar, dining-room
Credit cards MC, V
Children accepted
Disabled not suitable
Pets not accepted
Closed Sun, Mon, Sat lunch, Christmas Day, Boxing Day
Proprietors Jurg and Jane Bleiker

Eastern Dales

Inn, Wath-in-Nidderdale

Sportsman's Arms

The perfect country inn? The Sportsman's Arms certainly comes close. The long, rather rambling building – formerly a run-down pub – dates from the 17thC. The setting is as enchanting as the village name sounds: the river Nidd flows at the bottom of the lawn in front; Gouthwaite reservoir, a bird-watchers' haunt, is just behind; much glorious dales country spreads all around. The accommodation, as befits such a place, is modest but spotlessly clean and comfortable; the bedrooms are light and fresh, and the public rooms have now been brightened up as well. Best of all, the staff, headed by proprietor and chef Ray Carter, are hard-working, welcoming and friendly.

And then there is the food. The Sportsman's Arms is first and foremost a restaurant, and the large dining-room is the inn's focal point, dominated by the deep pink of its table-cloths and sparkling with silver cutlery and crystal table lights. You will not find fancy modern cooking here, but a lively menu of quality local produce, beautifully cooked. To back it up, there is a superb wine list – and an extremely reasonable bill.

Nearby Wharfedale, Wensleydale; Fountains Abbey, Bolton Abbey within easy reach.

Wath-in-Nidderdale, Pateley Bridge, near Harrogate, North Yorkshire HG3 5PP
Tel (0423) 711306
Location 2 miles (3 km) NW of Pateley Bridge, in hamlet; in 0.5-acre gardens, with ample car parking in front
Food & drink full breakfast, bar lunch, dinner (residents only on Sun); full licence
Prices B&B £17.50-£27; dinner £10-£18 (an £8.50 dinner available if staying more than one night)
Rooms 6 double, 2 with shower; all rooms have electric heating, tea/coffee kit, TV
Facilities 3 sitting-rooms, bar, dining-room; fishing
Credit cards AE, DC, MC, V
Children welcome **Disabled** access easy, but no ground-floor bedrooms
Pets welcome; own bedding must be provided
Closed Christmas and New Year (though open to non-residents)
Proprietors Jane and Ray Carter

North Yorkshire

Dweldapilton Hall

The modest Regency house that stands at the top of the village on the edge of the North York Moors was long ago dwarfed by a grand south-facing Victorian extension. The house was a girls' school, a home for evacuees and an old people's home before becoming a country hotel, and Richard Ambler's restoration has still got a little way to go to shake off all the reminders of the hall's recent past.

The public rooms, with lofty ceilings and big marble fireplaces, are old-fashioned. (Many pictures of sheep-strewn moorland scenes provide some visual entertainment throughout; but the local artist can evidently paint sheep only from behind.) Bedrooms – all nearly identical – are well equipped (including extra heaters and hot-water bottles) and have views. Outside, the grounds are beautifully maintained, with a sweeping lawn, flower beds and mature trees including some enormous copper beeches.

The menu has an enticing range of choices, including a 'Taste of Yorkshire' each day – such as jugged steak or Whitby cobble pie – complete with a culinary explanation. For after-dinner drinks, the tiny bar is bursting at the seams with whiskies.

Nearby Pickering Castle, 5 miles (8 km); Nunnington Hall, 6 miles (10 km); North York Moors.

Appleton-le-Moors, North Yorkshire YO6 6TF
Tel (07515) 227
Location 5 miles (8 km) NW of Pickering, one mile (1.5 km) N of A170, on edge of village; in gardens, with ample parking
Food & drink full breakfast, lunch, tea, dinner; restaurant and residential licence
Prices B&B £34.50; dinner £16.50; reduced weekly

rates; bargain breaks
Rooms 10 double, 2 single, all with bath; all rooms have central heating, colour TV, tea/coffee kit
Facilities 2 sitting-rooms, dining-room, bar
Credit cards MC, V
Children not accepted
Disabled access good – wide doors, lift **Pets** welcome, but not in public rooms
Closed Jan and Feb
Proprietor Richard Ambler

North Yorkshire

Inn, Coxwold

Fauconberg Arms

In the middle of a picturesque village street, this well-run 17thC stone inn – complete with traditional beams, horse-brasses and a sedan chair in one of its two bars, and a jumble of fresh and artificial flowers throughout – suffers from its own well-deserved popularity at times. The restaurant suffers too, with two rather frenetic sittings on Sunday for the roast-beef-and-Yorkshire-puddings lunch (the dinner menu is much more extensive and ambitious). The cottagey bedrooms are fresh and inviting; one bathroom is shared between three rooms.

Nearby Shandy Hall; North York Moors, York.

Coxwold, North Yorkshire YO6 4AD **Tel** (03476) 214 **Location** 7 miles (11 km) SE of Thirsk, between A19 and A170, in middle of village; car parking available **Food & drink** full breakfast, lunch (Tue to Sun), dinner (Tue to Sat); full licence **Prices** B&B £19-£20; dinner from £13	**Rooms** 4 double, one with shower; all rooms have central heating **Facilities** 2 bars, dining-room **Credit cards** not accepted **Children** welcome **Disabled** access easy to public rooms only **Pets** not accepted **Closed** never, but B&B only for 2 weeks each in Feb and Oct **Proprietors** Mr & Mrs Richard Goodall

Country hotel, Goathland

Mallyan Spout

This is walking country, and the Mallyan Spout, with its lattice windows peering out from a thick screen of ivy, has been welcoming walkers for almost a century. Three sitting-rooms, two of which have open fires, provide a relaxing haven, and the Heslops generate a friendly atmosphere. The bedrooms have all been recently refurbished in Laura Ashley 'cottage' style. Cooking and service are said to deteriorate badly under pressure on busy weekends.

Nearby Abbey and Pannett Art Gallery in Whitby; North Yorkshire Moors Railway.

Goathland, near Whitby, North Yorkshire YO22 5AN **Tel** (0947) 86206 **Location** 9 miles (14.5 km) SE of Whitby, off A169, in middle of village; in garden with ample car parking **Food & drink** full breakfast, lunch, tea, dinner; full licence **Prices** B&B £25-£35; dinner from £13.50; bargain breaks **Rooms** 19 double; one single; 2 suites; all with bath;	all rooms have central heating, colour TV **Facilities** 3 sitting-rooms, 2 bars, dining-room **Credit cards** AE, DC, V **Children** welcome if well behaved **Disabled** access easy, but no ground-floor bedrooms **Pets** welcome if well behaved, but not in public rooms **Closed** never **Proprietors** Peter and Judith Heslop

North Yorkshire

Ryedale Lodge

This former railway station has been transformed into a calm and well-ordered retreat. Once past the urns full of flowers either side of the door, you find yourself in the sitting-room, with its rich assortment of flowers and plants, its large comfy settees and restful blue-and-pink colouring – though some may find the baleful stares from the gloomy oils on the walls a little off-putting. The elegant dining-room looks out over the former platform and the farmland beyond, with not another building in sight. An extension of the house on to the platform is now complete. The bedrooms are immaculate and individual, with styles varying from country cane through floral-plus-antiques to functional white melamine. All are well equipped, with everything from TVs to trouser-presses and even the occasional spa bath; it might seem carping, then, to grumble about the lack of showers (only one bedroom has one).

Janet Leigh's dinner menu includes some tempting offerings, mainly in the French or international mould and the service is friendly and willing.

Nearby Nunnington Hall; Duncombe Park, 3 miles (5 km), Rievaulx Abbey, 6 miles (10 km), Castle Howard, 8 miles (13 km).

Nunnington, near Helmsley, York, North Yorkshire YO6 5XB
Tel (04395) 246
Location 4 miles (6 km) SE of Helmsley off B1257, one mile (1.5 km) W of village; in open countryside, with large car park
Food & drink full breakfast, dinner; residential and restaurant licence
Prices B&B £32.50-£42.50; dinner £19.45; bargain breaks
Rooms 7 double, all with bath; all rooms have central heating, colour TV, phone, radio alarm, tea/coffee kit hairdrier, trouser-press
Facilities sitting-room, dining-room, bar servery; fishing
Credit cards MC, V
Children welcome **Disabled** access easy to public rooms, one ground-floor bedroom
Pets not accepted, but may stay in cars
Closed 3 weeks Jan
Proprietors Janet and Jon Laird

North Yorkshire

Rangers House

The Butlers have adopted an unusual formula for their converted stables, built of mellow stone. Although the dining-room has elegant dark-wood tables and the lofty hall-cum-sitting-room is filled with antiques, the house has a lived-in, casual feel – some might even call it slightly tatty – which should suit families well. The Butlers are a charming, down-to-earth couple who are entirely flexible – breakfast any time, bring your own drinks if you prefer.

Nearby Sheriff Hutton Castle; Castle Howard, 5 miles (8 km).

The Park, Sheriff Hutton, York, North Yorkshire YO6 1RH
Tel (03477) 397
Location 9 miles (14.5 km) N of York between B1363 and A64; in garden surrounded by 200-acre parkland with ample car parking
Food & drink full breakfast, afternoon tea, dinner; restaurant and residential licence
Prices B & B £21-£23; dinner £15.50; DB & B £30 in spring and autumn
Rooms 4 double, one with bath, one with shower; one single with shower; one family room with bath; all rooms have central heating, tea/coffee kit, hairdrier
Facilities sitting-room, conservatory, dining-room; pergola, patio
Credit cards not accepted
Children welcome – high tea available
Disabled access difficult
Pets dogs may sleep in cars
Closed never
Proprietors Sid and Dorianne Butler

Judges' Lodgings

You might almost be in a dainty French chateau, so romantically is this 1700 red-brick townhouse decked out – with embroidery on the sheets and towels as well as rich floral drapes at every turn. So it is no surprise to learn that the lady of the house is a French comtesse, and that many of the antiques and paintings come from her family home. Naturally, there is a French emphasis to the ambitious menus. There is an equally French lack of a proper sitting-room.

Nearby Treasurer's House, Minster, National Railway Museum.

9 Lendal, York, North Yorkshire YO1 2AQ
Tel (0904) 38733
Location in middle of the town near Lendal Bridge; adequate car parking in forecourt
Food & drink full breakfast, lunch, dinner; full licence
Prices B & B £42.50-£47.50; dinner from £12.50
Rooms 11 double, 7 with bath, 4 with shower; 2 single, both with shower; 2 family rooms, both with bath; one suite; all rooms have central heating, TV, phone
Facilities bars, dining-rooms
Credit cards AE, DC, MC, V
Children welcome
Disabled access difficult
Pets accepted
Closed never
Proprietors Mr G C Mason MBE and Comtesse Mason de Diem

Town hotel, York

Mount Royale

Comprising two William IV houses only recently joined, the Mount Royale is the Oxtobys' home. The bedrooms are spacious, each individually decorated and furnished with some splendid antiques (many four-posters and half-testers), chintz drapes and armchairs. The public areas continue the traditional decoration, with some bold red colour schemes and more antiques. A modern extension provides a light and airy dining-room with views on to the neat and flowery garden. Cooking is ambitious and competent, and breakfast something of a feast.

Nearby Treasurer's House, Minster, National Railway Museum.

The Mount, York, North Yorkshire YO2 2DA
Tel (0904) 28856
Location on A1036 near racecourse; in large garden with parking for 30 cars
Food & drink full breakfast, dinner; residential and restaurant licence
Prices B&B £32.50-£67.50; dinner from £17.50
Rooms 19 double, 2 single, 2 suites; all with bath and shower; all rooms have central heating, colour TV, radio, phone, tea/coffee kit, hairdrier, trouser-press
Facilities 3 sitting-rooms, dining-room, bar, heated outdoor swimming-pool
Credit cards AE, DC, MC, V
Children welcome **Disabled** not suitable **Pets** small dogs only accepted, but must not be left alone in bedrooms
Closed 23 Dec to 7 Jan
Proprietors Christine and Richard Oxtoby

Restaurant with rooms, Aislaby

Blacksmith's Arms

What looks to the passing motorist like a rather care-worn road-side tavern is rightly described by the proprietors as a 'restaurant with accommodation' – it is the adventurous, generously served food and the friendly service that marks this place out. The rooms are cheerfully decorated, with the occasional 16thC beam to negotiate, but they are tiny, thinly-partitioned and have lacked finish (doors that shut, showers that shower...). However, the newly arrived Bullocks are aiming to improve matters – and prices are still modest.

Nearby Pickering Castle, 2 miles (3 km); North York Moors.

Aislaby, Pickering, North Yorkshire YO18 8PE
Tel (0751) 72182
Location 1.5 miles (2.5 km) W of Pickering on A170; with garden and ample car parking
Food & drink full breakfast, lunch, dinner; residential and restaurant licence
Prices B&B £13-£15; DB&B £22-£24
Rooms 4 double, one with bath, one with shower; one single with shower; all rooms have central heating, tea/coffee kit
Facilities sitting-room, bar, dining-room
Credit cards MC, V
Children welcome **Disabled** access good to public rooms only **Pets** accepted
Closed never
Proprietors Ken and Janet Bullock

Southern Lakes

Country hotel, Ambleside

Kirkstone Foot

This immaculately kept white-painted 17thC house, set amid large gardens, has had its critics in the past. But it has recently been refurbished, and there have been other changes behind the scenes. The kitchen, known for its plain English country cooking, has been strengthened by the arrival of Vic Sharrat; new vegetarian and fish dishes have resulted. The five-course dinner still starts promptly at 8pm, but there is now some choice of starter and main course as well as an array of desserts.

Nearby Townend, 3 miles (5 km); Lake Windermere.

Kirkstone Pass Road, Ambleside, Cumbria LA22 9EH
Tel (05394) 32232
Location on NE side of town, on road to Kirkstone Pass; parking for 40 cars
Food & drink full breakfast, dinner; residential licence
Prices DB&B £38; dinner £14.75; reductions for 3 nights or more and for children under 12 sharing parents' room
Rooms 12 double, 10 with bath, 2 with shower; one single, with bath; 2 family rooms, with bath; all rooms have central heating, colour TV, radio, tea/coffee kit
Facilities sitting-room, bar, dining-room
Credit cards AE, DC, MC, V
Children welcome; high tea provided **Disabled** access easy to public rooms
Pets not accepted in hotel
Closed Dec to first week Feb
Proprietors Simon and Jane Bateman

Country hotel, Ambleside

Nanny Brow

Built in 1908 by a London architect for his own use, Nanny Brow has a privileged setting at the foot of Loughrigg Fell; it was first converted to a hotel in 1952. The public rooms are immaculately and tastefully decorated in a modern but restrained style. No two bedrooms are alike but they share the high standards of the public rooms, and they also have excellent views. The garden wing has a number of luxury suites.

Nearby White Craggs Garden; Stagshaw, one mile (1.5 km), Rydal Mount, 2 miles (3 km), Dove Cottage, 2.5 miles (4 km).

Clappersgate, Ambleside, Cumbria LA22 9NF
Tel (05394) 32036
Location one mile (1.5 km) W of Ambleside on A593; in 5-acre grounds with ample car parking
Food & drink breakfast, dinner; residential and restaurant licence
Prices DB&B £33.50-£47.50
Rooms 18 double, 17 with bath, one with shower; one single; all rooms have central heating, TV, phone, tea/coffee kit, radio, alarm, hairdrier
Facilities sitting-room, bar (with snooker), dining-room, solarium, spa bath; fishing
Credit cards MC, V
Children welcome **Disabled** access possible – 2 steps to front door
Pets dogs accepted
Closed Dec/Jan
Proprietors Paul and Carolyn Fletcher

Southern Lakes

The Rothay Manor

This 1830s building in French colonial style seems far removed from the bustle of Ambleside when sitting in the comfort of one of the elegantly furnished rooms. The reputation of Rothay Manor was built up over 20 years by the late Bronwen Nixon, and it is a relief (though no surprise) to report that the standards she achieved are maintained by her two sons Nigel and Stephen. Bedrooms are neatly and subtly furnished with a full range of facilities unobtrusively accommodated, and the overall impression is one of quiet style and good taste. Food remains perhaps the key part of the hotel's appeal. The basic style of cooking is unfussy and distinctly English; but other influences are not excluded, and chef Jane Binns is allowed free rein on winter weekends, when the dishes (and wines) of different regions are explored in special Friday-night dinners. Our only criticism comes from a reporter who demands bigger plates at tea, so as to avoid "the shame of going back repeatedly for more of their amazing scones."

Nearby Townend, 1.5 miles (2.5 km), Rydal Mount, 2.5 miles (4 km), Dove Cottage, 3 miles (5 km); Lake Winderere.

Rothay Bridge, Ambleside, Cumbria LA22 0EH
Tel 05394 33605
Location 0.5 miles (0.75 km) S of Ambleside; in 2-acre grounds with ample car parking
Food & drink full breakfast, lunch, tea, dinner; residential and restaurant licence
Prices B&B £39-£56; dinner £15-£20; reduction for 4 nights or more; speciality winter breaks
Rooms 8 double, 2 single, 6 family rooms, 2 suites; all with bath and shower; all rooms have central heating, colour TV, phone, hairdrier
Facilities 3 sitting-rooms, dining-room; croquet
Credit cards AE, DC, MC, V
Children welcome; high tea, cots, baby-listening service
Disabled access good, with ground-floor bedrooms
Pets not accepted in hotel building, but may stay in car
Closed Jan to mid-Feb
Proprietors Nigel and Stephen Nixon

Southern Lakes

Wateredge Hotel

As its name suggests, the Wateredge is in a fine position, with its lawns leading to the very edge of Windermere; the several well-furnished sitting-rooms make the most of the exceptional views across the lake. The dining-rooms have no lake view, but do share the same high standards of decoration. Dinners comprise six splendidly filling courses. Bedrooms vary in size, but all are comfortable and stylishly decorated.

Nearby Stagshaw; White Craggs Garden, one mile (1.5 km), Townend, 1.5 miles (2.5 km), Dove Cottage, 3 miles (5 km).

Borrans Road, Waterhead, Ambleside, Cumbria
LA22 0EP
Tel (05394) 32332
Location 1 mile (1.6 km) S of Ambleside on lakeshore, on A591; with adequate car parking
Food & drink full breakfast, light lunch, tea, dinner; residential licence
Prices DB&B £45-£53; reductions for 3 nights or more; further off-season reductions
Rooms 19 double, 16 with bath, 3 with shower; 3 single, one with bath, 2 with shower; one family room with bath; all rooms have central heating, TV, phone, tea/coffee kit
Facilities 3 sitting-rooms (one with TV), bar, dining-rooms; rowing-boat, private jetty
Credit cards AE, MC, V
Children welcome over 7
Disabled access difficult
Pets by arrangement, but not in public rooms
Closed Dec and Jan
Proprietors Mr and Mrs Derek Cowap

Lindeth Fell Country House

This Edwardian villa enjoys a wonderful setting and views, and something of the atmosphere of a country house. Bedrooms are spacious, clean and well decorated, and the sitting-rooms have an appealing mixture of traditional styles. Sadly, a recent report suggests that the cooking and the welcome could be improved.

Nearby Lake Windermere.

Kendal Road, Bowness-on-Windermere, Cumbria
LA23 3JP
Tel (09662) 3286
Location On A5074 one mile S of Bowness; parking for 20 cars
Food & drink full breakfast, light lunch, tea, dinner; residential and restaurant licence
Prices DB&B £35-£40; dinner £16.50
Rooms 10 double, 6 with bath, 4 with shower; 2 single, one with bath, one with shower; 2 family rooms, both with bath; all rooms have central heating, TV, phone, tea/coffee kit, hairdrier
Facilities 2 sitting-rooms, 2 dining-rooms; croquet, tennis, fishing, putting
Credit cards AE, MC, V
Children welcome; special meals for under-5s
Disabled access easy to public rooms
Pets not accepted in house
Closed Nov to mid-Mar
Proprietors P and D Kennedy

Southern Lakes

Country house hotel, Bowness

Miller Howe

Twenty years ago, when the idea of eating well in a British hotel was not so much novel as fantastic, the dining-room of an otherwise dreary grand hotel in Windermere started serving, at a fixed hour, a fixed dinner of several exquisite courses. Before long, the chef responsible set up shop on his own. The rest is common knowledge: John Tovey has become one of the few British chefs to gain an international reputation, and Miller Howe a place of pilgrimage.

The Tovey act is essentially unchanged – dinner still involves a lowering of lights and a marshalling of countless perfectly prepared dishes. The same caring and thought that underlies the cooking goes into the the hotel-keeping, and despite the rich furnishings, the atmosphere remains informal and welcoming. The public rooms are slightly club-like, with leather chairs; the bedrooms employ luxurious fabrics but remain essentially home-like.

Although the official line is that Lutyens had a hand in the design of the house, it is no beauty; but who cares, when from its dining-room and terrace (and some of the bedrooms) you can gaze across sparkling Lake Windermere to the famous spikey outline of the Langdale Pikes, and dream of the days when you were fit enough to climb them?

We record with despair that the hotel's tariff does not make prices clear: a 12.5 per cent service charge is added.

Nearby Lake Windermere.

Rayrigg Road, Bowness-on-Windermere, Cumbria LA23 1EY
Tel (09662) 2536
Location on A592 between Bowness and Windermere; in 4-acre landscaped garden with ample car parking
Food & drink full breakfast, picnic lunch, tea, dinner; residential and restaurant licence
Prices DB&B £57–£105; dinner £26; weekend breaks
Rooms 13 double, 12 with bath, one with shower; all rooms have central heating, radio, trouser-press, hairdrier, hi-fi
Facilities 4 sitting-rooms, dining-rooms
Credit cards AE, DC, MC, V
Children welcome over 12
Disabled access difficult
Pets accepted if well behaved, but not allowed in public rooms
Closed mid-Dec to early Mar
Proprietor John Tovey

Southern Lakes

Country hotel, Cartmel

Uplands

'In the Miller Howe manner', declares Uplands' literature at every opportunity. Tom and Diana Peter spent 13 years working for John Tovey at his renowned hotel a few miles to the north – he as one of two head chefs, she as Tovey's assistant – and the man himself is their partner in this more modest enterprise. The sitting-room is notably spacious and welcoming, the bedrooms thoroughly civilised – and Tom's set dinners (four course, three offering a choice) do not disappoint.

Nearby Cartmel Priory, 1 mile (1.5 km); Lake District.

Haggs Lane, Cartmel, Cumbria LA11 6HD
Tel (05395) 36248
Location 1 mile (1.5 km) SE of Cartmel; in 2-acre garden with parking for 16 cars
Food & drink full breakfast; lunch, dinner Tue-Sun; residential and restaurant licence
Prices B&B, DB&B £44-£60; 20% reduction for 3 nights; spring and autumn breaks.
Rooms 4 double, one with bath, 3 with shower; all rooms have central heating, colour TV, phone; hairdrier
Facilities sitting-room, dining-room
Credit cards AE, MC
Children welcome over 12
Disabled access easy only to public rooms
Pets welcome, but not in public rooms
Closed 2 Jan to 25 Feb
Proprietors Tom and Diana Peter and John Tovey

Vegetarian country house hotel, Grasmere

Lancrigg

This secluded 17thC farmhouse, much modified in Georgian and Victorian times, and a favourite haunt of Wordsworth, was opened by the Whittingtons in 1985. A frequent visitor reports that the vegetarian dinners (no choice until the dessert) are "very imaginative, generous and appetizing". Although the cooking emphasizes wholefoods and organic produce, there is a wine list and the special luxury rooms include one with a spa bath.

Nearby Rydal Water, Langdale, Lake Windermere.

Easedale, Grasmere, Cumbria LA22 9QN
Tel (09665) 317
Location one mile (1.5 km) NW of Grasmere off the Easedale Road; in grounds with ample car parking
Food & drink full breakfast, packed lunch, dinner; restaurant and residential licence
Prices DB&B £25-£46; reductions in winter
Rooms 10 double, 6 with bath; one single; 2 family rooms; all rooms have TV, tea/coffee kit, hairdrier
Facilities sitting-room, dining-room; play area
Credit cards MC
Children welcome **Disabled** access easy to public rooms and one ground-floor bedroom **Pets** accepted in grounds, but not in hotel
Closed never
Proprietors Robert and Janet Whittington

Southern Lakes

Country house hotel, Grasmere

White Moss House

This fine country house, owned by the Wordsworth family until the 1930s, not only has the advantage of being close to some stunning countryside around Rydal Water, but also has an enviable reputation for the quality of its food. Peter Dixon, who cooks virtually single-handed, is considered to be in the forefront of 'modern English cooking'. The Dixons came here in 1981 to pursue full-time their long-standing love of food and wine. The main house has five comfortable bedrooms, each individually furnished, and there are two more in the secluded and peaceful cottage up the hill behind the hotel. The sitting-room is light and elegant, and the terrace overlooking the garden is pleasant. This is one of the few Lake District hotels with the genuine feel of a private house.

Nearby Rydal Mount; Dove Cottage, one mile (1.5 km); White Craggs Garden, 1.5 miles (2.5 km); Stagshaw, 1.5 miles (2.5 km); Townend, 4 miles (6.5 km).

Rydal Water, Grasmere, Cumbria LA22 9SE
Tel (09665) 295
Location one mile (1.5 km) S of Grasmere on A591; ample car parking
Food & drink full breakfast, dinner; residential and restaurant licence
Prices DB&B £49-£59; reductions for 3 nights or more
Rooms 7 double (2 part of a cottage suite), 6 with bath, one with shower; all rooms have central heating, colour TV, phone, radio, hairdrier, trouser-press
Facilities sitting-room, bar, dining-room; fishing
Credit cards not accepted
Children welcome over 10; 7-10 year olds by arrangement
Disabled access difficult
Pets not accepted in hotel; may stay in cars **Closed** mid-Nov to mid-Mar **Proprietors** Susan and Peter Dixon

Southern Lakes

Old Dungeon Ghyll

The Old Dungeon Ghyll is at the very heart of the Lake District – overshadowed by the famous Langdale Pikes. The three-storey slate and stone main building is in typical local style and is flanked by a Climber's Bar. Inside the house itself, the sitting-room is comfortably chintzy and traditional, with an open fire. Bedrooms have a pleasant, cottagey feel, with brass and iron bedsteads, but some are distinctly small. Food is filling and wholesome, in enormous portions to suit walkers' appetites.

Nearby high fell walks into the heart of the Lakes.

Great Langdale, Ambleside, Cumbria LA22 9JY
Tel (09667) 272
Location 7 miles (11 km) NE of Ambleside off B5343; in countryside with ample car parking
Food & drink breakfast, packed lunch, dinner, bar meals; full licence
Prices B&B £18-£21; dinner £12; reductions mid-week for 2 nights or more; reduced weekly rates; reductions for children

sharing parents' room
Rooms 6 double, one with shower; 3 single; 5 family rooms, 3 with shower; all rooms have central heating
Facilities sitting-room, 2 bars, dining-room
Credit cards not accepted
Children welcome **Disabled** access difficult **Pets** welcome, but not allowed in dining-room
Closed 24 to 26 Dec
Proprietors Neil and Jane Walmsley

Nab Cottage

If you want to sample some of the literary associations of the Lake District and enjoy a sensation of time-travel, it is hard to beat Nab Cottage – once the home of Hartley Coleridge, son of Samuel T, and much visited by Thomas de Quincey, essayist and opium-user on the periphery of the Wordsworth clan. It is not a large building – with a full complement of guests things must be a little crowded – and the main road runs unpleasantly close; but the views across Rydal Water, the warmth of the Mellings' welcome, and the atmosphere which they sensitively preserve more than make up for these short comings. Bedrooms are very simple, sitting-rooms are tiny with many original features such as built-in cupboards.

Nearby Rydal Mount; Lake Windermere.

Rydal, Ambleside, Cumbria LA22 9SD
Tel (09665) 311
Location 1.5 miles (2.5 km) N of Ambleside on A591; with parking for 10 cars
Food & drink breakfast, dinner; residential licence
Prices B&B £13.50-£15.50; DB&B £21-£23

Rooms 4 double; one single; 2 family rooms; some rooms have central heating
Facilities sitting-room, TV room, dining-room; fishing
Credit cards not accepted
Children welcome **Disabled** access difficult **Pets** welcome
Closed Christmas week
Proprietors T and L Melling

Southern Lakes

Country hotel, Spark Bridge

Bridgefield House

What sets Bridgefield apart from others of its ilk is the care its owners take to look after their guests without (as they put it) "fussing" them. Two of the house's three acres form a miniature parkland of mature conifers; on the third, David Glister grows the vegetables that Rosemary later cooks with great skill and imagination. Furnishings are comfortably in sympathy with the house, and the spacious bedrooms are well equipped.

Nearby Rusland Hall, 3 miles (5 km), Coniston Water.

Spark Bridge, Ulverston, Cumbria LA12 8DA	bath; all rooms have central heating, radio/alarm, hairdrier, phone
Tel (022985) 239	
Location 5.5 miles (9 km) N of Ulverston, off A5092; in 3-acre grounds with parking for 10 cars	**Facilities** dining-room, bar, sitting-room
	Credit cards MC
	Children very welcome; high-chairs, cots, laundry, high tea at no extra charge
Food & drink full breakfast, dinner; residential and restaurant licence	
	Disabled not suitable **Pets** well-behaved dogs welcome, but not in public rooms
Prices B&B £27.50-£30; dinner £15; reduction for children; reduction for 4 nights or more, Sep to Feb	
	Closed never
Rooms 5 double, all with	**Proprietors** David and Rosemary Glister

---

Country hotel, Underbarrow

Greenriggs

'The kitchen is the heart of a good home' is Sarah Smithson's motto, and she puts it soundly into practice with her unpretentious but wide-ranging five-course dinners (which allow some choice except at the soup stage); there is no shortage of local diners ready to take any seats not filled by hotel guests. Since they took it over in 1984, the Smithsons have given a new lease of life to this established, mainly Victorian country hotel in one of the most charming margins of Lakeland; they are of the dedicated amateur school of hotel-keepers, for whom home and hotel are one and the same.

Nearby The Lakes.

Underbarrow, near Kendal, Cumbria, LA8 8HF	rooms with bath; all rooms have tea/coffee kit
Tel (04488) 387	**Facilities** bar, sitting-room, TV room, restaurant; croquet
Location 2.5 miles (4 km) W of Kendal; ample car parking; close to A591	
	Credit cards MC, V
	Children welcome if well-behaved
Food & drink full breakfast, dinner, residential and restaurant licence	
	Disabled access difficult
	Pets accepted if well trained but not in public rooms
Prices B&B £25-£32.50; dinner £13.50; reductions for children	
	Closed Jan to Feb
Rooms 8 double, 4 with bath, 2 with shower, 4 family	**Proprietors** D and S Smithson

Southern Lakes

Country hotel, Witherslack

The Old Vicarage

The Old Vicarage would offer peace and seclusion even if sleepy Witherslack found itself invaded by the Lake District hordes, hidden as it is in a large wooded garden. But it offers much else besides. The building is not exceptional – its Georgian vintage is scarcely evident from its proportions – but it is furnished with great care and some style, successfully combining antiques with new cane and pine to create warm and relaxing surroundings.

The Reeves and the Burrington-Browns, like so many of the best hotel-keepers in Britain, are amateurs who simply seek to provide accommodation which they would enjoy themselves. They devote equal care and enthusiasm to the meals they serve, which are justly recognized to be among the best in the area. The secret is excellent local ingredients in fresh and thoughtful combinations. Although vegetarians are admirably catered for, there is no choice until the puddings, which have been described by a higher authority than us as "breathtaking". Fortunately there are plenty of splendid local walks to mitigate the damage.

Nearby Levens Hall, 3 miles (5 km), Sizergh Castle, 5 miles (8 km), Holker Hall, 6 miles (10 km); Lake Windermere.

Church Road, Witherslack, near Grange-over-Sands, Cumbria LA11 6RS
Tel (044852) 381
Location 5 miles (8 km) NE of Grange off A590; in 5-acre garden and woodland with ample car parking
Food & drink breakfast, dinner; residential and restaurant licence
Prices B&B £31.50-£45.50; dinner £18.50; bargain breaks
Rooms 7 double, 3 with bath, 4 with shower; all rooms have central heating, radio/alarm, phone, colour TV, hairdrier, tea/coffee kit
Facilities breakfast room, dining-room, sitting-room, lounge bar
Credit cards AE, DC, MC, V
Children accepted only by arrangement if under 10
Disabled not suitable
Pets dogs accepted by arrangement, but not allowed in public rooms
Closed one week at Christmas
Proprietors Jill and Roger Burrington-Brown, Irene and Stanley Reeve

Farm guest-house, Blawith

Appletree Holme

The Carlsens came here in 1979 after years of running a much bigger and glossier (and in its way very successful) hotel on the shores of Ullswater – because they wanted, in Roy's words, 'to go back to looking after people again'.

The farm enjoys a lovely setting on the fringe of Lakeland, with nothing but fells in view. The low, stone-built house has been lovingly restored and sympathetically furnished with antiques; pictures and books abound, and open fires on stone hearths supplement the central heating. Two of the equally welcoming bedrooms have the unusual luxury of double-size baths.

Roy believes in tailoring his menus (whether for breakfast or dinner) to suit guests' tastes and the local fruits of the land – home-grown vegetables, meat, poultry and dairy produce from neighbouring farms. And anyone whose appetite needs a lift can enlist the help of Pip and Pooch, father-and-son sheepdogs, who will gladly take you for a walk over the fells.

In the interests of their guests the Carlsens discourage casual callers, so do phone ahead if you want to look around.

Nearby Rusland Hall, 4 miles (6.5 km); Coniston Water; Lake Windermere

Blawith, near Ulverston, Cumbria LA12 8EL
Tel (022985) 618
Location 6 miles (10 km) S of Coniston off A5084, in open countryside; in extensive grounds, with ample car parking
Food & drink full breakfast, dinner; residential and restaurant licence
Prices DB&B £43-£46
Rooms 4 double, all with bath and shower; all rooms have central heating, phone, radio, tea/coffee kit, colour TV
Facilities 2 sitting-rooms, dining-room
Credit cards AE
Children not suitable
Disabled access difficult
Pets not allowed in the house
Closed Christmas and New Year
Proprietors Roy and Shirley Carlsen

Northern Lakes

Inn, Bassenthwaite Lake

Pheasant Inn

Tucked away behind trees just off the A66, the Pheasant was originally an old coaching inn and there are many reminders of this within, particularly in the old oak bar, which does not seat many, but is full of dark nooks and crannies – a real piece of history, little changed from its earliest days. The building is a long, low barn-like structure that has been exceptionally well maintained, and it has a small but well-kept garden to the rear with a couple of small lawns and fine views up the hill to the forest. One of the great attractions – unusual in a smart hotel, never mind a roadside inn – is the generous sitting space. There are two residents' sitting-rooms to the front, both low ceilinged with small windows and plenty of small prints on the walls. A third, with easy chairs before an open log fire, juts out into the garden and has the advantage of its own serving hatch to the bar. Bedrooms are modern, light and well equipped. The dining-room is a long, uncomfortably shaped room, but its furnishings have recently been improved and the food – no-nonsense stuff with few concessions to modern fashions – is competently cooked, and service is outstandingly friendly.

Nearby Bassenthwaite Lake; Keswick, 5.5 miles (9 km).

Bassenthwaite Lake, near Cockermouth, Cumbria CA13 9YE
Tel (059681) 234
Location 5 miles (8 km) E of Cockermouth, just off A66
Food & drink breakfast, lunch, tea, dinner, bar snacks; full licence
Prices B&B £32-£35; DB&B £42-£47; reduced weekly rates
Rooms 16 double, 15 with bath, one with shower; 4 single, 3 with bath, one with shower; all rooms have central heating, hairdrier
Facilities bar, sitting-rooms, dining-room
Credit cards not accepted
Children welcome, but not allowed in main bar
Disabled access easy only to public rooms **Pets** not allowed in bedrooms
Closed Christmas Day
Proprietor W Barrington-Wilson

Northern Lakes

Seatoller House

It should be said at the outset that a stay at Seatoller House is something quite different from the run-of-the-mill hotel experience. You eat communally at set times, and to get the best out of the place must be prepared to take part in the social life of the house. If you do, the 'country house party' effect, much vaunted elsewhere, really does come about.

Seatoller House is over 300 years old and has been run as a guest-house for over 100 years; the first entry in the visitors' book reads 23 April 1886. The long, low building is part of a row of cottages in the tiny village of Seatoller, built in the traditional Lakeland style at the head of Borrowdale and the foot of Honister Pass. Bedrooms are simple and comfortable, and all now have their own bathrooms (although some are physically separate from the bedrooms). The dining-room is in a country-kitchen style, with a delightfully informal atmosphere – one that spills over into the two sections of the low-ceilinged sitting-room. Food is excellent; and if you are thirsty, just wander to the fridge, take what you like, and sign for it in the book provided.

Several times a year the house is taken over entirely by members of the Lakes Hunt, who enjoy running up and down the surrounding fells in pursuit not of foxes (the traditional quarry of local hunts), but of one another.

Nearby Derwentwater, 4 miles (6 km), Buttermere, 6 miles (10 km), Keswick, 7 miles (11 km).

Borrowdale, Keswick, Cumbria CA12 5XN
Tel (059684) 622
Location 8 miles (13 km) S of Keswick on B5289; parking for 10 cars
Food & drink full breakfast, packed lunch, dinner (not Tue); residential licence
Prices DB&B £23.50–£25
Rooms 3 double, 6 family rooms; all with bath or shower, or separate bathroom; all rooms have central heating
Facilities sitting-room, library, dining-room, tea room, drying-room
Credit cards not accepted
Children welcome over 5
Disabled access easy; 2 downstairs bedrooms
Pets welcome, but not in public rooms
Closed Dec and Jan
Managers Ann and David Pepper

Northern Lakes

Country hotel, Howtown

Howtown Hotel

This mid-18thC building was originally a licensed farmhouse but was extended and converted to a hotel in the late 19thC. The Howtown is a long, low stone building in traditional Lakeland style close to the shores of Ullswater.

The Howtown has been in the Baldry family for four generations and this in part accounts for its home-like atmosphere. The public bar to the rear is small and intimate, with dark panelling in the best town-pub tradition; the several sitting-rooms for hotel guests are crammed with bric-a-brac and *objets d'art*. The food has attracted favourable reviews from all quarters.

Nearby Dalemain, Lowther Castle, 5.5 miles (9 km); Ullswater.

Howtown, Ullswater, Penrith, Cumbria, CA10 2ND
Tel (08536) 514
Location 4 miles (6.5 km) SW of Pooley Bridge
Food & drink full breakfast, cold lunch (hot on Sun), dinner; full licence
Prices DB&B £22.25
Rooms 13 double, 4 with bath; 3 single
Facilities 3 sitting-rooms (one with TV), bars; fishing, sailing, other water sports
Credit cards not accepted
Children accepted
Disabled no special facilities
Pets welcome
Closed Nov to mid-Mar
Proprietors Jacqueline Baldry and David Baldry

Country guest-house, Mungrisdale

The Mill

The Mill (not to be confused, as it often is, with the Mill Inn next door) is a cottagey guest-house offering good value for money, despite minor niggles. The main sitting-room is chintzy, relaxing and well cared for; the dining-room is more simply furnished, and the soft background muzak is not to everyone's taste. The food is increasingly ambitious and generally successful, with little choice of early courses but a range of tempting puddings. Bedrooms, are light and airy, and newly carpeted.

Nearby Derwentwater, Ullswater; Hadrian's Wall.

Mungrisdale, Penrith, Cumbria CA11 0XR
Tel (059683) 659
Location 9.5 miles (15 km) W of Penrith close to A66, in village; in wooded grounds with parking for 15 cars
Food & drink breakfast, lunch, dinner; residential and restaurant licence
Prices B&B £17; dinner £12.50; reductions for 5 nights or more, and for children sharing parents' room
Rooms 8 double, 5 with bath; one single; one family room; all rooms have tea/coffee kit; 4 rooms have colour TV
Facilities sitting-room, TV room, dining-room, games room, drying-room
Credit cards not accepted
Children welcome; cots, high-chairs, laundry facilities
Disabled access difficult **Pets** dogs accepted if well behaved, but not allowed in public rooms
Closed Nov to Feb
Proprietors Richard and Eleanor Quinlan

Northern Lakes

Inn, Wasdale

Wasdale Head

The Wasdale Head is in a site unrivalled even in the consistently spectacular Lake District. It stands on the flat valley bottom between three major peaks – Pillar, Great Gable and Scafell Pike (England's highest) – and only a little way above Wastwater, England's deepest and perhaps most dramatic lake.

Over the last twelve years the old inn has been carefully and thoughtfully modernized, adding facilities but retaining the characteristics of a traditional mountain inn. The main lounge of the hotel is comfortable and welcoming, with plenty of personal touches. Bedrooms are not notably spacious but are adequate, with fixtures and fittings all in good condition. The dining-room is heavily panelled, and decorated with willow pattern china and a pewter jug collection. Food is solid English fare, served by young, friendly staff.

There are two bars. The one for residents has some magnificent wooden furniture, while tasty bar meals are served in the congenial surroundings of the public bar, much frequented by walkers and climbers.

Nearby Hardknott Castle Roman Fort, 5 miles (8 km), Ravenglass and Eskdale Railway, 5.5 miles (9 km); Wastwater, Scafell.

Wasdale Head, Gosforth, Cumbria CA20 1EX
Tel (09467) 26229
Location 9 miles (14.5 km) NE of Gosforth at head of Wasdale; ample car parking
Food & drink full breakfast, bar and packed lunches, dinner; full licence
Prices DB&B £37-£44; reduction for 4 nights or more
Rooms 7 double, 6 with bath, one with shower; 2 single, one with bath, one with shower; 2 family rooms, both with bath; all rooms have central heating, tea/coffee kit, phone
Facilities sitting-room, dining-room, 2 bars
Credit cards MC, V
Children welcome, but under 7 not allowed in dining-room during evening
Disabled access easy to ground floor, but not to bedrooms **Pets** tolerated, in bedrooms, but not allowed in public rooms
Closed mid-Nov to mid-Mar; open 2 weeks for New Year
Proprietor Edwin Hammond

Northern Lakes

Country hotel, Watermillock

Old Church

There are many hotels with spectacular settings in the Lakes, but for our money there are few to match that of this white-washed 18thC house on the very shore of Ullswater, reached by a long private drive through well-kept gardens.

Over the last decade, Kevin and Maureen Whitemore have developed the hotel carefully and stylishly. The three sitting-rooms, one of which is formed by the entrance hall, are all very well furnished with clever touches in their decorations that give some hint of Maureen's interior design training. They also have the natural advantage of excellent views across the lake. The bedrooms are all different in decoration, but they too show a confident but harmonious use of colour. Most have lake views; the absence of modern gadgetry is a deliberate part of the White-mores' desire to provide a peaceful retreat.

Ex-accountant Kevin does more than keep the books in order: his daily-changing dinners are enterprising and expertly prepared, with a reasonable choice at each course.

Nearby Dalemain, 3 miles (5 km), Penrith Castle, 5.5 miles (9 km), Brougham Castle, 7 miles (11 km); Ullswater.

Watermillock, Penrith, Cumbria CA11 0JN
Tel (07684) 86204
Location 5.5 miles (9 km) SW of Penrith on A592; in own grounds on lakeshore with ample car parking
Food & drink breakfast, dinner; residential licence
Prices DB&B £65
Rooms 10 double, all with bath; all rooms have central heating, phone

Facilities bar, TV room, 2 sitting-rooms, dining-room; boat, fishing
Credit cards not accepted
Children welcome; not allowed at dinner under 8 – cots, high-chairs, high tea available **Disabled** access difficult **Pets** not accepted
Closed Dec to Feb
Proprietors Kevin and Maureen Whitemore

Cumbria

Farm guest-house, Alston

High Fell Old Farmhouse

Running what may or may not be the highest hotel in England (on the high Pennine moorland between the upper Tyne and Penrith) is a demanding business, and the Chapmans have at last given it up. Peter and Val Dow have taken over after many years of working in Africa and the Pacific. Val is the cook, specializing in French dishes in 'generous' proportions, prepared on an Aga and chosen from a short 'carte'. A house in this position needs to be warm and inviting, and High Fell is, with its abundance of beams, exposed stone walls, open fires and warm welcome (the Dows cultivate a house-party atmosphere).

Nearby Yorkshire Dales; the Lakes.

Penrith Road, Alston, Cumbria CA9 3BP **Tel** (0434) 381597 **Location** 2 miles (3 km) SW of Alston on A686; in grounds with ample car parking **Food & drink** full breakfast; dinner; residential and restaurant licence **Prices** B&B £17.50-£25; DB&B £27.50-£37.50	**Rooms** 5 double, 4 with bath, one with shower; all rooms have central heating **Facilities** sitting-room, bar, restaurant **Credit cards** MC, V **Children** welcome over 14 **Disabled** access difficult **Pets** not accepted **Closed** never **Proprietors** Peter and Val Dow

---

Country house hotel, Alston

Lovelady Shield Country House

The Rosiers have been here since 1983 and by now have got their handsome 1830-ish house pretty much as they want it – quietly and comfortably furnished in harmony with its style, but with all modern amenities. Its setting is captivating – in a rambling garden beside the babbling Nent. Annie does the cooking; she is French, and knows a thing or two about salads and daubes.

Nearby Pennine Way; Hadrian's Wall; Lake District.

Nenthead Road, near Alston, Cumbria CA9 3LF **Tel** (0498) 81203 **Location** 2.5 miles (4 km) E of Alston, close to A689; in secluded gardens with parking for 20 cars **Food & drink** full breakfast, dinner; Sun lunch; residential and restaurant licence **Prices** B&B £24-£34; DB&B £40-£50; reduced weekly rates; reductions for children sharing parents' room **Rooms** 9 double, 7 with bath, 2 with shower; 2 single, both	with shower; one family room, with bath; all rooms have central heating, TV, hairdrier, phone **Facilities** dining-room, bar, sitting-room, library; croquet, tennis **Credit cards** AE, DC **Children** welcome; high tea served – not allowed at dinner **Disabled** access difficult **Pets** dogs welcome if well behaved, but not allowed in public rooms **Closed** mid-Dec to early Mar **Proprietors** Barry and Annie Rosier

Cumbria

Country house hotel, Brampton

Farlam Hall

For over a decade now the Quinions have been assiduously improving their solid but elegant Border country house. A recent reporter could find no flaw: "charming family, quiet surroundings, excellent food, tastefully furnished bedroom". Bedrooms vary widely – some decidedly large and swish. Barry Quinion's dinners range from plain country dishes to mild extravagances, and there is a notable cheeseboard.

Nearby Naworth Castle, 2.5 miles (4 km); Hadrian's Wall.

Brampton, Cumbria CA8 2NG
Tel (06976) 234/359
Location 3 miles (5 km) SE of Brampton on A689, NE of Farlam village; ample car parking
Food & drink full breakfast, dinner; restaurant and residential licence
Prices DB&B £50-£80; winter and spring reductions
Rooms 12 double, 11 with bath, one with shower; one single with shower; all rooms have central heating, colour TV, phone, hairdrier
Facilities 2 sitting-rooms, bar; croquet
Credit cards AE, MC, V
Children accepted over 5
Disabled access reasonable – 2 steps to restaurant, 2 ground-floor bedrooms **Pets** welcome, but not in dining-room or left alone in bedroom
Closed Christmas week, Feb
Proprietors Quinion and Stevenson families

Country hotel, Ravenstonedale

The Black Swan

The Stuarts are sticking to their predecessors' successful formula – offering a relaxing and good-value home away from home, with particular emphasis on food of the first quality. The atmosphere is, however, more formal than that of a country inn. There is a choice of a daily fixed menu (ending with some indulgent puddings and excellent British cheeses) or a small 'carte', and a welll balanced wine-list. The dining room is appropriately polished, the sitting room more lived in with plenty of reading matter and an open fire. Breakfasts are a home-made feast.

Nearby Brough Castle, 8 miles (13 km); Eden valley.

Ravenstonedale, Kirkby Stephen, Cumbria CA17 4NG
Tel (05873) 204
Location 6 miles (10 km) E of M6, off A685; ample car parking
Food & drink full breakfast, lunch, dinner (except Sun); full licence
Prices B&B £19-£33; dinner from £14.50; bargain breaks
Rooms 13 double, 10 with bath, 6 also with shower; all rooms have central heating, tea/coffee kit, hairdrier, phone
Facilities sitting-room, lounge bar, dining-room; fishing, tennis, bowling
Credit cards AE, MC, V
Children welcome if well behaved; early tea provided
Disabled access difficult
Pets welcome if well behaved, but not in public rooms
Closed Jan
Proprietors Gordon and Norma Stuart

Durham

Manor house hotel, Gainford

Headlam Hall

"Extraordinary house, fine grounds, reasonable rates" was the telegraphic message that came back from one of our scouts about this mansion in a peaceful hamlet just north of the Tees. And so it is: a grand Jacobean house on three floors, its mellow stone all but hidden by creepers, with substantial Georgian additions – standing in four acres of beautiful formal gardens, with mellow stone walls, massive hedges and a canalised stream. As for the rates – by comparison with the prices of many well known grand houses in other parts of the country they look positively cheap. But is is equally true that Headlam is not among the best-furnished country hotels in the land – and therein lies part of its appeal, for us at least. Although there are abundant antiques alongside the reproductions (the Robinsons furnished the place from scratch after they took it over in the late 1970s) there is a comfortable ordinariness about the place which is refreshing. The food is relatively unexciting – but again much more affordable than is the norm in such places.
Nearby Barnard Castle, 8 miles (13 km).

Gainford, Darlington,
Durham DL2 3HA
Tel (0325) 730238
Location 7 miles (11 km) W
of Darlington off A67; in
4-acre gardens surrounded
by farmland, which ample
car parking
Food & drink breakfast,
lunch, dinner; restaurant
and residential licence
Prices B&B £25-£50;
dinner £10.50-£15.50
Rooms 16 double all with
bath and shower; 3 suites; all
rooms have central heating,
TV, phone, tea/coffee kit
Facilities sitting-room, bar,
dining-room, restaurant,
snooker room; tennis,
fishing **Credit cards** MC, V
Children welcome **Disabled**
access easy to ground floor
only **Pets** welcome, but dogs
not allowed in bedrooms,
loose boxes available
Closed Christmas to New
Year
Proprietors John Robinson,
Clare Robinson

Northumberland

The Coach House

Lynne Anderson (an ex-singer, with a beautiful voice still) is a charming hostess who devotes herself to the care of guests in this group of converted farm buildings. Some bedrooms are in the old outbuildings around a sunny courtyard, others in a separate stone house. The four-course dinners (with a choice of starter and dessert) are wholesome affairs employing much local produce, as are the breakfasts.

Nearby Northumberland National Park.

Crookham, Cornhill-on-Tweed, Northumberland TD12 4TD
Tel (089082) 293
Location 4 miles (6 km) E of Cornhill-on-Tweed on A697; with ample car parking
Food & drink full breakfast, tea, dinner (except Tue); residential licence
Prices B&B from £19; DB&B from £29.50; reductions for children under 10
Rooms 9 double, 4 with bath, 4 with shower, one with bath and shower; one single, with bath and shower; all rooms have central heating, tea/coffee kit; some rooms have fridge
Facilities 3 sitting-rooms, dining-room, music room, TV room, games rooms
Credit cards not accepted
Children accepted; cots and high-chairs provided
Disabled excellent facilities
Pets welcome in bedrooms, but not allowed in public rooms
Closed Nov to Feb
Proprietors Jamie and Lynne Anderson

Breamish House

In an area where there is precious little competition, it is a relief to come upon Graham Taylor's establishment – originally an 18thC farmhouse, converted to a hunting lodge in the 19thC and opened as a hotel in 1982. It is a thoroughly good all-rounder, which stands comparison with many of the best hotels in parts of the country more popular with visitors – a welcoming, informal atmosphere, solid, comfortable furniture in well-decorated bedroooms (those at the front notably spacious. The staff are charming and thoughtful, the cooking excellent.

Nearby Callaly Casstle, 4 miles (6.5 km).

Powburn, Alnwick, Northumberland, NE66 4LL
Tel (066578) 266
Location 7.5 miles (12 km) NW of Alnwick in middle of village; ample car parking
Food & drink breakfast, tea, dinner, Sun lunch, residential and restaurant licence
Prices B&B £26-£35; dinner £16.50
Rooms 9 double, 8 with bath, one with shower; one single with shower all rooms have central heating, colour TV, tea/coffee kit, radio
Facilities 2 sitting-rooms, dining-room
Credit cards not accepted
Children welcome over 12
Disabled access easy
Pets considered **Closed** Jan
Proprietors Alan and Doreen Johnson

Inn, Canonbie

Riverside Inn

For over a decade now the Phillipses have been improving and extending this country-house-turned-inn to the point where it scores highly whether viewed as a pub, a restaurant or a hotel. Retailing and nursing, whence they came, are obviously an excellent preparation for the business of catering for travellers – and we guess that passing motorists remain the mainstay of the Riverside's trade, despite the fact that the A7 from Carlisle to Edinburgh has recently been shifted westwards to by-pass Canonbie. For those who do pause there, Canonbie and the Riverside are, not surprisingly, more attractive now that very little traffic separates the Riverside from the public park it faces, and from the river Esk it pretends to be beside.

Inside, the comfortable bars and sitting-rooms have occasional beams and are furnished in traditional, chintz, country style, while the dining-room is less pub-like. Both in the bars and dining-room, the food is way above normal pub standards, both in ambition and execution.

Nearby Hadrian's Wall and the Borders.

Canonbie, Dumfries and Galloway DG14 0UX
Tel (03873) 71512
Location 11 miles (18 km) N of M6 on A7, in village by river; with garden and ample car parking
Food & drink full breakfast, lunch, dinner; full licence
Prices B&B £25-£40; dinner £16.50; winter breaks
Rooms 6 double, 4 with bath, 2 with shower; all rooms have storage heater, tea/ coffee kit
Facilities 2 sitting-rooms, bar, dining-room; fishing, tennis, green bowls
Credit cards MC, V
Children welcome
Disabled access easy – one ground-floor bedroom
Pets not accepted
Closed Christmas Day, Boxing Day, New Year, 2 weeks Feb
Proprietors Robert and Susan Philips

Dumfries & Galloway

Country house hotel, Portpatrick

Knockinaam Lodge

Galloway is very much an area for escaping the hurly-burly, and Knockinaam Lodge complements it perfectly (as well as being the ideal staging post for anyone bound for the ferry to Northern Ireland). Succeeding proprietors of the Lodge have had a reputation for fine food and warm hospitality, and the tradition is thoroughly maintained with the help of an enthusiastic young staff by newcomers Marcel and Corinna Frichot – professional hotel-keepers, he of Seychellois extraction, she coming from Cheshire.

The house is a low Victorian villa, built as a holiday home in the late 19th century and extended a few years later. Its rooms are cosy in scale and furnishings, the bedrooms varying from the stylishly simple to the quietly elegant. A key part of the appeal of the place is its complete seclusion – down a wooded glen, with lawned garden running down to a sandy beach.

Dinner is obligatory, but this is not a hardship; there is a small choice of dishes at each course, and the cooking is competent and stylish modern French.

Nearby Logan Botanic Gardens, 9 miles (14.5 km), Glenluce Abbey, 11 miles, (17.5 km).

Portpatrick, Wigtownshire, Dumfries and Galloway DG9 9AD
Tel (077681) 471
Location 3 miles (5 km) SE of Portpatrick, off A77; in 30-acre grounds with parking for 25 cars
Food & drink full breakfast, lunch, dinner, high tea for children; full licence
Prices DB&B £57-£77; reductions for children sharing parents' room
Rooms 9 double with bath; one single with bath; all rooms have central heating, TV, phone
Facilities bar, 2 sitting-rooms, dining-room, croquet
Credit cards AE, DC, MC, V
Children welcome; cots and baby-sitting available
Disabled access easy to ground floor, but no ground-floor bedrooms
Pets accepted, but not allowed in public rooms; have own kennels
Closed Jan to Apr
Proprietors Marcel and Corinna Frichot

Lothian

Howard Hotel

Edinburgh is a city of big hotels, and even the Howard is not small by our standards; nor is it cheap. But it conforms to our basic requirements in offering personal service in surroundings that have some character – it consists of three houses in a Georgian terrace – and its position in the heart of the New Town is quiet but central. Bedrooms on the first floor are bigger in every dimension than those on the second. The competent cooking includes a two-course 'chef's supper' at a reasonable price.

Nearby Castle, Holyrood Palace, botanic gardens.

32-36 Great King Street, Edinburgh, Lothian EH3 6QH **Tel** 031-557 3500 **Location** off Dundas St in New Town; parking for 14 cars at rear **Food & drink** full breakfast, lunch, dinner; full licence **Prices** B&B £37.50-£60; dinner from £12.50; winter breaks **Rooms** 15 double, all with bath; 8 single, one with bath, 7 with shower; 2 family rooms, both with bath; all rooms have central heating, colour TV, tea/coffee kit, phone, hairdrier **Facilities** sitting-room, cocktail bar, lounge bar **Credit cards** AE, DC, MC, V **Children** welcome **Disabled** not suitable **Pets** welcome, but not allowed in public rooms **Closed** Christmas and New Year **Manager** Michael Gilbert

Greywalls

Greywalls is right at the top of our price-range and our size-range, but we cannot resist such a distinctive place – a classic turn-of-the-century product of Sir Edwin Lutyens with a garden laid out by Gertrude Jekyll, overlooking the 18th green of the famous Muirfield golf links. The feel is still very much one of a private house, furnished largely with period pieces; the large panelled library is a particularly appealing room. The ambitious young chef uses fine local produce.

Nearby Countless golf courses.

Muirfield, Gullane, East Lothian EH31 2EG **Tel** (0620) 842144 **Location** 17 miles (27 km) E of Edinburgh on A198 to North Berwick; ample car parking **Food & drink** breakfast, lunch, dinner; full licence **Prices** B&B £42.50-£55; dinner £25; reductions for long stays **Rooms** 19 double, 2 with bath, 17 with bath and shower; 4 single, all with bath; all rooms have central heating, TV, phone, radio **Facilities** 2 sitting-rooms, library, bar; croquet, putting, tennis **Credit cards** AE, DC, MC, V **Children** welcome **Disabled** access good – no steps to public rooms and 8 ground-floor bedrooms **Pets** accepted, but not public rooms **Closed** Nov to Apr **Proprietor** Jim Lennox

Strathclyde

Country hotel, Kilchrenan

Taychreggan

Visitors are appreciative of the privileged lochside setting of this much-enlarged old drovers' inn – many of the rooms have fine views. The new owners will have refurbished the public rooms by the time this edition is published, we hope matching the standard of the pretty bedrooms, some of which are admirably spacious. Dinner is a five-course affair with a modest choice of interesting dishes.

Nearby Loch Awe, forest walks; Inveraray Castle within reach.

Kilchrenan, by Taynuilt, Argyll PA35 1HQ
Tel (08663) 211
Location 8 miles (13 km) S of Taynuilt, at end of B845 on lochside; in 25-acre grounds with ample car parking
Food & drink full breakfast, lunch, dinner; full licence
Prices DB & B £52-£68; reductions for children sharing parents' room
Rooms 14 double, 8 with bath, 6 with bath and shower; 2 single, one with bath; all rooms have central heating, radio, hairdrier
Facilities dining-room, bar, 3 sitting-rooms, TV lounge; boating, fishing
Credit cards AE, DC, MC, V
Children welcome; baby-listening service
Disabled access easy to bar and dining-room **Pets** dogs accepted but not in dining-room
Closed mid-Oct to Easter
Proprietors John and Monika Tyrrell

Inn, Tarbert

West Loch

After a dozen or so years at this black-and-white 18thC coaching inn, Janet and Alastair Thom have moved on; Sandy Ferguson took over at the beginning of 1988. The house is simply furnished and decorated, and warmed by log and peat fires; there are no fancy frills or pretences to luxury. But the food served in the small dining-room overlooking the loch aims higher – Mrs Ferguson has devised ambitious five-course menus making good use of local fish and game, and supplements the best local vegetables with more exotic fare brought in from Glasgow. Simpler steak and fish dishes are also available.

Nearby Knapdale, Kintyre; islands of Arran, Gigha.

Tarbert, Argyll, Strathclyde PA29 6YF
Tel (08802) 283
Location 1 mile (1.5 km) SW of Tarbert, on A83; with ample car parking
Food & drink breakfast, lunch, dinner; restaurant and residential licence
Prices B & B £16-£22; dinner £14.50
Rooms 3 double; 1 single; 2 family rooms
Facilities 2 sitting-rooms, one with TV; 2 bars, dining-room
Credit cards not accepted
Children welcome
Disabled access possible
Pets welcome, but not in public rooms
Closed never
Proprietor Mrs Sandy Ferguson

Tayside

Country hotel, Cleish

Nivingston House

We have good reports of this amiable country house, once a restaurant with rooms but now a full-scale hotel with a calm atmosphere, friendly service (despite the presence of patience-testing children), freshly prepared food and exemplary house keeping. Decoration is largely in the hands of Laura Ashley and friends, except in the more formal dining-room.

Nearby Loch Leven, 3 miles (5 km); Edinburgh within reach.

Cleish, Kinross-shire,
Tayside KY13 7LS
Tel (05775) 216
Location 4.5 miles (7 km) SW
of Kinross, off B9097; in 12
acres of landscaped gardens
with ample car parking
Food & drink full breakfast,
lunch, dinner; full licence
Prices B&B £30-£47.50;
dinner £20; weekend breaks
Rooms 13 double, 2 single
and 2 family rooms, all with
bath and shower; all rooms
have central heating, colour
TV, phone, radio/alarm,
tea/coffee kit, hairdrier
Facilities 2 sitting-rooms,
bar; pitch and putt, croquet
Credit cards AE, DC, MC, V
Children welcome
Disabled access easy, 6
ground-floor bedrooms
Pets welcome in bedrooms
but must not be left
unattended
Closed never
Proprietor Allan Deeson

Farm guest-house, Pitlochry

Auchnahyle Farmhouse

This is a friendly working sheep farm within walking distance of the popular tourist town of Pitlochry where the Howmans have been taking guests since 1982. Game is reared on the farm, and there are several family pets, including a donkey, three dogs, English lop-eared rabbits and ornamental pheasants. Penny Howman's satisfying four-course dinners are served by candle-light – you are welcome to take your own wine – and for those going to the theatre a simpler two-course supper is available.

Nearby Falls of Tummel, Pass of Killiecrankie; Blair Castle.

Pitlochry, Perthshire,
Tayside PH16 5JA
Tel (0796) 2318
Location on E edge of town,
towards Moulin; in large
gardens with ample car
parking
Food & drink full breakfast,
picnic lunch, dinner; no
licence
Prices B&B £17-£25;
dinner £12.50; reductions
for 3 nights or more
Rooms 3 double, one with
bath, 2 share bathroom;
family cottage available; all
rooms have central heating,
tea/coffee kit
Facilities sitting-room with
TV
Credit cards MC
Children welcome over 12
Disabled access good – one
ground-floor bedroom
Pets well-behaved dogs
welcome
Closed Oct to Mar
Proprietors Alastair and
Penny Howman

Inner Hebrides

Inn, Gigha

Gigha Hotel

A reporter who makes something of a speciality of staying on islands describes this cottagey Victorian hotel, subject of an award-winning process of renovation in the 1970s, as "quite the nicest hotel I have ever stayed in – attractively furnished, comfortable, excellent home-cooked food and exceptionally friendly atmosphere". And she is not alone in appreciating the hospitality of the Roebucks, who have been running the hotel for many years now. The island is only three miles off the mainland, and not much longer from end to end.

Nearby Achamore Gardens.

Isle of Gigha, Argyll, Strathclyde PA41 7AD
Tel (05835) 254
Location 3 miles (5 km) off W coast of Kintyre (ferry from Tayinloan); with garden and adequate parking
Food & drink full breakfast, lunch, dinner; full licence
Prices B&B £22; DB&B from £35; reductions for children under 12

Rooms 9 double; all rooms have central heating
Facilities 2 sitting-rooms (one with TV), public bar
Credit cards MC, V
Children welcome
Disabled not suitable
Pets welcome, but not allowed in dining-room
Closed never
Managers Mr and Mrs K L Roebuck

Country hotel, Dervaig

Bellachroy Hotel

This solid white-painted inn is not far short of its fourth centenary, and can scarcely have been more popular in any earlier age. The bar meals are a key attraction for non-residents, along with musical entertainments in the season (and late opening). Residents find simple but spick-and-span bedrooms, and excellent wholesome breakfasts – as well as satisfying set dinners.

Nearby Mull Little Theatre; Old Byre Heritage Centre.

Dervaig, Isle of Mull, Argyllshire, Strathclyde PA75 6QW
Tel (06884) 314
Location in village, 8 miles (13 km) SW of Tobermory on main road; in 1.5-acre grounds with ample car parking
Food & drink breakfast, dinner; bar lunches; full hotel licence
Prices B&B £14.50; dinner £10.50; reductions for children under 12 sharing parents' room
Rooms 6 double and 2 family

rooms, none with bath or shower; all rooms have wash basins and heaters
Facilities dining-room, sitting-room, TV room, 2 bars
Credit cards not accepted
Children accepted, with facilities provided **Disabled** no special facilities **Pets** discouraged – not accepted in public rooms
Closed Christmas week
Proprietors Andrew and Anne Arnold

189

Inner Hebrides

Tiroran House

Tiroran House is a converted shooting-lodge, now very much a home. From the moment you arrive (when Wing Commander Blockey may require you to park your car with military precision) there is almost nothing to indicate that you are in a hotel; no room numbers, no lift, no contrived interior decoration.

Particularly appealing are the two comfortable sitting-rooms, furnished mainly with antiques and filled with books, ornaments and family photographs. Bedrooms are also comfortable and welcoming, and the two smallest ones have been amalgamated to form the grand Yellow Room. The small dining-room has a delightful conservatory extension with lovely views towards the loch. Mrs Blockey's food is delicious, with fresh, traditional ingredients imaginatively prepared and presented. There is a wide-ranging, reasonably priced wine-list. Do not expect service to be speedy.

Fuelled by a generous breakfast, guests are encouraged to get out and about – and there is plenty of scope.

Nearby Loch Scridain; Ben More, 3,169 ft (966 m); islands of Iona and Staffa.

Isle of Mull, Argyll, Highland PA69 6ES
Tel (06815) 232
Location 23 miles (37 km) W of Craignure ferry, on W side of island, one mile (1.5 km) off B8035; in 40-acre grounds with ample car parking
Food & drink full breakfast, light or packed lunch, dinner; residential and restaurant licence
Prices DB&B £65-£79; reductions for 3 nights or more; ferry fares repaid in part or full for longer stays
Rooms 8 double, one single; all with bath; all rooms have central heating, tea/coffee kit, radio, hairdrier
Facilities dining-room, 2 sitting-rooms, games room; croquet
Credit cards not accepted
Children welcome over 10
Disabled access possible; one ground-floor bedroom
Pets dogs accepted by arrangement, but not allowed in public rooms
Closed early Oct to early May
Proprietors Sue and Robin Blockey

Inner Hebrides

Town hotel, Mull

The Tobermory Hotel

This long-established guest-house was relaunched as a hotel in 1985, and the Gibbons arrived in 1988. Bedrooms and public rooms alike are now light and bright, and if there is some lack of character in the furnishings there is no lack of comfort or facilities. There is a proper emphasis on quality ingredients in the cooking (seafood is the speciality).

Nearby walking, golf, beaches.

53 Main Street, Tobermory, Isle of Mull, Argyll, Strathclyde PA75 6NT
Tel (0688) 2091
Location on waterfront; ample car parking on street and quayside
Food & drink full breakfast, dinner, lunch from May to Sep; residential and restaurant licence
Prices DB&B £28.50-£49; reduced weekly rates; reductions for children sharing parents' room
Rooms 10 double, 2 with bath, one with shower; 3 single; 2 family rooms, one with bath, one with shower; all rooms have tea/coffee kit
Facilities 2 sitting-rooms (one with TV), dining-room
Credit cards not accepted
Children welcome **Disabled** access easy to public rooms only
Pets dogs welcome, but not in public rooms
Closed never
Proprietors Jackie and Reg Gibbons

Inn, Skye

Ardvasar Hotel

The Fowlers' double act – Bill in the kitchen, Gretta managing the front of house – has proved its worth since they took over this 18thC coaching inn several years ago. With the able assistance of local ladies, they have created a warm and welcoming ambience and gained a reputation for serving good food. The house is solid and low-built, simply and cosily furnished; a log fire blazes in the sitting-room, which (like the front bedrooms) gives splendid views across the Sound of Sleat.

Nearby Clan Donald Centre, 1 mile (1.5 km).

Ardvasar, Sleat, Isle of Skye, Highland IV45 8RS
Tel (04714) 223
Location in tiny village, 0.5 miles (one km) SW of Armadale ferry; on roadside, with parking for 30 cars
Food & drink breakfast, bar lunch and supper, fixed-menu dinner; full licence
Prices B&B £19-£27.50; dinner from £14
Rooms 8 double, 6 with bath, 2 with shower; one single, with shower; all rooms have tea/coffee kit
Facilities sitting-room, TV room, two bars, dining-room
Credit cards V
Children welcome **Disabled** access easy to public rooms but not to bedrooms **Pets** well-behaved dogs accepted, but not allowed in public rooms
Closed Nov to Mar
Proprietors Bill and Gretta Fowler

Inner Hebrides

Country hotel, Skye

Kinloch Lodge

This white-painted stone house, in an isolated position at the southern extremity of the Isle of Skye, was built as a farmhouse around 1700 and subsequently became a shooting lodge. But it escaped the baronial treatment handed out to many such houses – "thank goodness," says Lady Macdonald, whose style is modern interior-designer rather than dark panelling and tartan.

The Macdonalds have been running the house as a hotel and restaurant for many years; it has always had that easy-going private-house air, but it is now also their home – though they have separate quarters at one side of the house. The guests' sitting-rooms are comfortably done out in stylishly muted colours, the dining-room more elegant, with sparkling crystal and silver on polished tables at dinner. All but three of the bedrooms are undeniably small, but this does not deter fans, who go here for an unaffectedly warm welcome and for the excellent food – three courses with a choice at each stage, cooked by Lady M along with Peter Macpherson. Desserts are particularly notable.

Nearby Clan Donald Centre, 6 miles (10 km).

Sleat, Isle of Skye, Highland IV43 8QY
Tel (04713) 214
Location 6 miles (10 km) S of Broadford, one mile (1.5 km) off A851; in 60-acre grounds with ample car parking
Food & drink full breakfast, lunch by arrangement, dinner; residential and restaurant licence
Prices B&B £50-£60; dinner £24
Rooms 10 double, 8 with bath; all rooms have central heating, tea/coffee kit, hairdrier
Facilities 2 sitting-rooms, games room, dining-room; fishing
Credit cards MC, V
Children welcome if well behaved; special meals under 8 **Disabled** access reasonable – one ground-floor bedroom **Pets** dogs accepted, but not allowed in public rooms
Closed 1 Dec to 10 Mar
Proprietors Lord & Lady Macdonald

Inner Hebrides

Viewfield House

This formidable Victorian country mansion, as the name suggests, has some fine views from its elevated position. The need for costly repairs to the roof prompted Evelyn Macdonal (now retired) to open Viewfield to guests. The delight of it is that the distinctive character of the house was preserved; and though you will not lack for comfort or service, a stay here is likely to be a novel experience. The rooms are original, right down to the wallpaper and there is – a classic Victorian parlour; a grand dining-room; and the original bathrooms complete with all their Victorian wares and accoutrements.

Nearby Trotternish peninsula.

Portree, Isle of Skye, Highland IV51 9EU
Tel (0478) 2217
Location on outskirts of town, 10 minutes' walk S of middle
Food & drink full breakfast, packed lunch, dinner
Prices B&B £16; DB&B £24
Rooms 10 double; 4 single; 2 family rooms; all rooms have tea/coffee kit
Facilities sitting-room, dining-room
Credit cards not accepted
Children welcome
Disabled access difficult
Pets welcome but not allowed in public rooms
Closed Nov to Apr
Proprietors Mr and Mrs Hugh MacDonald

Isle of Colonsay Hotel

Colonsay is not one of the most remote Scottish isles, but nevertheless a two to three-hour steamer trip from Oban. The island's old inn is a warmly civilized place serving sophisticated fixed meals based on fresh ingredients – and the Byrnes, who have been here since 1978, are still finding ways to improve this focus of island life.

Nearby Colonsay House gardens; walking, wildlife, fishing, golf.

Scalasaig, Isle of Colonsay, Argyll, Strathclyde PA61 7YP
Tel (09512) 316
Location on E coast of island; in large gardens with car parking; car can be left at Oban
Food & drink breakfast, bar/packed lunch, high tea, dinner or bar supper; full licence
Prices DB&B £35-£50; reductions for one week or more, and for children sharing parents' room
Rooms 6 double, all with shower; 3 single; 2 family rooms both with bath and shower; all rooms have central heating, tea/coffee kit; phone, TV on request
Facilities sitting-room, sun room, 2 bars; sea and loch fishing, golf, bicycles, sailing
Credit cards AE, DC, MC, V
Children welcome; high tea provided **Disabled** access good, some ground-floor rooms
Pets dogs welcome if well behaved, but not allowed in public rooms
Closed Nov to Feb except 2 weeks at New Year
Proprietors Kevin and Christa Byrne

Highland

Inn, Arisaig

Arisaig

Not to be confused with the much grander Arisaig House nearby, this lochside inn has been meeting the needs of travellers on the road to the isles for almost 200 years. The Stewarts have given it a new lease of life. It is their hospitality that is at the heart of the hotel's appeal, but they have also invested heavily in recent improvements. Janice and son Gordon cook dinners with a pronounced local emphasis – particularly strong on fish and seafood which comes in by boat.

Nearby Mallaig (for ferries to Skye); white sands of Morar.

Arisaig, Inverness-shire
PH39 4NH
Tel (06875) 210
Location 10 miles (16 km) S of Mallaig on A830, on edge of village; with ample car parking
Food & drink breakfast, bar lunch, dinner; full licence
Prices B&B £24.50-£34; dinner £17
Rooms 9 double, with bath; 4 family rooms, one with bath; all rooms have

radio, tea/coffee kit phone
Facilities 2 bars, sitting-room, TV area
Credit cards not accepted
Children welcome; cots and baby listening
Disabled access easy only to public rooms
Pets dogs accepted, but not allowed in public rooms
Closed Nov to mid-Mar
Proprietors George, Janice and Gordon Stewart

Country house hotel, Fort William

Factor's House

A factor is the manager of a Scottish estate, and the estate in question here is that of the famous Inverlochy Castle hotel, excluded from these pages by its sky-high prices. This much more modest (though still not cheap) establishment is run by the son of Inverlochy's Grete Hobbs. The turn-of-the-century house has been smartly modernised and extended, and is furnished in an informal mix of antique and modern styles, with Peter Hobbs' interest in expeditions reflected in the ornaments. Dishes at dinner range from the traditionally Scottish to the mildy experimental.

Nearby Ben Nevis, the Great Glen.

Torlundy, Fort William, Inverness-shire, Highland
PH33 6SN
Tel (0397) 5767
Location 3.5 miles (5.5 km) NE of Fort William on A82; parking for 25 cars
Food & drink full breakfast, light lunch, dinner; residential and restaurant licence
Prices B&B £34.50-£63.25; dinner £17.50

Rooms 7 double, 5 with bath, 2 with shower; all rooms have central heating, colour TV, phone
Facilities 2 sitting-rooms
Credit cards AE, DC, MC, V
Children welcome over 6
Disabled access easy – one ground-floor bedroom
Pets not accepted
Closed Dec to Mar/Apr
Proprietor Peter Hobbs

Highland

Country hotel, Glen Cannich

Cozac Lodge

This Edwardian shooting lodge is a splendid base for walkers and watchers of wildlife, and looks the part. It has rich mahogany panelling in the hall, and floor-to-ceiling windows looking out over loch and forest from the sitting-room (where there are plenty of books and a log fire when the weather closes in). The Butlers took over here from Pam Hall and John Wood in early 1989, and we lack reports on the new regime. Food remains wildly unconventional in range – New England chowder may be followed by rogan josh and Queen of Puddings.
Nearby Glen Affric; Loch Ness.

Glen Cannich, by Beauly, Inverness-shire, Highlands IV4 7LX
Tel (04565) 263
Location 8 miles (13 km) W of Cannich village in remote glen; in 3-acre grounds amidst 25,000-acre deer forest, with ample car parking
Food & drink breakfast, lunch, dinner; residential and restaurant licence
Prices B&B £22-£30; dinner £17; reductions for children under 12 in family room; bargain breaks
Rooms 5 double, 2 with bath, 3 with shower; one family room, with bath; all rooms have central heating, TV, tea/coffee kit
Facilities sitting-room, dining-room; fishing, stalking
Credit cards AE, MC, V
Children welcome if well behaved
Disabled access easy; one ground-floor bedroom
Pets well behaved accepted by arrangement
Closed mid-Oct to Easter, except Christmas and New Year
Proprietors Brian and Enid Butler

Invereshie House

Andrew and Patricia Hamilton, who took over in 1987, seem just the people to realize the potential of this spacious, mainly Georgian country house, given his long experience as a chef and her background in marketing for the Scottish Tourist Board. Both the public rooms and the bedrooms are split between the grander Georgian style and the cosier style of the older part (17thC/early 18thC). Cooking concentrates on traditional Scottish fare, and special attention is paid to breakfast.
Nearby Cairngorm mountains.

Kincraig, Kingussie, Inverness-shire, Highland PH21 1NA
Tel (05402) 332
Location 1 mile (2 km) E of Kincraig across River Spey; in 40-acre grounds with ample car parking
Food & drink breakfast, lunch on request, dinner; residential and restaurant licence
Prices B&B £24.50; dinner £15
Rooms 8 double, 5 with bath, 3 with shower; all rooms have central heating, TV, phone
Facilities sitting-room, bar, dining-room, drying-room; stalking, shooting, fishing
Credit cards V
Children accepted, but no special facilities **Disabled** access possible but no special facilities **Pets** dogs accepted but not in public rooms; kennels for working dogs
Closed never
Proprietors Andrew and Patricia Methven-Hamilton

Ard-na-Coille

The Cottams took over this 1920s millionaire's shooting lodge, in an elevated position on the flank of Strathspey, early in 1988. They are refugees from academic life, intent upon preserving the warm and welcoming character of the place while improving and refurbishing it. Pictures and books still abound; rooms are still mainly antique-furnished. Food is 'Modern British'.
Nearby Cluny Castle; Cairngorm mountains.

Kingussie Road, Newtonmore, Inverness-shire, Highland PH20 1AY
Tel (05403) 214
Location on N edge of town, off A86; in 2-acre grounds with ample car parking
Food & drink breakfast, packed lunch, dinner; restaurant and residential licence
Prices B&B £15-£30; DB&B £30-£45; reductions for children under 12 sharing parents' room; winter breaks
Rooms 6 double, 2 with bath, 4 with shower; 3 single, one with shower; all rooms have central heating
Facilities 2 sitting-rooms, dining-room, games room
Credit cards not accepted
Children very welcome if well behaved
Disabled access difficult
Pets dogs accepted, but not allowed in public rooms
Closed Nov and Dec
Proprietors Nancy Ferries and Barry Cottam

Highland

Country hotel, Drumnadrochit

Polmaily House

Nick Parsons travelled the world for Reuters before coming to Polmaily House in 1982, while Alison honed her cooking skills by catering for embassy dinners and other formal functions. They run their tall, completely secluded Edwardian-style house almost as if it was a private home, but there is a dining-room open to non-residents. Alison's cooking, in the modern British style and making the most of highland seafood and game supplies, has won considerable acclaim, and Nick takes credit for assembling an interesting cellar. The public rooms are comfortably lived-in – particularly the sitting-room, where pre-dinner drinks are served in front of an open fire.

Nearby Urquhart Castle, 1.5 miles (2.5 km); Loch Ness.

Drumnadrochit, Inverness-shire, Highland, IV3 6XT
Tel (04562) 343
Location 2 miles (3 km) W of Drumnadrochit on A831; with ample car parking
Food & drink breakfast, snack lunch, dinner; residential and restaurant licence
Prices B&B £30-£60; dinner from £15; children under 14 sharing parents' room free; reductions for 7 nights or more, 4 nights or more in winter
Rooms 5 double, all with

bath; 2 single; 2 family rooms both with bath; all rooms have central heating, radio
Facilities 2 sitting-rooms, bar, restaurant, tennis, swimming pool, croquet
Credit cards MC, V
Children welcome
Disabled access to dining-room good, but not to bedrooms
Pets not accepted
Closed mid-Oct to Easter-early April
Proprietors Alison and Nick Parsons

Highland

Country hotel, Achiltibuie

Summer Isles

Robert Irvine, who ran this very remote, cottagey hotel for 15 years or more, is still around – not least, growing vegetables at amazing speed in his new-fangled soil-less greenhouse – but the Summer Isles is now in the hands of the next generation. The decorations and furnishings remain simple but satisfactory, the food wholesome and interesting (a different five-course set dinner each night), the views across Loch Broom and the Summer Isles themselves riveting.

Nearby walking, beaches, boat cruises.

Achiltibuie, by Ullapool, Ross-shire, Highland IV26 2YG
Tel (085482) 282
Location close to village post office; car parking
Food & drink full breakfast, lunch, dinner; full licence
Prices B&B £20-£42; dinner £21; reductions for 6 nights or more
Rooms 12 double, 9 with bath, one with shower; one single; one family room, with bath; all rooms have central heating
Facilities dining-room sitting-room, 2 bars, TV room/reading-room, sun room; fishing
Credit cards not accepted
Children welcome over 8
Disabled access difficult
Pets dogs allowed, but not in dining- or sitting-rooms
Closed mid-Oct to Easter
Proprietors Mark and Geraldine Irvine

Town hotel, Kingussie

Osprey

This modest hotel without any grounds stands on a corner of the village street at a distance from the main road to Aviemore, so it is not too noisy. The Osprey's bedrooms are clean and cosy, decorated with light floral wallpapers and furnished in various styles. The heart of the place is the tiny dining-room, refurbished for the 1988 seasons where Pauline Reeves's excellent home-cooked food (including vegetarian dishes and a notable cheese board) is served by the chatty Duncan. His wines are, as he puts it, "of more than passing interest". The sitting-room is small but welcoming.

Nearby Highland Folk Museum (in Kingussie).

Ruthven Road, Kingussie, Inverness-shire, Highland PH21 1EN
Tel (05402) 510
Location in middle of village on A86; herb garden and parking for 10 cars
Food & drink breakfast, packed lunch, dinner; residential and restaurant licence
Prices B&B £15-£28; DB&B £30-£44
Rooms 7 double, one with bath, 3 with shower; one single; all rooms have central heating
Facilities sitting-room, TV room, dining-room
Credit cards AE, DC, MC, V
Children welcome **Disabled** access difficult **Pets** dogs accepted by arrangement
Closed Nov and Dec
Proprietors Duncan and Pauline Reeves

Highland

Clifton

It is not unusual to come upon small hotels with a theatrical touch, but the Clifton is in a different league: it actually is a theatre, staging plays and recitals in the dining room during the winter months, to the delight of locals and visitors alike. The hotel has been run by Gordon Macintyre for over 35 years. His hotel-keeping act is by now thoroughly polished.

The Victorian house is richly furnished to ensure not only the comfort but also the amusement of guests; paintings fill the walls (which are themselves works of art), flowers fill antique vases, books fill shelves, knick-knacks fill every other nook and cranny – and a welcoming calm fills the air. Whatever your mood, one of the several public rooms should suit. The bedrooms are individually decorated and furnished in what Gordon modestly calls 'a mixture of good antiques and painted junk'.

The cooking, supervised by Mr Macintyre, imposes French provincial techniques on the best local produce – particularly seafood, upon which lunch in the smaller Green Room is largely based – with huge success, and there is a fine, long wine-list. Typically breakfast is served without time limit.

Nearby Cawdor Castle, 5 miles (8 km), Fort George, 8 miles (13 km); Moray Firth; Inverness within reach.

Nairn, Highland IV12 4HW
Tel (0667) 53119
Location on sea-front in middle of town, close to A96; with own parking
Food & drink full breakfast, lunch, dinner; full licence
Prices B & B £34-£43; dinner about £15
Rooms 9 double, all with bath; 7 single, 6 with bath, one with shower; all rooms have central heating

Facilities 2 sitting-rooms, writing-room, 2 dining-rooms
Credit cards AE, DC, MC, V
Children welcome, but no special facilities **Disabled** access difficult – no ground-floor bedrooms **Pets** well behaved dogs accepted but not allowed in restaurant
Closed Nov to Feb
Proprietor J Gordon Macintyre

Highland

Altnaharrie Inn

There are good hotels in many unlikely-sounding places in Britain, but this one takes first prize. Ullapool itself is pretty remote, but to get to Altnaharrie you have to make a 10-minute crossing of Loch Broom in the inn's private ferry – or tackle it from Little Loch Broom and hike 2 miles over the mountains.

Such complete seclusion has a powerful appeal in itself, at least to some – there can hardly be a better way to appreciate the wild grandeur of this north-western extremity of the British mainland than to explore it on foot from this remote spot. But the really remarkable thing about staying here is that it involves no compromises whatever. The inn is as welcoming a house as you will find anywhere; what is more, the food is stunningly good.

Gunn does the cooking, and brings to it the same originality she employs in painting and weaving. Fresh local ingredients – including superb seafood and game in season – form the basis of her set menus, which defy classification but have achieved wide acclaim. There are no better restaurants in the highlands, and few in the whole of Britain.

The centuries-old white-painted stone house, only a stone's throw from the loch, is warmly and prettily decorated, with woven wall-hangings, Middle Eastern rugs and a sprinkling of antiques.

Nearby walking, birdwatching; Loch Broom Highland Museum, Ullapool; Inverewe gardens.

Ullapool, Highland
IV26 2SS
Tel (085483) 230
Location SW of Ullapool across Loch Broom – reached by private launch; private car park in Ullapool
Food & drink full breakfast, light lunch (residents only), dinner; residential and restaurant licence
Prices DB&B £74-£79
Rooms 6 double, 5 with bath, one with shower;
Facilities sitting-room, dining-room
Credit cards not accepted
Children welcome if well behaved, but not suitable for small children **Disabled** access difficult **Pets** dogs may be accepted by prior arrangement
Closed late Oct to Easter
Proprietors Fred Brown and Gunn Eriksen

Highland

Country guest-house, Ullapool

Ceilidh Place

A 'ceilidh' (pronounced kaylee) is a sort of party – an evening of music, song, dance and story-telling; and the name gives a clue to the social and cultural vitality of the Urquharts 'hotel'. It started as a coffee shop in a cottage, spread into adjacent cottages to provide bedrooms, and then into other 'clubhouse' buildings nearby, where there is more basic accommodation as well as a bookshop, gallery and auditorium, and by now possibly several other things too. The essentials are all there too – simple but comfortable rooms with plenty of pictures, wholesome, largely vegetarian cooking, "no telly, no teasmaids".
Nearby mountains, walks.

West Argyle Street, Ullapool, Wester Ross, Highland IV26 2TY
Tel (0854) 2103
Location in middle of village; 0.5-acre garden with parking for 25 cars
Food & drink breakfast, lunch, high tea, dinner; full licence
Prices B&B £15-£35; dinner £10-£16
Rooms 10 double, 6 with bath; 5 single, 2 with bath; 7 family rooms; all rooms have central heating
Facilities sitting-room, bar, coffee shop, dining-room, games room
Credit cards AE, DC, MC, V
Children welcome
Disabled access difficult
Pets welcome
Closed never
Proprietors Jean and Robert Urquhart

Country house hotel, Whitebridge

Knockie Lodge

The Milwards must have had vision to see the potential in this 200-year-old shooting-lodge – then a distinctly lacklustre hotel – which they quit London to take over in 1983. In less than a year they had transformed it, creating the kind of welcoming atmosphere that its romantic setting demands, and improvements continue in the same vein. Dinner is a satisfactory set meal of five 'simple but imaginative' dishes.
Nearby Great Glen Museum, 6 miles (10 km); Loch Ness.

Whitebridge, Inverness, Highland IV1 2UP
Tel (04563) 276
Location 8 miles (13 km) NE of Fort Augustus on B862; in open country with ample car parking
Food & drink breakfast, bar lunch, dinner; residential licence
Prices DB&B £48-£64; reductions for 7 nights or more
Rooms 8 double, all with bath, 4 also with shower; 2 single, both with bath; all rooms have central heating
Facilities sitting-room with bar, dining-room, billiard-room; fishing
Credit cards AE, DC, MC, V
Children welcome over 10
Disabled access difficult
Pets dogs accepted, but not allowed in public rooms
Closed Nov to Apr
Proprietors Mr and Mrs Ian Milward

Outer Hebrides

Country guest-house, Harris

Scarista House

Harris has little in the way of hotels, but Scarista would stand out even among the country houses of the Cotswolds. It is not uncommon to discover that several of the guests at Scarista have re-arranged their holiday itineraries to be sure of a stay.

The converted Georgian manse stands alone on a windswept slope overlooking a wide stretch of tidal sands. The decoration is quite formal, with antiques throughout, but the atmosphere is relaxed, and by the open peat fires, conversation replaces television. The Johnsons, who escaped Oxford for the solitude of Harris's western shores, are welcoming hosts from the moment you are greeted at your car. But service is never intrusive, and you are likely to feel more like a guest in a private home than in an hotel. One of Scarista's greatest attractions, particularly rewarding after a long walk over the sands, is the meals. The combination of imaginatively prepared fresh farm produce and an impressive wine list ensure a memorable dinner. The bedrooms, all with private bathrooms, have selected teas, fresh coffee, and home-made biscuits.

All this civilized luxury did not come easily. The story of how this particular phoenix was dragged from the ashes is told in Alison Johnson's own book, 'A House By The Shore'.

Nearby swimming, walking, bird-watching.

Harris, Western Isles
PA85 3HX
Tel (085985) 238
Location 15 miles (24 km) SW of Tarbert on A859, overlooking sea; in 2-acre garden, with ample car parking
Food & drink full breakfast, packed/snack lunch, dinner; residential licence
Prices B & B £33-£45; dinner £17

Rooms 7 double, all with bath; all rooms have central heating, tea/coffee kit
Facilities library, sitting-room, dining-room
Credit cards not accepted
Children welcome over 8
Disabled access easy, but no ground-floor toilets **Pets** welcome if well behaved
Closed Oct to Easter
Proprietors Andrew and Alison Johnson

Outer Hebrides/Shetland

Baile-na-Cille

Discovered in a ruinous state by the Gollins, this beautifully set 18thC manse has been lovingly restored and the adjacent stables converted into light, pretty rooms. Many discarded antiques were restored and given new life in this friendly, relaxed guest-house. The home-cooked meals, which include freshly baked bread, are served around communal tables in a lofty dining-room. It is essential to book well ahead.

Nearby Walking, climbing, birdwatching, sailing, fishing.

Timsgarry, Uig, Isle of Lewis, Outer Hebrides PA86 9JD
Tel (085175) 242
Location 32 miles (51 km) W of Stornaway, close to end of B8011; in countryside, with ample car parking
Food & drink full breakfast, dinner, packed lunch; residential licence
Prices B&B £16-£21.50; dinner £14
Rooms 9 double, 5 with bath; 3 single; 2 family rooms; all rooms have storage heater
Facilities 2 sitting-rooms, dining-room, TV room; dinghy, wind-surfing, boat trips
Credit cards not accepted
Children welcome; climbing frames/playroom
Disabled some ground-floor bedrooms
Pets welcome
Closed Nov to Feb
Proprietors Richard and Joanna Gollin

Burrastow House

If remoteness appeals, Burrastow makes the ideal goal – a calm, solid stone house, romantically isolated on a rocky shore, reached down a long single-track road. The new proprietors, Ann Prior and Bo Simmons, have set out to preserve the honest character and simple style of the place established under their pre-decessors, the Tuckeys. They share the cooking, and now offer light lunches on the premises.

Nearby walking, swimming, boating, bird-watching, fishing.

Walls, Shetland Islands ZE2 9PD
Tel (059571) 307
Location 3 miles (5 km) W of Walls; in spacious grounds with ample car park
Food & drink breakfast, light lunch, dinner; residential and restaurant licence
Prices B&B £27-£32; DB&B £36.50-£41.50; reduction for 4 nights or more; spring weekend breaks; big reductions for children
Rooms one double, one family suite of 2 rooms with lobby and bath; all rooms have central heating, hairdrier, tea/coffee kit; TV on request
Facilities dining-room, 2 sitting-rooms; golf practice area, dinghy, fishing
Credit cards not accepted
Children welcome **Disabled** access difficult **Pets** dogs accepted, but not in public rooms **Closed** Oct to Feb
Proprietors Bo Simmons and Ann Prior

Kerry

Caragh Lodge

A hundred-year-old house furnished with antiques and log fires, a 300-yard lake frontage, nine acres of parkland with a fine planting of rare and sub-tropical shrubs, views of some of Ireland's highest mountains, abundant facilities for children and outdoor types, quick access to the sea and glorious sandy beaches: Caragh Lodge offers a heady combination, attractive to all the family.

The hotel was established many years ago by the German Schaper family, and has lately been run by daughter Ines and her husband Michael Braasch. But in mid-1989 it was taken over by Mary Gaunt, an ex-Aer Lingus stewardess. She immediately set about a thorough redecoration, which we hope will extend to refurbishment of the previously rather ordinary annexe bedrooms, and promises good home cooking based largely on home-grown fruit and vegetables. Reports on the new regime welcome.

Nearby Killarney, 15 miles (24 km); Ring of Kerry.

Caragh Lake, Co Kerry
Tel (066) 69115
Location 22 miles (35 km) NW of Killarney, one mile (1.5 km) off Ring of Kerry road, W of Killorglin; in 9-acre gardens and parkland, with ample car parking
Food & drink full breakfast, dinner, restaurant licence
Prices B & B £29-£37.50; dinner £20
Rooms 7 double, 2 with family room (mainly in annexes); all with bath; all rooms have central heating
Facilities 2 sitting-rooms, dining-room; table tennis, tennis, swimming in lake, fishing, boating, sauna, bicycles
Credit cards AE, MC, V
Children welcome
Disabled access easy – some ground-floor bedrooms
Pets not accepted
Closed mid-Oct to Easter
Proprietors Mary Gaunt

Cork

Assolas Country House

This historic, mellow country house, in a fairy-tale setting of award-winning gardens beside a slow-flowing river, has been in the Bourke family since the early years of this century. The familiar story of escalating maintenance costs and dwindling bank balances led to their taking in guests in 1966, and since then they have never looked back. Assolas is still their family home, and the business of sharing it has obviously turned out to be a pleasure.

The house was built around 1590, and had unusual circular extensions added at two corners in Queen Anne's time; beyond the expanses of lawn at front and back are mature woods, and then hills and farmland. Inside, the public rooms are richly decorated and elegantly furnished, almost entirely with antiques, and immaculately kept. The bedrooms have recently been redecorated, and many have newly enlarged luxury bathrooms. The rooms are notably spacious – particularly the 'circular' rooms at the corners of the house.

The food is in what might be called modern Irish style – country cooking of fresh ingredients (many home-grown) with progressive overtones.

Nearby Killarney, Limerick, Blarney within reach.

Kanturk, Co Cork
Tel (029) 50015
Location 12 miles (19 km) W of Mallow, NE of Kanturk, signposted from N72; in extensive gardens with ample car parking
Food & drink full breakfast, light or packed lunch, dinner; wine licence
Prices B&B £35-£55; dinner about £20; reductions for children under 12

Rooms 7 double/family rooms, 3 suites; all with bath and shower, all rooms have central heating, phone
Facilities sitting-room, dining-room, TV room, games room; fishing, tennis, boating, croquet
Credit cards AE, DC, MC, V
Children welcome **Disabled** access fair **Pets** welcome, but must stay in stables
Closed Nov to Mar
Proprietors Bourke family

Cork

Arbutus Lodge

Arbutus Lodge is a substantial suburban house, well known for its food (and for its terraced gardens planted with rare trees and shrubs, including an arbutus tree). Superb shellfish, fish and game are the specialities of the suitably grand restaurant – and there is a top-notch wine list. We are pleased to hear that the public rooms have recently been redecorated, and that there have been major improvements to several bedrooms; though those in the main house have more character than the ones in the modern extension.

Nearby Blarney Castle, 6 miles (10 km).

Middle Glanmire Road, Montenotte, Cork, Co Cork
Tel (021) 501237
Location 0.25 miles (0.4 km) NE of middle of Cork; with garden and ample car parking
Food & drink breakfast, lunch, dinner; full licence
Prices B&B £34.50-£75; dinner £18-£25
Rooms 12 double, all with bath, 4 also with shower; 8 single, 4 with bath, 4 with shower; all rooms have central heating, TV, phone, radio, minibar
Facilities sitting-room, bar, dining-room
Credit cards AE, DC, MC, V
Children welcome if well behaved **Disabled** access difficult – 5 steps at entrance
Pets not accepted
Closed 24 to 30 Dec; restaurant only Sun
Proprietors Ryan family

Longueville House

The O'Callaghans' imposing white Georgian country house is full of beautifully ornate plastered ceilings, elaborately framed ancestral oils and graceful period furniture. But the house is not the stiff place it might be in Britain. Equally important, it does excellent food (particularly local lamb and fish), served in the marvellous Victorian conservatory in summer.

Nearby Blarney castle, 12 miles (19 km).

Longueville, Mallow, Co Cork
Tel (022) 47156
Location 4 miles (6 km) W of Mallow on Killarney road; on 500-acre wooded estate with ample car parking
Food & drink full breakfast, lunch, dinner; full licence
Prices B&B £39-£49; dinner £20
Rooms 13 double, all with bath, 11 also with shower; 4 single, 2 with bath, 2 with shower; all rooms have central heating, TV, radio, phone, hairdrier
Facilities sitting-room, library, TV room, bar, dining-room, conference room; billiards/table tennis
Credit cards AE, DC, V
Children welcome over 10
Disabled access easy to public rooms only
Pets not accepted in house
Closed Christmas to early Mar
Proprietors Michael and Jane O'Callaghan

Cork

Country house hotel, Shanagarry

Ballymaloe House

Thirty bedrooms would rule out any normally attractive hotel, but our inspector's verdict on Ballymaloe dictates otherwise: "You must put Ballymaloe right at the top of your list: other Irish hotels have their pros and cons, but this is just about perfect."

It is an amiable, rambling, creeper-clad house in rolling green countryside, largely Georgian in appearance but incorporating the remains of a 14thC castle keep. The Allens have been farming here for 40 years, opened as a restaurant in 1964, started offering rooms three years later, and since then have added more facilities and more rooms – those in the main house now outnumbered by those in extensions and converted out-buildings. Throughout all this – and despite quite elegant and sophisticated furnishings – they have managed to preserve intact the warmth and naturalness of a much-loved family home. At the heart of it is the kitchen, the province of Myrtle Alen – a self-taught cook whose genius has gained an inter-national reputation. Classic French and Irish dishes are pre-pared alongside original creations, all based on home produce and fish fresh from the local quays. However, just as much care is lavished on breakfast, and the famous children's high tea, as on dinner.

Nearby Beaches, cliff walks, fishing, golf

Shanagarry, Midleton, Co Cork
Tel (021) 652531
Location 20 miles (32 km) E of Cork, 2 miles (3 km) E of Cloyne on the Ballycotton road, L35
Food & drink breakfast, lunch, dinner; full licence
Prices B&B £31.50-£50; dinner £20; reductions for children, bargain breaks
Rooms 27 double, 25 with bath, 2 with shower; 3 single, one with bath, one with shower; one family room; all rooms have central heating, phone
Facilities 2 sitting-rooms, conference/TV room; table tennis, tennis, golf, heated outdoor swimming-pool
Credit cards AE, DC, MC, V
Children welcome; high tea provided **Disabled** access to main building easy, with some bedrooms built for wheelchairs **Pets** accepted
Closed 24 to 26 Dec
Proprietors I and M Allen

Tipperary

Country house hotel, Ballinderry

Gurthalougha House

By the time you reach the end of the mile-long drive which twists and turns through the forest on the way to this hotel beside Lough Derg, it is easy to believe you have travelled back to an altogether more peaceful and graceful era.

Michael and Bessie Wilkinson have, since they arrived in 1981, managed to create an atmosphere as civilized and serene as the hotel's setting. The spacious, high-ceilinged public rooms have plenty of pictures and antiques, but the search for style has not got in the way of comfort. The long, well-lit sitting-room, with its two open fireplaces and big, cosy armchairs, is notably relaxed, while the enormous panelled library has a substantial collection of books about the locality. The restraint continues into the bedrooms, which are spacious and carefully (though fairly sparsely) furnished, with no modern trimmings.

Bessie, who has long experience of the hotel business, looks after the front of house, while Michael does the cooking, producing a smallish 'table d'hote' menu each evening, which may include locally-caught pike and smoked eel.

Nearby Birr Castle gardens, 12 miles (19 km); Limerick.

Ballinderry, Nenagh,
Co Tipperary
Tel (067) 22080
Location just W of village, 10 miles (16 km) N of Nenagh off L152; in 100-acre woodland on lakeside, with ample car parking
Food & drink full breakfast, dinner, snack (or packed) lunch; wine licence (though other drinks available)
Prices B&B £27.50; dinner £18; bargain breaks
Rooms 8 double, 6 with bath, 2 with shower; all

rooms have central heating
Facilities dining-room, sitting-room, library; rowing-boats, table tennis, croquet, fishing
Credit cards MC, V
Children accepted if well behaved; high tea available
Disabled access not easy – 2 sets of steps on ground floor
Pets accepted if well behaved
Closed a few days at Christmas
Proprietors Michael and Bessie Wilkinson

Tipperary

Country house hotel, Cashel

Cashel Palace

We make few apologies for straying well beyond our normal upper price limit to include this magnificent Georgian bishop's palace – built in 1730 and used for its original purpose until 1960 – nestling below the historic Rock of Cashel and its ruined abbey. (Other considerations apart, prices are in practice not necessarily as high as they seem: if you don't make a reservation but ring up late in the day, you may well find that you are able to negotiate a hefty reduction.)

The hotel is mercifully not quite as grand as you might expect from the stately avenue which links it to the heart of the small hilltop town of Cashel and the main Dublin-Cork road. The pillared and panelled entrance hall is imposing enough, with its grand marble fireplaces; but the main public rooms, though superbly furnished in keeping with the house, are on a happily human scale. The handsome Four Seasons restaurant is where the serious eating goes on (and at a serious price too); there is also a more modest buttery and bar in the basement. Some bedrooms are quite small, others palatial, but the standard of furnishings – which often include antiques – is very high, and the general style impeccable. There are fine leafy gardens at the back, including colourful old mulberry trees, planted in 1702 to commemorate the coronation of Queen Anne.

Nearby Rock of Cashel, Longfield House, 6 miles (10 km); Cahir Castle, 8 miles (13 km); Tipperary, 13 miles (21 km).

Main Street, Cashel, Co Tipperary **Tel** (062) 61411 **Location** close to middle of town, on main N8 (Dublin-Cork) road; in gardens with ample car parking **Food & drink** breakfast, lunch, dinner; full licence **Prices** B&B £55.50-£94.75; dinner from £26	**Rooms** 18 double, 2 single; all with bath; all rooms have central heating, TV, phone **Facilities** sitting-room, 2 dining-rooms, bar **Credit cards** AE, DC, MC, V **Children** welcome **Disabled** access difficult **Pets** not welcome **Closed** never. **Proprietor** Ray Carroll

Clare/Kildare

Gregans Castle

Peter and Moira Haden have created a hotel which is impeccably civilized throughout. Pictures of local flora adorn the walls of the cosy, book-filled sitting-room; big, floral-covered armchairs, well-chosen antiques and a large open fireplace grace the big hall at the centre of the house; and the subtly extended, elegant dining-room makes excellent use of fresh local produce. Bedrooms range from relatively simple, to distinctly sumptuous, with lots of space.

Nearby The Burren; Cliffs of Moher, 14 miles (22 km).

Ballyvaughan, Co Clare
Tel (065) 77005
Location 3.5 miles (5.5 km) S of Ballyvaughan, on N67, in open countryside; in large gardens, with ample car parking
Food & drink full breakfast, lunch, dinner; full licence
Prices B&B £38-£56; DB&B £50; suites £65-£75; reduced rates for longer stays
Rooms 11 double, all with bath; 4 mini-suites, one extra large suite, all with bath; all rooms have central heating, hairdrier
Facilities 2 sitting-rooms (one with TV), bar, dining-room
Credit cards V
Children accepted **Disabled** access easy – some ground-floor suites
Pets not accepted
Closed Nov to Feb
Proprietors Peter and Moira Haden

Curryhills House

Only half an hour from Dublin, this ample Georgian house stands in the rich, open pastureland of a county famous for its racehorse breeding. Bill and Bridie Travers have converted it over the years from a farm guest-house into a comfortable country house hotel, most notably through the additon of a discreet modern wing in 1980, which now houses all the bedrooms. The long, pot-holed drive from the main road is off-putting, but both the house and its interior are well cared for, a particular attraction being the large, carefully furnished sitting-room, which boasts antiques and a big open fireplace. Meals in the restored cellar restaurant are simple though imaginative.

Nearby Castletown House, The Curragh, Dublin.

Prosperous, Naas,
Co Kildare
Tel (045) 68150
Location 8 miles (13 km) NW of Naas, one mile (1.5 km) from village; in 100-acre grounds, with ample car parking
Food & drink full breakfast, lunch, dinner; full licence
Prices B&B £25.50-£32; dinner from £15.50
Rooms 10 double, all with bath and shower; all rooms have central heating, phone
Facilities 2 sitting-rooms, bar, dining-room
Credit cards AE, DC, MC, V
Children welcome
Disabled access possible
Pets accepted by arrangement
Closed Christmas week
Proprietors Billy and Bridie Travers

Connemara

Cashel House

A modern extension has increased the size of this immaculate white-painted Victorian establishment, set in luxuriant and exotic grounds – but it is still a comfortable and relaxed country house. The antique-laden sitting-rooms are notably cosy, the greatly extended dining-room, and the bar less so – but furnishings and decoration are of a high quality throughout. Some of the bedrooms are quite palatial.

Nearby Kylemore Abbey, 21 miles (35 km); Clifden, 12 miles (19 km); Lough Corrib, Connemara National Park.

Cashel, Connemara, Co Galway
Tel (095) 31001
Location 35 miles (56 km) NW of Galway, 3 miles (5 km) S of N59; on seashore, with ample car parking
Food & drink full breakfast, snack lunch, dinner; full licence
Prices B&B £38-£41; dinner £19.95
Rooms 16 double, 3 single, 13 mini-suites; all with bath and shower; all rooms have central heating, phone, hairdrier
Facilities 2 sitting-rooms, TV room, library, bar, dining-room; tennis, private beach, boat, horse-riding
Credit cards AE, DC, MC, V
Children not accepted
Disabled access easy – several ground-floor bedrooms **Pets** not accepted in public rooms
Closed Dec to Feb
Proprietors D and K McEvilly

Rosleague Manor

The Georgian builder who erected this fine, square house had a superb eye for scenery. But the brother-and-sister Foyles have just as good an eye for what makes a hotel. Paddy supervises the kichen, which specialises in Connemara lamb and seafood, and makes much use of home-grown fruit and vegetables. Anne takes charge of the front of house, including the large, elegant dining-room, decked out with antiques and chandeliers. Bedrooms have recently been refurbished throughout.

Nearby Connemara National Park, Joyce Country.

Letterfrack, Connemara, Co Galway
Tel (095) 41101
Location one mile (1.5 km) W of Letterfrack, on shores of Ballinakill Bay; in 30-acre grounds, with ample car parking
Food & drink breakfast, light lunch, tea, dinner; full licence
Prices B&B £25-£45; dinner from £18.50
Rooms 15 double, all with bath; all rooms have central heating, phone
Facilities 3 sitting-rooms, bar, dining-room, conservatory
Credit cards AE, MC, V
Children accepted, but not specially catered for
Disabled ramp to public rooms and access at rear to ground-floor bedroom
Pets dogs accepted in bedrooms by arrangement
Closed Nov to Easter
Proprietors Patrick and Ann Foyle

Connemara

Country guest-house, Moyard

Crocnaraw

A long, low, white-painted Georgian building on a small hilltop, Crocnaraw has won prizes for its lush, well-tended gardens sloping down to the main coast road; nevertheless it is the simple, elegant modernity of the interior that is its most striking feature. Plain white walls, bright rugs and stylish modern furniture predominate – the large, light drawing-room on the corner of the house is almost austere. The same can hardly be said of the food, which is adventurous and often includes local seafood, and vegetables and fruit from the garden.

Nearby Kylemore Abbey, 5 miles (8 km); Joyce Country.

Moyard, Connemara,
Co Galway
Tel (095) 41068
Location 6 miles (10 km) N of Clifden, on shores of Ballinakill Bay; in 20-acre grounds, with ample car parking
Food & drink full breakfast, lunch, dinner; full licence
Prices B&B £27-£30; dinner £16.50; reduced DB&B rates for 3 or 7 nights
Rooms 6 double with bath,
2 also with shower; 2 single; all rooms have central heating
Facilities 2 sitting-rooms, dining-room; fishing, riding and golf nearby
Credit cards AE, V
Children accepted by arrangement **Disabled** access easy to one ground-floor bedroom **Pets** dogs welcome except in dining-room
Closed Nov to Apr
Proprietor Lucy Fretwell

Country house hotel, Oughterard

Currarevagh House

This solid country house on the quiet, leafy shores of Lough Corrib has been in the Hodgson family for five generations, since it was built 150 years ago. From the moment you set foot inside, the sense of traditional styles and standards meticulously preserved is quite overpowering – you almost expect Lord Peter Wimsey to turn up for afternoon tea in the airy, spacious sitting-room. Many of the guests come back again and again for the fishing on the lough.

Nearby Connemara, Joyce Country.

Oughterard, Connemara,
Co Galway
Tel (091) 82313
Location 4 miles (6 km) NW of Oughterard; in 150-acre woodlands beside Lough Corrib, with ample car parking
Food & drink breakfast, lunch, tea, dinner; licence
Prices B&B £31.90-£46.20; dinner £16
Rooms 11 double, 9 with bath,
2 with shower; 2 single, one with bath; one family room, with bath
Facilities 3 sitting-rooms (one with TV), bar, dining-room; tennis, boats, croquet
Credit cards not accepted
Children accepted
Disabled not ideal
Pets accepted
Closed Oct to Easter
Proprietors Harry and June Hodgson

Mayo

Country Hotel, Crossmolina

Enniscoe House

Susan Kellett's family home, opened to guests since 1982, is a Georgian country house, set in wooded parkland on the shores of Lough Conn. The public rooms, with their open fires and family portraits, are lived-in and welcoming. Of the five period-style bedrooms, three have canopy and four-poster beds, and for those who prefer to cook for themselves there are sympathetically converted units around the old courtyard. Mrs Kellett produces fine, unfussy Irish country house food (including Irish cheeses).

Nearby Moyne Abbey, 10 miles (16 km); Lough Conn.

Castlehill, near Crossmolina, Ballina, Co Mayo	**Rooms** 3 double, 2 with bath, 3 family rooms, 2 with bath,
Tel (096) 31112	one with shower; all rooms
Location 12 miles (19 km)	have central heating
SW of Ballina, 2 miles (3 km)	**Facilities** sitting-room,
S of Crossmolina on	dining-room; boating,
Castlebar road; in parkland	fishing
on 300-acre estate, with	**Credit cards** AE, MC, V
ample car parking	**Children** welcome
Food & drink breakfast,	**Disabled** not suitable
dinner; wine licence	**Pets** accepted only by special
Prices B&B £35-£37; DB&B	arrangement
£48-£52; reduced weekly,	**Closed** Oct to Mar
weekend and family rates	**Proprietor** Susan Kellett

Country house hotel, Newport

Newport House

Fishing is the preoccupation of most visitors to Newport House, though it is by no means the only attraction. The Georgian house is gracious and elegant, but the Thompsons encourage a caring, friendly attitude rather than super-slick professionalism in their staff. The bedrooms are spacious and individually decorated. Simplicity is the hallmark of the food, making full use of local Clew Bay seafood – and the kitchen does its own butchering as well as baking. Wines are Kieran's hobby.

Nearby Lough Conn, Joyce Country.

Newport, Co Mayo	annexes adjacent to main
Tel (098) 41222	house; all rooms have phone
Location on edge of town,	**Facilities** 3 sitting-rooms,
overlooking Newport river;	bar, dining-room; fishing
ample car parking	**Credit cards** AE, DC, MC, V
Food & drink breakfast,	**Children** accepted **Disabled**
light lunch, dinner; full licence	access possible – some
Prices B&B £38-£47; dinner	ground-floor bedrooms
£23	**Pets** accepted, but not in
Rooms 16 double, 15 with	main house or public rooms
bath, one with shower; 2	**Closed** Oct to mid-Mar
single, one with bath, one	**Proprietors** Kieran and
with shower; 2 four-poster	Thelma Thompson
bedrooms; some rooms in	

Sligo

Country house hotel, Riverstown

Coopershill

Joan O'Hara's 14 years at the helm of this delightful country house were rounded off in 1986 by another guide-book which singled out Coopershill for its "outstanding Irish country hospitality". We could scarcely have put it better ourselves.

Mrs O'Hara's son Brian has come back from the UK to take over the running of the house along with his wife Lindy. The house, though not a pretty one by Georgian standards, has splendidly large rooms (including the bedrooms), and is furnished virtually throughout with antiques; but it is emphatically a home, with no hotel-like formality – and there is the unusual bonus of a playroom to keep children amused. The grounds are big enough not only to afford complete seclusion, but also to accommodate a river on which there is boating and coarse fishing.

Lindy cooks honest country dinners based on English and Irish dishes, entirely in harmony with the nature of the place, while Brian knowledgeably organizes the cellar.

Nearby Sligo, 10 miles (16 km); Lough Arrow, Lough Gara.

Riverstown, Co Sligo
Tel (071) 65108
Location 1 mile (1.5 km) W of Riverstown, off N4 Dublin-Sligo road; in large garden on 500-acre estate, with ample car parking
Food & drink full breakfast, dinner, light or packed lunch; restaurant licence
Prices B&B £30-£38; dinner £16; reductions for 3 or more nights; 50% reduction for children under 12
Rooms 6 double, 4 with bath, one with separate bath, one with shower; one family room, with bath; all rooms have tea/coffee kit
Facilities sitting-room, dining-room; boating, coarse fishing
Credit cards AE, MC, V
Children welcome if well behaved **Disabled** access difficult **Pets** welcome if well behaved, but not allowed in public rooms
Closed Nov to mid-Mar
Proprietors Brian and Lindy O'Hara

Leitrim

Country house hotel, Dromahair

Drumlease Glebe House

The American proprietors who brought this house into the guide, Barbara Flanagan Greenstein and Andrew Greenstein, have moved on. But many of the elements of the peaceful, cultured, cordial Irish experience they offered to guests are still to be found here.

Each room is decorated in keeping with the Georgian house, but employing rich colours and 'modern' fabrics. All the public rooms have Adam fireplaces, the floors are old pine with oriental carpets, drapes are from Liberty and the house has a fine collection of art and antiques. Every little luxury and comfort is provided in the rooms, and there are many personal touches. In the smaller sitting-room, there are lots of books about Ireland (and a television), while the larger sitting-room is the social focus of the house.

We have no reports on the cooking under the new regime, but the approach is encouraging: a set dinner served at a fixed time, employing only fresh local produce (some of it from the garden).
Nearby Sligo town, 9 miles (14.5 km); Lough Gill.

Dromahair, Co Leitrim
Tel (071) 64141
Location 9 miles (14.5 km) SE of Sligo, 1.5 miles (2.5 km) E of Dromahair; in 10-acre grounds with ample car parking
Food & drink full breakfast, dinner, packed lunch; wine licence
Prices B & B £34.50-£38.50; dinner £18.50
Rooms 7 double, 3 with bath and shower, 4 with shower; 2 single, both with separate bath or shower; all rooms have central heating, hairdrier
Facilities sitting-room, study (with TV), dining-room; outdoor swimming-pool, fishing
Credit cards AE, MC, V
Children welcome over 15
Disabled no special facilities
Pets not accepted
Closed Feb
Manager Walter A Beatty

Reporting to the guide

Please write and tell us about your experiences of small hotels, guest houses and inns, whether good or bad, whether listed in this edition or not. As well as hotels in Britain, we are interested in hotels in Italy, France, Spain, Portugal, Austria, Switzerland, Germany and other European countries, and those in the eastern United States.

The address to write to is:
Chris Gill,
Editor,
Charming Small Hotel Guides,
The Old Forge,
Norton St Philip,
Bath, BA3 6LW,
England.

Checklist
Please use a separate sheet of paper for each report; include your name, address and telephone number on each report.

Your reports will be received with particular pleasure if they are typed; and if they are organized under the following headings:
Name of establishment
Town or village it is in, or nearest
Full address, including post code
Telephone number
Time and duration of visit
The building and setting
The public rooms
The bedrooms and bathrooms
Physical comfort
(chairs, beds, heat, light, hot water)
Standards of maintenance and housekeeping
Atmosphere, welcome and service
Food
Value for money

We assume that in writing you have no objections to your views being published unpaid, either verbatim, or in an edited version. Names of outside contributors are acknowledged, at the editor's discretion, on the final page of each guide.

If you would be interested in looking at hotels on a professional basis on behalf of the guides, please include on a separate sheet a summary of your travel experience and hotel-going.

Index of hotel names

Index of hotel names

Index of hotel names

Index of hotel names/place names

An index of cities, towns and
villages at which, or near
which, hotels in the guide are
located.

A

B

C

Index of place names

Index of place names

Index of place names

Acknowledgements

The editor is particularly grateful to:

Stephen Locke, Jo King, Fiona Duncan, Lindsey Bareham, Paul Kitchen, Paul Manias, Susie Bolton, Martin Hitchcock, Will Peskett, Gill de Bono, Paul Turtle, Barbara Canter, Nigel Fox, Sue Harris, Nina Kent, David Dickinson, Ingrid Morgan and Francis Roxburgh

for assistance with hotel inspection and writing reports. Also to the many people – too numerous to mention by name – who sent in reports about their hotels, guest-houses and inns. He is also indebted to the staff of the 200 Tourist Information Centres around Britain for supplying valuable local information.